JUSTICE, POSTERITY, AND THE ENVIRONMENT

Justice, Posterity, and the Environment

Wilfred Beckerman and Joanna Pasek

OXFORD
UNIVERSITY PRESS

OXFORD

UNIVERSITY PRESS

Great Clarendon Street, Oxford OX2 6DP

Oxford University Press is a department of the University of Oxford.
It furthers the University's objective of excellence in research, scholarship,
and education by publishing worldwide in

Oxford New York

Athens Auckland Bangkok Bogotá Buenos Aires
Cape Town Chennai Dar es Salaam Delhi Florence Hong Kong Istanbul
Karachi Kolkata Kuala Lumpur Madrid Melbourne Mexico City Mumbai
Nairobi Paris São Paulo Shanghai Singapore Taipei Tokyo Toronto Warsaw
and associated companies in Berlin Ibadan

Oxford is a registered trade mark of Oxford University Press
in the UK and in certain other countries

Published in the United States
by Oxford University Press Inc., New York

British Library Cataloguing in Publication Data

Data available

Library of Congress Cataloging in Publication Data
Beckerman, Wilfred.
Justice, Posterity, and the Environment/Wilfred Beckerman
and Joanna Pasek.
p. cm.
Includes bibliographical references and index.
1. Environmental ethics. I. Pasek, Joanna. II. Title.
GE42 .B43 2001   179'.1—dc21   00–068612
ISBN 0–19–924509–6
ISBN 0–19–924508–8 (pbk)

1 3 5 7 9 10 8 6 4 2

Typeset in Stone Sans and Stone Serif by
Cambrian Typesetters, Frimley, Surrey
Printed in Great Britain
on acid-free paper by
Biddles Ltd
Guildford & King's Lynn

PREFACE

It would be going much too far to suggest that Amartya Sen's (1987: 9) call for greater collaboration between economists and philosophers has been responsible for the marriage between the two authors of this book, Wilfred Beckerman, who is an economist, and Joanna Pasek, who is a philosopher. But, to switch to the first person, the most important result of the marriage has been our daughter, Beatrice, without whose help this book would have been finished much sooner. Whenever we are walking with her past the Oxford University Museum of Natural History, which is only a short distance from our house, she likes to call in. One of the objects in it that she finds particularly fascinating is a stuffed dodo—a photograph of which is on the front cover of this book. This is a bird that once inhabited the forests of the Mauritius. At first Beatrice used to ask whether we could go to see a live dodo somewhere, like in the Cotswold Wild Life Park. But we have tried to explain that this is impossible since the dodo has been extinct for about three centuries. In so far as she understands this idea, she gets quite indignant about it.

Should we feel that the settlers and visiting seamen who were responsible for the extinction of the dodo violated Beatrice's right to see a live dodo? After all, the extinction of the dodo around that time was largely their fault. For some of them probably killed some of the dodos, and some of the animals that they brought to the island escaped from captivity and ate the dodo's eggs, if not the dodos themselves. It is true that the dodo was a stupid bird that was on its way out anyway. It acquired the name 'dodo' from the Portuguese word *duodo*, which means 'silly' or 'stupid', because, like the panda today, it was not the sort of animal cut out for survival against the odds. It laid only a single large egg and it could not fly, so left the eggs on the ground.

What, you may ask, does this have to do with this book? The answer is, 'plenty'. For one of the issues that has aroused a lot of interest lately, on account of growing awareness of our impact on the environment, is the nature of our obligations to future generations. Public figures and politicians can hardly ever make any pronouncement these days about global issues, such as climate change, without proclaiming their passionate concern with the welfare of their children and grandchildren. Concern with the interests of future generations is often translated into assertions about the 'rights' of future generations to inherit the environment as it stands today and to the corresponding dictates of 'intergenerational justice', or 'equity', or 'sustainable development'. But one only has to pose the question—did the settlers in the Mauritius three centuries ago violate our rights to see a live dodo?—to recognize that, perhaps, the concept of the rights of future generations and the associated concepts of intergenerational justice and so on are not as clear-cut as they may at first sight appear. One of our main aims in this book, therefore, has been to raise doubts about the moral force of such concepts in general and in environmental policy in particular.

As it happens, we, too, are passionately concerned with the interests of all our children and grandchildren, and even—if far less passionately—with the interests of more distant generations. We would greatly regret it if our children or grandchildren grow up in a world in which there were no more Bengal tigers or certain other endangered species of animals. But the prospect for the future that most alarms us is that they may grow up in a world in which countless millions of people live in fear of death, oppression, suffering, and humiliation because basic human rights are violated in most countries of the world and are threatened in the others by the recent widespread resurgence of xenophobia and intolerance. In 1974 one of us wrote that the real prospective conflicts would not be between man and the environment but between man and man. Since then the world has witnessed the savagery of ideological, religious, or ethnic conflicts all over the world: in Cambodia, Bosnia, Indonesia, Kosovo, and in various African states, as well as brutal repression in some South American countries, continued conflict in the Middle East, Northern Ireland, parts of the Indian sub-continent, and violent manifestations of endemic ethnic intolerance even in Western Europe.

The central message of this book, therefore, is that the most important bequest we can make to posterity is to bequeath a decent society characterized by greater respect for human rights than is the case today. Furthermore, while this by no means excludes a concern for environmental developments—particularly those that many people believe might seriously threaten future living standards—policies to deal with these developments must never be at the expense of the poorest people alive today. One could not be proud of policies that may preserve the environment for future generations if the costs of doing so are born mainly by the poorest members of the present generation.

Wilfred Beckerman
Joanna Pasek
October 2000

ACKNOWLEDGEMENTS

We are particularly grateful to John Broome, Ruth Chang, Avner de-Shalit, Andrew Dobson, John O'Neill, Onora O'Neill, Joseph Raz, Paul Streeten, and Marcel Wissenburg who helped, in correspondence or in person, to improve our understanding of problems that had a bearing on Chapters 2 through 4 of our book and/or made invaluable comments on these chapters. We have also learnt much from David Miller and David Pearce, both of whom made important comments on Chapters 8 and 9 that considerably influenced the balance of our discussion therein of environmental valuation.

Our greatest debt is to Jerry Cohen, Roger Crisp, and Larry Temkin. All three commented in considerable detail on one or more of the Chapters 2 through 4, and went to great trouble trying to educate us in the intricacies of theories of equality and justice, without ever allowing us to feel either intimidated by their outstanding expertise in these areas or that we were wasting their time. Their interest in our work was a source of great encouragement. Larry Temkin was even willing to stop and discuss it whenever one of us would waylay him outside our house as he tried to cycle past unobtrusively on his way to All Souls College.

We have also greatly benefited from comments by participants at conferences or seminars at the Accademia Nazionale dei Lincei in Rome; Trinity College, Dublin; the University of California at Davis; the University of Columbia, New York; the University of Keele; and seminars on intergenerational justice organized at Trinity College, Cambridge, by Peter Laslett, who more or less invented the subject. We have no doubt benefited from discussing, at one time or another, most of the topics covered in this book, with other economists and philosophers to whom we would like to extend our collective thanks.

To all of the people indicated above we can only apologise if, as a result either of our failure to understand some of their arguments or an obstinate unwillingness to be convinced by them, we have persisted with some views or passages of text of which we know they would disapprove and which may even horrify them. And, of course, we are entirely responsible for all the shortcomings of the book.

Finally, we are most grateful to Dominic Byatt and Amanda Watkins, of Oxford University Press, for the speed and efficiency with which they have handled the administrative side of publication, and to Michael James for the outstanding professionalism of his copy-editing. We are also grateful to the International Food Policy Research Institute, the Oxford University Press, and the editors of *Environmental Values* for permission to use in this book material written by one or both of us and published by them.

ACKNOWLEDGEMENTS

CONTENTS

LIST OF FIGURES

1

Introduction: Ethics and Economics in Environmental Policy

1. Introduction

In rich countries, environmental problems are seen as problems of prosperity. In poor countries they are seen as problems of poverty. How can this be explained? The answer is that the environmental problems in poor countries, such as lack of clean drinking water or decent sanitation, are problems that affect them here and now, whereas in rich countries the environmental problems that people worry about most are those that—largely as a result of current prosperity and economic growth—seem likely to harm mainly posterity. What has most captured the public's imagination in rich countries is the widespread fear that continued economic growth will damage the environment in ways that are inconsistent with our obligations to future generations.

But what exactly are our obligations to future generations? Are these determined by the some ethical system, such as the 'rights' of future generations, or justice between generations, or intergenerational equity, or sustainable development? For if resources are used in ways that benefit future generations, the present generation has to bear the burden. If more resources are devoted to environmental protection, fewer can be devoted to competing claims for, say, health care or education or housing, not to mention the urgent claims in poor countries for better food, sanitation, drinking water, shelter, and basic infrastructures to prevent or cure widespread disease. It cannot serve the interests of justice if the burden of protecting the environment for the benefit of posterity is born mainly by poorer people today. Generations are not homogeneous entities.

Hence, one cannot divorce the question of intergenerational justice from the question of how the costs of any policy are to be shared out between different people alive today, particularly between poor and rich nations. Any government policy, including a policy of doing nothing about some problem, creates winners and losers, even if the overall effect is beneficial. This applies as much to environmental policy as to any other. For example, regulations to prevent some factory from polluting a river with its effluent may be beneficial for some people, and perhaps for society as a whole, but if the prices of the factory's product have to rise and customers are lost, some of the employees may lose their jobs.

As well as affecting differently individual members of any given generation, some environmental policies can also affect differently whole generations. For example, if, in the interests of future generations, we were to cut the use of fossil fuels as a source of energy before cheaper substitutes were available, there would be a net loss of welfare for the present generation taken as a whole. On the other hand, an attempt to increase reliance on nuclear energy could impose serious harm on future generations unless the nuclear waste can be safely stored.

Of course, some environmental policies may, on balance, benefit both present and future generations, such as policies to preserve some recreational or aesthetic amenity: beautiful scenery, clean rives or lakes, clean air, and so on. But, at any point in time, the total output of goods and services that any society can produce is limited by its supply of basic resources—labour, capital, raw materials—its technology, and certain social constraints—for example, hours worked. Hence, anybody who believes that we should spend more on preserving the environment, whether for the present or future generations, must presumably believe that too much is being spent on other purposes. This view can be justified only if it is also believed that, at the margin, the value of these other uses to the people who use them is less than the value of protecting the environment. It is a view that is hardly likely to be shared by the vast majority of the world's population.

How then should we balance the welfare of the different groups affected? How do we resolve these conflicts of interest—between different generations, between rich and poor nations, and between different groups within the same nation—when environmental policy decisions have to be made? These are the questions to which this book is mainly addressed. Although economics provides well-developed techniques for assessing the relative value of different forms of expenditure to different members of the present generation, these questions also raise ethical issues. Hence, it is the ethical aspects of these questions that predominate in this book. Indeed, in many respects the economics and the ethics of these questions are inextricably linked.

2. Some Ethical and Psychological Assumptions in Economics

It is well-known, particularly among economists, that so-called 'normative economics'—the economics of what *ought* to be done to increase economic welfare—and even 'positive economics'—which seeks only to describe and analyse economic behaviour without prescribing what ought to be done—are both founded on ethical assumptions.[1] This is not surprising given that economics started out life in the English-speaking world as a branch of ethics. Adam Smith, after all, was a professor of moral philosophy. And the most significant ethical contributions to economics have been made by economists themselves.[2]

One of the ethical questions that is particularly relevant to environmental policy is *which society* are we talking about when we discuss the society whose economic welfare we are seeking to maximize. How far should we extend the boundaries of the society, the welfare of which we want to maximize, to encompass distant strangers, non-human species, or future generations? Should we treat people who are not yet born as having the same moral status as people alive today? And if so, what then are our obligations towards them? These are problems in ethics, not economics.

A second major limitation on 'normative' economics is that it can contribute very little to the distributional problems discussed above. For what economics essentially provides, and with great sophistication, is an analysis of the 'efficient' distribution of resources—land, labour, capital, and so on— between different uses *given whatever happens to be the initial distribution of assets—wealth, skills, and so on—among people, and taking peoples' preferences as given*. It can also often tell us something about the effects any particular policy will have on the distribution of income among people. But it cannot tell us much about whether the initial distribution of assets, or the changes in it, were equitable or not. Yet, as we have indicated, environmental policy raises precisely this kind of distributional question, particularly insofar as it affects the distribution of well-being among different generations.

Another important issue that frequently crops up in environmental policy is the extent to which the market mechanism provides an adequate guide to the value that people attach to environmental preservation. For example, how far should expenditures on environmental projects depend on some sort of cost-benefit analysis? This question highlights a third limitation on conventional economic theory. This is the presumption that the satisfaction of peoples' preferences has some overriding moral force.[3] This presumption underlies the conventional economics view that, since the expression of consumers' self-interest is reflected in their preferences, we ought to allow such preferences to determine social choices.

But perhaps we may need to make ethical distinctions between alternative

---

[1] Among many works on the relationship between economics and ethics, one might single out for special mention Hahn and Hollis (1979), Sen (1987), and Hausman and McPherson (1993).

[2] Hausman and McPherson (1993) provide what is probably the best survey of these contributions.

[3] See, in particular, Sen (1987). Other economists, such as Arrow (1951), Graaff (1967), and Little (1950) had, of course, also made important contributions to the general problem of arriving at compelling social choices on the basis of individual preferences.

ways in which consumers may obtain satisfaction. For example, it is quite likely that a cost-benefit analysis in ancient Rome of the spectacle of throwing Christians to the lions in the Colosseum would have come up with a positive result. On the one hand, the satisfactions to the spectators as measured by their willingness to pay might have been considerable. And the costs would have been very small: the lions would have been nourished and society would have disposed of a lot of people regarded at the time as troublemakers. However, virtually everybody today would believe, as no doubt did many people at the time, that this violation of basic human rights was totally abhorrent, degrading, and immoral, and the fact that the monetary value of consumer satisfactions may have outweighed any corresponding measure of the relevant costs would be totally irrelevant. We would take this view even if many early Christians had welcomed martyrdom as a quick route to paradise, so that the situation would have corresponded to what economists would define as a 'Pareto-optimal move', namely, a move which makes some people better off without making anybody worse off.

Another criticism of the use of cost-benefit analysis in environmental decision-making is that much of economic theory rests on deliberately simplified models of the way that people make decisions. In standard economic theory, a working assumption is that people make choices in some 'rational' manner between the options available to them, all of which can be made commensurate with each other in units of 'utility'. However, there are well-known limitations on this model of consumer behaviour.[4] No doubt people frequently make choices between options that, however hard they are pushed, they could not compare in any common units. In a world of plural values, including such values as liberty, compassion, justice, and, perhaps above all, personal relationships, most people would be simply unable to base their choices on any clear-cut ranking of the value to them of the various options open to them. Thus, the role that economic techniques should play in the way that institutions reach decisions on environmental policy raises unavoidable ethical questions; and later chapters of this book discuss how much force there is in the various criticisms made of these techniques.

3. The Scope of This Book

It is clear that certain ethical assumptions underlying standard welfare economics—all well known, of course, to many professional economists—

---

[4] Some of these were elaborated in pioneering work by economists over 20 years ago. Harvey Leibenstein brought together work that he had been developing and publishing over a period of many years in his *Beyond Economic Man* (1976). See also Herbert Simon (1982). A comprehensive critical guide to the problem of rationality in economics is provided by Hargreaves Heap *et al.* (1992).

have a major bearing on environmental policy. First, there is the way we draw the boundary around the society whose welfare we wish to promote. Second, there are the distributional problems, such as how one should approach the problem of the distribution of costs and benefits between generations, or how the burden of international action to combat global environmental problems ought to be shared among rich and poor nations. Third, we have to ask whether a preference for environmental preservation, whether for future generations or for any groups in society, has some special moral value, and how far environmental preferences are intrinsically incommensurate with the values people attach to ordinary goods and services.

This book is mainly about these particular aspects of certain environmental problems, though, as will be seen in various chapters, this inevitably leads us to discuss some basic concepts such as 'justice' or the intrinsic value of the environment. Thus, this book is not intended to be a textbook of environmental ethics.[5] In the first place, there is some economics input. Second, no attempt is made to survey the environmental pronouncements of everybody whose views on environmental ethics are worth mentioning. And, third, we do not adopt an entirely neutral 'textbook' stance, limiting ourselves to enumerating the pros and cons of alternative points of view. Instead we concentrate on raising questions about the selected topics mentioned above and on presenting our own particular view of them.

Furthermore, although we are primarily concerned with the distributional dimension of environmental policy—across generations and within generations—we do not discuss what is often described as 'environmental justice'. This is because we do not think that the concept of 'environmental justice' makes much sense. In our view, the term 'environmental ethics' makes sense since it refers merely to those ethical considerations that arise in the analysis of environmental problems, in the same way that, say, the term 'medical ethics' would describe the ethical issues arising in medicine. But the term 'environmental justice' has no such clear meaning and is probably a confusing misnomer.[6] It tends to be used to mean two different things, both of which are misleading.

The first is a reference to the fact that poorer people tend to suffer more

---

[5] There are several wide-ranging anthologies of environmental ethics, such as Elliot (1995) and Elliot and Gare (1983). But the serious student of the subject could hardly do better than begin with Passmore's (1974) classic.

[6] See the careful survey and classification of concepts of 'environmental justice' and a description of the development, particularly in the USA, of the environmental justice movement, in Dobson (1998: Ch. 1), as well as David Miller's scrutiny of the concept of environmental justice in Miller (1999: 151–5). According to Dobson (1998: 17), 'the starting point for considerations of environmental justice as I characterised it . . . . [is] the observation that "poor people live in poor environments" '. Dobson also provides various references to statements by leading figures in the 'environmental justice' movement that confirm their central concern with the way that the costs and benefits of environmental pollution and its prevention are distributed between rich and poor people.

from environmental pollution, or from measures to reduce it, than do rich people (for example, Bryant 1995). For example, the people living near smelly factories tend to be poorer than others.[7] But it happens that rich people tend to enjoy more of all sorts of 'goods' and less of 'bads' than do poorer people. It is consequently inevitable that they will also tend to have fewer 'bads', such as pollution. Indeed, there is no conceptual difference between, say, the 'bad' of living near a smelly factory and the 'good' of living in an environment free of smells. The rich also tend to have better food, bigger cars and houses, better health care, smarter clothes, and so on. But one does not talk about 'food justice', or 'clothes justice', and so on. We may well have views concerning what is a 'just' distribution of incomes, or welfare, or whatever, between people. This will then determine how we think that environmental goods and 'bads', like other goods, should be distributed among people. But this will not require any special theory of 'environmental justice'.

The second common usage of the term 'environmental justice' is a reference to justice between human beings, on the one hand, and 'nature'—animals or trees or mountains and so on—on the other hand. But the conception of justice to which we subscribe refers to relationships between *people*. After over two thousand years of scrutiny of the concept of justice, philosophers have made some progress in clarifying the main serious theories of 'just' relationships between human beings. For example, useful distinctions have been made between those theories of justice that are in terms of mutually advantageous contracts that people may make, or have inherited, and theories based on the notion of 'fairness' or 'impartiality'. But we find it difficult to conceive of a serious theory of justice in terms of a contract between human beings and animals, or in terms of how 'unfair' it is on mountains if too many people are allowed to ski down them. Of course, it may well be that theories of justice should be interpreted more widely to encompass the relationship between humans and other species or cherished natural features. But, meanwhile, we prefer to leave such relationships to that part of morality that lie outside the domain of 'justice'.

4. The Moral Basis of Environmentalism

It is easy to adopt a high moral tone in discussing almost any social problem. But it is not so easy to justify it. And many people seem to find it impossible to engage in a discussion of the long-run effects of alternative environmental

---

[7] Indeed, it is well-known that one of the main reasons why the west side of most cities in western Europe, particularly in Britain, tend to be the more expensive and fashionable areas is that the prevailing winds are from the west so that in the days when factories were located in, or near, city centres it was the eastern sides of the cities that tended to suffer most from air pollution.

policies without appeal being made to the overriding moral claims of future generations in general, or to our concern with our children and grandchildren in particular, or the sanctity of nature. For example, a leading environmentalist, Bryan Norton, states that 'Environmentalists are moralists, and one of the ways they show this is by taking an active concern for both the options for experiences and the values of future people' (Norton 1994: 323). This is all highly commendable. But this does not mean that people who have different views are not equally motivated by moral considerations.

Furthermore, claiming to be a moralist is no guarantee that one's particular views are, in fact, justified, or even 'moral' by most peoples' standards. Human history is only too full of horrific suffering inflicted on some human beings by other human beings acting out of what they thought were the highest moral considerations, such as saving the victims' souls. At various stages throughout this book, therefore, we shall be raising questions concerning the claims to occupy the moral high ground that are commonly made by many environmental activists and by public figures.

5. Outline of the Book

In Chapters 2 through 5, we discuss how far our moral obligations to future generations can be derived from theories in terms of their 'rights', intergenerational justice, sustainable development, and intergenerational equity. We contrast the claims of such theories with the claims of the simple, if vague and old-fashioned, concepts of beneficence or 'virtue' or compassion, that lie outside the normal domain of theories of rights and justice. But whatever ethical approach one adopts to tackle the problem of our obligations to posterity, it seems incumbent on us to make some prediction, however rough and ready, concerning long-run developments in order to identify what are likely to be the most important interests that future generations will have and how these compare with the interests of people alive today.

Chapters 6 and 7, therefore, comprise an attempt to predict what, in the very long run, are likely to be the most important interests of future generations. This covers not only the prospects for continued economic growth and environmental constraints but also the prospects for conflicts between people and the extent to which these can be resolved in a tolerant and peaceful manner. On the whole we are optimistic about the former but pessimistic about the latter.

We then turn, in Chapters 8 and 9, to the problems of how the burden of environmental protection ought to be distributed among different people alive today. First, we discuss the possible limitations on economic appraisal mentioned above, and their implications for the way that resources ought to be distributed between environmental preservation and other claims. And finally, in Chapters 10 and 11, we consider the way that the burden of international efforts to combat global environmental problems ought to be shared out between rich and poor countries.

Needless to say, we cannot hope to provide simple and decisive answers to the sort of questions raised in this book. Even economists are known to often hold major legitimate differences of opinion. And there can never be definite final answers to the ethical questions that predominate in this book. By their very nature the main function of ethical considerations is to stimulate the imagination rather than to provide any straightforward answers. At best their study brings out the difficulties in the way of reaching facile conclusions. Hence, our ambition is mainly to show that there are objections to some of the more popular positions currently adopted in environmental discourse. The most that we can hope for is that we have brought out some of the reasons why the many 'simple and decisive' ethical assumptions that are so widespread in the field of environmental debate today need to be challenged. And if some of our challenges turn out to be justified it may well be that they will have some small impact on the priorities that many people give to different obligations we may have towards future generations.

PART 1
Justice between generations

2

The Rights of Future Generations

1. Justice Between Generations: A New Problem

Most of the questions that are asked by philosophers are the sort that children are frequently asking, like 'How can I know that I am not really dreaming?' or 'What is fairness?' Children frequently complain that it is not 'fair' that they cannot stay up late to watch the TV, or that they are given less pocket money than some other children, or a smaller portion of ice-cream than somebody else, and so on. In fact their most common complaint about most constraints on their pleasures or activities is that they are 'unfair'. Sometimes we can find simple and convincing answers to their questions about fairness, but sometimes the answers are not obvious or are not convincing, even to ourselves.

Many grown-up philosophers are also preoccupied with the question of what is 'fairness', though this tends to be subsumed under the heading of what is 'just'. In particular, the conception of 'justice as fairness' has become very widely discussed, largely under the stimulus of the work of John Rawls, although many philosophers who by no means give unqualified approval to Rawlsian philosophy still take 'fairness' as the bedrock of their own particular conceptions of justice in general and 'distributive justice'—that is, the justice of the way that certain things are shared out among people—in particular.

But whereas the problem of distributive justice within any given society at any point in time has occupied philosophers for over 2,000 years, its extension to intergenerational justice is relatively recent.[1] It has no doubt been provoked by the increasing concern, over the last three or four decades, with the possibility that we are seriously depleting the Earth's resources and damaging the environment. In this way, it is often believed, we are violating

[1] According to Laslett and Fishkin (1992: 1), 'The revival of political theory over the past three decades has taken place within the grossly simplifying assumptions of a largely timeless world . . . [it] is limited, at most, to the horizons of a single generation who make binding choices, for all time, for all successor generations'. There have, however, been some exceptions, such as Rawls, who discussed intergenerational distributive justice at some length back in 1972, and others, such as Partha Dasgupta (1974), or the contributors to the volumes on the subject edited by Sikora and Barry (1978) or Partridge (1981).

the rights of future generations and hence not behaving in a way that would pass the tests of any principles of intergenerational justice.

Questions such as 'What is a just distribution of the Earth's resources between us and future generations?' or 'Do we have obligations to future generations?' or 'Do future generations have rights to inherit the same environment as exists now?' are not what most of us mean by factual questions to which there may be definite answers, at least in principle. We cannot strip-search future generations to check whether or not they have some rights concealed about their persons, or even search present generations to check whether they are carrying any obligations in their baggage, perhaps quite innocently and unaware of their presence.

Philosophical considerations can rarely provide clear answers to practical policy issues, so that most philosophers do not attempt to provide them.[2] And for many people the extent of our obligations to future generations need not to be grounded in some coherent ethical system, any more, say, than their feeling that we have obligations to treat other people or animals decently or to respect works of art. They may say that concern for the preservation of the environment and the interests of future generations is just one part of our moral intuition and one cannot get very far in trying to incorporate it into some articulated ethical system. In other words, they just adopt the value judgement to the effect that decent human beings ought to be concerned with posterity and that is the end of it.

Up to a point this is the conclusion that is reached in this book. However, it is reached somewhat reluctantly, and after having rejected the most popular alternatives. We would have preferred to be able to identify some precise criteria that could be used to judge the weight that should be attached to one's concern with future generations as compared with the interests of people alive today. But unfortunately very few of the ethical systems that are taken seriously provide us with a formula for trading off conflicting values against each other.

The main exception, perhaps, is utilitarianism, which is important chiefly in the English-speaking world. Utilitarianism does purport to provide a simple rule for trading off the moral value of different courses of action, namely, that we should pursue the course of action that will maximize total utility, provided—and this is a major proviso—one can predict the likely consequences of any action. But, quite apart from various well-known objections to utilitarianism, it is of very little use as far as intergenerational distributive justice is concerned.[3] This is chiefly because utilitarianism does not attach *intrinsic* value to any particular equality of distribution of anything, and it

---

[2] The limited, but nevertheless valuable, role of philosophical considerations in the environmental context is well set out by Williams (1992). His comments on this apply equally, of course, over the whole range of applied ethics.

[3] We have surveyed some of the arguments in Pasek (1992) and Beckerman (1995a).

often conflicts with the way that most people would, and probably should, regard their relationships to other people. It also seems unable to handle problems involving changes in the size of the population, which cannot, of course, be ignored in framing environmental policy (for example Mirrlees 1982; Parfit 1984).

Thus, finding some clear compelling ethical principles of justice that apply to contemporaries is difficult enough. Finding some that apply to different generations encounters new and special difficulties. The conclusions we arrive at here concerning our obligations will thus not emerge from any elegant 'system'. But it is hoped that a discussion of the problems will at least help dispel some widely held exaggerations and misconceptions concerning our obligations to future generations as well as putting such obligations as we do have on a firmer footing than has been the case so far.

2. The Structure of the Argument

The general status of moral 'rights' is a central topic in ethics. Indeed, some philosophers see 'rights' as the foundation of political morality and possibly of morality in general.[4] It is not surprising, therefore, that all our moral obligations to future generations are often thought of as being simply the counterpart of their 'rights'. Nevertheless it is argued in this chapter that any attempt to establish all our moral obligations to future generations on the basis of their rights is a dangerous, and probably fatal, enterprise. It is argued that this is because future generations cannot be said to have any rights. And, as is then argued, this means that it is difficult to construct any coherent theory of intergenerational justice.

There are many different conceptions of 'rights' and of 'justice' as well as of the relationship between them. It would be beyond the scope of this book as well as outside our competence to try to present and appraise the arguments that have been put forward over the ages in favour of one conception of justice or rights rather than another. All we shall try to do here is to show that the conceptions of rights and justice that we adopt are widely accepted. Our only 'original' contribution is to argue that, if these conceptions of rights and justice are adopted, then, taken together, they do seem to lead to a somewhat surprising conclusion, namely, that there is no place for a theory of justice between generations. Indeed, John Dunn, Professor of Political Theory at Cambridge University, almost suggests that the opposite conclusion is 'obvious'![5]

---

[4] See Dworkin (1984) and Mackie (1984).

[5] Dunn (1999: 77) writes that 'The reasons for supposing that an understanding of justice should drastically inhibit the harm which we knowingly inflict on the human future are simple and intuitively obvious'. But Dunn does not go as far as do Rawls and Barry in actually proposing explicit principles of intergenerational justice.

Our argument is really very simple and can be summarized in the following syllogism:

(1) Future generations—of unborn people—cannot be said to have any rights.

(2) Any coherent theory of justice implies conferring rights on people.

Therefore, (3) the interests of future generations cannot be protected or promoted within the framework of any theory of justice.

Of course, both of the first two propositions can be challenged. The first of them, which is the subject of this chapter, is not new and may be thought by many people to be non-controversial, or even obvious, and to correspond to what is generally understood by most people to be implied by the concept of 'rights'. Nevertheless, as indicated below, some reputable philosophers do explicitly claim that future generations have rights, as do most environmentalists. Furthermore, certain philosophers who do not explicitly claim that future generations have rights must implicitly believe that they do insofar as they believe—as do John Rawls (1972: 284ff.) and Brian Barry (1999: Ch. 3), for example—both that theories of justice imply the attribution of rights and that it is possible to construct some theory of intergenerational justice.

The second proposition also reflects a particular conception of justice, which, following Rawls, is essentially that justice is a virtue of institutions and consists of defining the rights and duties of the members of the institutions in question, notably their rights over the way that the fruits of their cooperation ought to be shared out. This conception of justice is discussed further in the next chapter. But other conceptions of justice are certainly plausible. In particular, some philosophers subscribe to conceptions of 'natural justice'— and natural 'fairness'—according to which an injustice exists insofar as somebody is worse off than somebody else for no fault of her own, even if this state of affairs has not been imposed by anybody else and does not reflect a failure of any institution to act according to principles of justice.

Given the conceptions of rights and justice that we have adopted, the conclusion to which it seems to lead means that attempts to locate our obligations to future generations in some theory of intergenerational justice are doomed to fail. But this would not necessarily mean that future generations have no 'moral standing' and that we have no moral obligations towards them. For we share the widely held view that rights and justice by no means exhaust the whole of morality.[6] After setting out in the next chapter our reasons for ruling out intergenerational justice as a guide to our obligations to future generations, we argue, in the succeeding chapters, that neither intergenerational 'equity' nor 'sustainable development' provides a substitute. We then set out some suggestions concerning our obligations towards future generations.

[6] Recent lucid reminders of this include, notably, Rawls (1972), Raz (1986: Ch. 8), and particularly the recent extensive and lucid discussion of this topic in O. O'Neill (1996).

3. Do Future Generations Have Rights?

It should be made clear at the outset that, first, we are talking about future generations *of unborn people* and are abstracting from the case of over-lapping generations. Thus, we are not concerned with what we may feel inclined to bequeath to our children or their descendants on account of bonds of affection, or what they may feel obliged to do for us for the same reason. This is because we are concerned here with identifying what are our *moral obligations* to future generations, not what we would like to do for them anyway. We adopt the Kantian view that what is morally right is a matter of duty and cannot be determined by one's sentiments or self-interest. Hence, crudely speaking, doing what you fancy is nothing to do with moral duty. [7] Indeed, many of the things that most of us would like to do from time to time are probably quite immoral.[8]

Second, we are talking about *moral* rights, not *legal* rights. And, third, we do not wish to enter into discussion of the general problem of how widely one should draw the boundary around the 'rights', if any, that the present generation can be said to possess, or the particular problem of how far these rights include rights over the environment.

The Essential Conditions for Having Rights to Something

The crux of our argument that future generations cannot have rights to anything is that properties, such as being green or wealthy or having rights, can be predicated only of some subject that exists. Outside the realm of mythical or fictional creatures or hypothetical discourse, if there is no subject, then there is nothing to which any property can be ascribed.[9] Propositions such as 'X is Y' or 'X has Z' or 'X prefers A to B' make sense only if there is an X. If there is no X then all such propositions are meaningless.[10] If we were to say 'X has a fantastic collection of CDs' and you were to ask us who is X and we were to reply 'Well, actually there isn't any X', you would think we had taken leave of our senses—as each of us, that is, the authors, has long suspected

---

[7] At one point Kant (1964: 99) explicitly says that the categorical imperatives 'did by the mere fact that they were represented as categorical, exclude from their sovereign authority every admixture of interest as a motive'.

[8] There may, of course, be routes by which one can arrive at some sort of contract between overlapping generations that dispenses with bonds of affection, notably that followed by Gauthier (1986: 298ff.). But his proposal does not seem to be able to handle satisfactorily the problem of sharing out resources over distant generations, which is what the environmental debate seems to be mainly about. See Temkin's (1995: 79–87) critique.

[9] When rights are attributed to mythical or fictional creatures, for example, they are not believed to be rights that exist in the real world and that hence impose any obligations on real world people, such as us.

[10] We are here using the term 'meaningless' to describe propositions such as 'X is Y' when there is no X, although such propositions could be transposed into longer and clumsy propositions that are meaningful, such as 'X exits and if there is an X it has Y', but are false if, in fact, there is no X.

about the other for some time. And you would be right. Thus the general proposition that future generations cannot have anything, including rights, follows from the meaning of the present tense of the verb 'to have'.[11] Unborn people simply cannot *have* anything. They cannot have two legs or long hair or a taste for Mozart.

In connection with the more specific proposition, namely, that future generations have rights to specific assets, such as the existing environment and all its creatures, a second condition has to be satisfied. This is that even people who do exist cannot have rights to anything unless, in principle, the rights could be fulfilled (Parfit 1984: 365). In the case of rights to particular physical objects, for example, like a right to see a live dodo, it is essential that the dodo exist. In the case of, say, a right to have a clause in a mutually agreed contract to be carried out, it must be feasible for the contracting parties to carry it out. In the same way that it does not seem to make sense to say 'X has Y' or 'X is Z' if X does not exist, it does not make sense even when X does exist to say 'X has a right to Y' if Y is not available or beyond the power of anybody to provide.

Thus for the proposition 'X has a right to Y' to be valid, where Y refers to some tangible object, two essential conditions have to be satisfied. First, X must exist, and second, it must be possible, in principle, to provide Y.

In the case of our right to see live dodos, for example, one of these two conditions is not satisfied. We exist, but dodos do not exist. And before the dodos became extinct, the dodos existed but we did not exist, so we could not have any rights to its preservation. Hence, insofar as it is implausible to say that we *had* the right to the preservation of live dodos before we existed it must be implausible to say that non-existent unborn generations have any rights now to inherit any particular asset.

Thus, however widely society wishes to draw the boundary around the rights that future generations *will* have, they cannot *have* any rights now. Nor, when they come into existence, can the rights that they will have include rights to something that will no longer exist, such as an extinct species.

This conception of rights may appear clearer if we consider some examples. As regards the most important condition, namely that the rights-holder exists, we can agree that you have a right not to be killed, so that everybody has a counterpart obligation not to kill you. But suppose somebody kills you nevertheless. Can we say next week, when you no longer exist, that your right not to be killed has been violated? Yes, why not? It will be perfectly true to say that, in the previous week, when you existed, somebody violated your right to life. The fact that you no longer exist is irrelevant. What is relevant is

---

[11] This fundamental and in our opinion decisive point was made by De George (1981) and, if less forcibly, by Macklin (1981). But with some exceptions, notably de-Shalit (1995; 2000: 137), it does not seem to have been given due weight in the literature on this subject. The same point is also set out very effectively in Merrills (1996: 31).

that at the time you were killed you *did exist, as did your life*, so your right to life could be violated. But this does not mean that it makes sense to say that you have a right to life a week later, when you no longer exist—and hence, by definition, nor does your life.

Consider now the more specific proposition, namely, that one cannot have a right that cannot be fulfilled. Consider, for example, the case where some naughty boy, Billy, takes Tommy's toy dodo and burns it. Most people, and courts of law, would accept that, in taking away and destroying Tommy's slightly battered but beloved toy dodo, he did a wicked thing and should be punished. But they would not agree that Tommy has a right to get the very same toy dodo back. One can imagine the scene if Tommy made such a claim. A kindly and sympathetic judge would lean over the bench and say, 'But Tommy, your dodo has been burnt. Wicked little Billy cannot give you back the same one. The best I can do is to order him or his mummy to buy you a new one'. And Tommy would say, tearfully, 'No, no! I want my own dodo back. I have a right to it, don't I?'

A corollary of the two conditions for the existence of a right follows from the fact that one traditionally accepted interpretation of the term 'rights' is that all rights imply obligations—though not vice versa (for example, Hohfeld 1923; Hart 1982: 80, fn.7; Rawls 1972: 113; O. O'Neill 1996: Ch. 5).[12] Most rights—and certainly those that are relevant in the context of rights to specific environmental assets—are what are known, following Hohfeld, as 'claim rights'. They are the counterpart of valid claims, on legal or moral grounds, to have or obtain something, or to act in a certain way. This implies that somebody or some institution is under an obligation to provide or permit whatever is claimed. If *X* has a universal right, such as a right to free speech, everybody has an obligation to allow him to say what he likes. If *X* has a right to a specific object or service, some person or institution has an obligation to ensure that *X* can exert his right. In other words, the existence of a right is a sufficient condition for the existence of an obligation.

But it is not a necessary condition. In the above example of the destruction of the toy dodo, it may well be that Tommy has a moral right to compensation for the destruction of his toy dodo and it may well be that somebody, such as Billy's parents, had a moral obligation to provide the compensation. We do not dispute any of that. But since the right, if there is one, cannot be to the object that has been destroyed, the obligation cannot be to restore it.

What are the implications of this view of rights for certain long-range environmental problems? Suppose somebody had made preparations to set off a bomb in, say, two hundred years' time, or buried some radioactive nuclear waste in an unsafe location. This would harm a lot of people who do not yet

---

[12] Reference is sometimes made to the concept of 'manifesto rights' introduced by Feinberg in 1970, which need not be correlated with counterpart duties (see for example see Baier 1981: 182, fn3, and Feinberg 1970/1998: 612).

exist. But it would be wrong to say that their rights not to be harmed had been violated. For since they did not exist when the delayed-action bomb was planted they could not be said to have any rights.

Of course, it would still be a very wicked thing for anybody to do. One has a moral obligation not to behave in a way that might inflict grievous harm on people, however removed from us they may be in time or space. But violating this moral obligation does not necessarily imply violating somebody's rights. Like many others we do not subscribe to the special view of rights according to which rights, and their counterpart obligations, exhaust the whole of morality. We would accept that a rights-based morality is seriously deficient in many respects. One can think of innumerable situations in which one's behaviour will be influenced by some conception of what our moral obligations are, without necessarily believing that somebody or other must have some corresponding rights.

To start with a trivial example, one may allow one's neighbour to use one's telephone or toilet if his own is out of order without believing that he has any 'right' to do so. We would do so out of simple benevolence and neighbourly helpfulness and fraternity. At a more dramatic extreme, if we are walking along the beach and see somebody in danger of drowning in the sea we have a moral obligation to go to his assistance if we can, even though the person in danger may not have any 'right' to expect such assistance.

In a classic article on rights Herbert Hart (1984: 82) argued that

. . . we should not extend to animals and babies who it is wrong to ill-treat the notion of a right to proper treatment, for the moral situation can be simply and adequately described here by saying that it is wrong or that we ought not to ill-treat them . . . If common usage sanctions talk of the rights of animals or babies it makes an idle use of the expression 'a right', which will confuse the situation with other different moral situations where the expression 'a right' has a specific force and cannot be replaced by the other moral expressions which I have mentioned.

Thus one may be justified in believing that the failure of past generations to take adequate account of the effect of their activities on our welfare was morally deplorable. But that is not the same as saying that all such past acts of commission or omission represented ancient violations of our rights. We may deplore somebody refusing to allow a neighbour to use his telephone to make an urgent call but this does not mean that we believe the neighbour had a right to do so. Whatever rights future generations may have in the future they have none now, and such rights as they will have to any asset or resources must be restricted to rights over what is available when they are alive.

Furthermore, as we shall argue at greater length in later chapters, the moral obligations that any generation has towards future generations do not, anyway, include an obligation to bequeath to them specific assets (Parfit 1984). Insofar as the Mauritians had any moral obligations towards unborn generations it was an obligation not to behave in a way that condemned them to poverty or were likely to inflict serious harm on them. Depriving them of clean drinking water or breathable air or other primary resources for which no substitutes could conceivably become available would indeed be a violation of their moral obligations to posterity. But depriving them of the opportunity to see live dodos would not.

The Non-existence of Future People

The consequences of ignoring the significance of the non-existence of future generations is clearly seen in many of the arguments used to justify attributing rights to unborn people. For example, one widely quoted authority on intergenerational equity, Edith Brown-Weiss, refers to the Preamble to the Universal Declaration of Human Rights, which states that 'Whereas recognition of the inherent dignity and of the equal and inalienable rights of all members of the human family is the foundation of freedom, justice and peace in the world'; she then goes on to argue that the 'reference to all members of the human family has a temporal dimension, which brings all generations within its scope' (Brown-Weiss 1989: 25). But future generations—of unborn people—are not 'members of the human family'. They are not members of any family, or of any tennis club or national legislature or of anything at all. They do not exist. In the absence of some global catastrophe there *will* be members of the human family in the future, but whether or not they can be said to *have* rights here and now is the whole problem and cannot be simply side-stepped in the way that Professor Brown-Weiss tries to do.

The same objection applies to Annette Baier's (1981: 174) conclusion that 'So far I have found no conceptual reason for disallowing talk of the rights of future persons. Neither their nonpresence, nor our ignorance of *who* exactly they are, nor our uncertainty concerning how many of them there are, rules out the appropriateness of recognizing rights on their part'. In fact Baier is mistaken. There is no uncertainty at all as to how many future persons there *are*. There aren't any. It is true that, in the future, there probably *will* be very many. (In fact, one objection to according rights to people who are not yet born is that there may be so many of them!). But, by definition, future people have not arrived yet.

The notion that unborn people can have rights is rather like thinking about unborn people as some special class of people waiting out in the wings for the cue for them to enter on to the stage and play their many parts. But there is no such class of people as unborn people. In his devastating critique of the notion of attributing rights to future generations Hillel Steiner (1983: 159) put it admirably in saying that 'In short, it seems mistaken to think of future persons as being already out there, anxiously awaiting either victimization by our self-indulgent prodigality or salvation through present self-denial'.

It is true that there are borderline cases of beings who do exist but to whom the attribution of rights may be debatable. For example, in the case of babies or animals or seriously handicapped people anywhere it may often be impossible for them to exercise any of the prerogatives that normally ought to accompany the possession of rights. Consequently there is legitimate room for debate as to whether handicapped people or babies or animals can be said to have rights or only interests that moral considerations require to be respected. This means that it is not clear-cut how far one should attribute rights only to people who are able to claim to them or exercise them or complain if they are denied the exercise of them or authorize somebody else to exercise them in their place, or even waive them.

As Feinberg (1974/1981: 140) says, 'In between the clear cases of rocks and normal human beings . . . is a spectrum of less obvious cases, including some bewildering borderline ones. Is it meaningful or conceptually possible to ascribe rights to our dead ancestors? To individual animals? To whole species of animals? To plants? To idiots and madmen? To foetuses? To generations yet unborn?'

But some of these categories—namely, 'dead ancestors' or 'generations yet unborn'—do not seem to be borderline cases. Surely they fall into a different logical category. It may be *physically* impossible for a small child or a handicapped person to claim a right or to delegate it to somebody else, but it is *logically* impossible for a member of a distant future generation to do so.[13]

Indeed, insofar as ordinary adults can be said to have a moral right to something or other, it must presumably mean that they have a moral right to choose whether to exercise the right, or claim to exercise it, or complain if they are denied the exercise of that right, or authorize somebody else to exercise the right in their place, or even waive the right. In practice, of course, many people today are unable to exercise their moral rights. But it would not be impossible for them to do so if the regimes in which they live changed. There is no logical obstacle. But given the flow of time it is not *logically* possible for us to insist that inhabitants of Mauritius three centuries ago refrain from hunting the dodo or take action to preserve it, on the grounds that its extinction around the end of the seventeenth century deprived us of our right to see it. Similarly, we could not, if we so wished, waive our right to see a live dodo by saying 'OK. Go ahead. Hunt it if you like. We think it is a rather silly bird anyway'.[14] Again, this is a logical impossibility, not a question of whether, in practice, one can exercise some right.

---

[13] Readers may need to be reminded that we are abstracting here from the problem of overlapping generations and hence the rights that younger members of any generation may have in relation to older people alive at the same time—their parents, for example.

[14] This point was developed by Hillel Steiner (1983).

The Defence of the Rights of Future Generations

In spite of the argument of the last two sections, some eminent philosophers or authorities on intergenerational 'equity' explicitly or implicitly believe that future generations can be said to have rights.[15] Most of the defenders of the rights of future generations base their argument partly on the fact that future generations *will* have 'interests', interpreted very widely to mean anything that might be believed, rightly or wrongly, to add to one's sense of well-being. For example, the distinguished philosopher, Joel Feinberg, who is also the author of authoritative articles on the concept of 'rights', writes of the interests of future generations that, 'The identity of the owners of these interests is now necessarily obscure, but the fact of their interest-ownership is crystal clear, and that is all that is necessary to certify the coherence of present talk about their rights'. He concludes by saying that, 'Philosophers have not helped matters by arguing that animals and future generations are not the kinds of beings who can have rights now, that they don't presently qualify for membership, even "auxiliary membership", in our moral community' (Feinberg 1974/1981: 148–9).[16]

But there seem to be two objections to the argument that because future generations *will* have interests they must *have* rights now.[17] First, having interests is, at best, merely a necessary condition for having rights contemporaneously, not a sufficient condition. Many people have an interest in seeing the horse they have backed to win a race winning it. But they have no right to such an outcome and, indeed, it would be internally inconsistent to maintain that they did. It is not necessary to scrutinize the border-lines between 'interests', 'needs', 'desires' and so on in order to see that 'If we had rights to all that is necessary for the good life, rights would be too extensive' (Griffin 1986: 227).

Second, the fact that future generations will have interests in the future, and may well have rights in the future, does not mean that they can have interests today, that is, before they are born. It may well be that having certain interests implies having certain rights. But future generations do not at this point in time—as politicians like to say—*have* any interests.

And the weakness in the argument that future generations have 'rights' because they have interests cannot be dispelled by the assertion that their rights or interests are being represented today by environmentalist pressure groups and the like. It is *logically* impossible, as well as physically impossible, for future generations to delegate the protection of their rights to somebody

---

[15] The selection of previously published articles brought together in Partridge (1981) contains several arguing for rights of future generations by, for example, G. K. Pletcher, Annette Baier, Mary Ann Warren, and others, notably Joel Feinberg.

[16] The same argument is advanced at length by James Sterba (1980; 1998).

[17] See, in particular, Feinberg (1974/1981) and Elliot (1989).

alive today. Unborn people cannot delegate anything, in the same way that they cannot *do—in the present tense*—anything. Even if we thought that our moral right to see a live dodo had been violated by people living in Mauritius three centuries ago, we doubt if we could find a lawyer, even in the USA, to lodge a complaint about this violation of our right.

Of course, anybody can *claim* to represent the interests of future generations, but that is another matter. As it happens we claim to do so. But our view of what is in the best interests of future generations happens to differ considerably from the view advocated by environmental activists.[18] In later chapters we set out what policies, in our opinion, are likely to be in the best interests of future generations. These policies attach very different priorities to those usually stressed in environmental discourse. Roughly speaking, and recognizing that it makes little sense to rank broad aggregative objectives, we believe that, by and large, the most valuable bequest we can make to future generations would be decent societies characterized by just institutions and respect for the basic human rights enumerated in international conventions. But we do not claim that, in advocating such policies, we are representing the 'rights' of future generations, let alone that our mere advocacy demonstrates that future generations do have any rights today.

Indeed, one feature of having 'rights' is that they confer a degree of freedom and power to shape one's own life according to one's own view of what makes life worth living. In other words, they give one choice and freedom to act in pursuit of one's chosen goals. We should not, therefore, prejudge how future generations will want to exercise their choices. The policy most be consistent, therefore, with respect for the rights that future people will have is one that concentrates on bequeathing institutions that give members of future generations as much freedom in their lives as is compatible with maximum freedom for others.[19]

Some weak arguments against conferring rights to future generations have been effectively criticized by some pro-rights advocates, and we wish explicitly to disassociate ourselves from them. In particular, we would not want to make use of the argument that rights are usually rights of identifiable individuals: for example, the basic prima facie moral right to life or liberty of everybody living today, or the moral right of certain classes of people to special consideration on account of their needs or functions that society has

---

[18] As de-Shalit (2000: 136–7) rightly points out, this is the weakness in the suggestion often made to appoint proxy representatives of future generations in the interests of ensuring that decisions affecting future generations are made on a more 'democratic' basis. For we believe that *real* future generations are more likely to prefer our view of what will be in their interests than those of the Green activists who claim to represent them.

[19] This follows a point made by Steiner, who goes further than this and says that 'Thus it is self-contradictory to identify a present person's act as obligatory within a future person's domain, and then to remove it from that domain by denying that future person the choice as to whether or not it should be performed' (Steiner 1983: 155–6).

vested in them. We accept that, strictly speaking, 'rights' can be attributed only to individuals. But, as most defenders of the rights of future generations have correctly argued, this is not a reason for rejecting those rights.[20]

Similarly, we do not wish to deploy the argument that the tastes and preferences of future generations may not be the same as ours. We are also quite ready to assume that they will have preferences that, in essentials, are likely to be similar to ours so that they will also have interests that, within limits, we can anticipate. It is also true that the policies that we adopt now will affect their interests one way or another. In our view this suffices to impose on us a moral obligation to take account of how far our policies will do so. But that is not the same as saying that this moral obligation has to be based on any 'rights' that future generations may be believed to have and which, therefore, must have the hierarchical status usually attached to rights and that can override some of the interests of people alive today.[21]

4. Rights or Obligations?

One tradition in ethics is that rights and obligations—or duties—are just two sides of the same coin.[22] Not merely do all rights imply obligations—which, as indicated above, is virtually uncontroversial—but all obligations imply counterpart rights, which is far more controversial. According to this tradition it does not matter much which side one chooses. Both terms describe a particular kind of relationship between people. The obligations and rights do not arise out of the independently moral character of any particular actions to be taken but out of the relationship between the parties in question. For example, we may be under an obligation to keep a promise to perform a certain action that might not, in itself, be desirable. It is our relationship to the specific person to whom we have made the promise that imposes an obligation on us.

On this view, therefore, the choice between the 'rights' approach and the 'obligations' approach is basically a matter of from whose point of view one looks at this relationship. Or, depending on the context, one approach may be more useful than the other. It may be politically more persuasive to talk

---

[20] This is lucidly argued in Baier (1981), Dunn (1999: 77), and Sterba (1998: 56–7), and the general question of rights and obligations to people whose identity is not known is dealt with fully by O. O'Neill (1996: sec. 4.5). Any number of examples can illustrate the point, such as the fact that the police may not know the identity of any member of the public who may need their services to protect some right that is being threatened (Sterba 1998: 56).

[21] Thus we can accept the first part but not the last part of Mary Anne Warren's (1981: 271) argument that 'To say that merely potential people are not the sort of things which can possibly have moral rights is by no means to imply that we have no obligation toward people of future generations, *or that they (will) have no rights that can be violated by things which we do now*' (emphasis added).

[22] This tradition is clearly set out, and challenged, in O. O'Neill (1996: 128ff.).

about rights rather than obligations. Or it may be preferable from the point of view of expository convenience. For example, if we are walking on the grass in a park where this is permitted and some officious busybody rebukes us for doing so, we are quite likely to reply 'But we have a right to walk on the grass here'. We are unlikely to reply 'Everybody has a universal obligation not to prevent our walking on the grass here'. Many of the people we meet in our local park in Oxford would understand the latter formulation, but might still give us a funny look if we were to use it.

If one accepted the view that all obligations imply counterpart rights, then if future generations cannot be said to have any 'rights' it would be a waste of time thinking about our obligations towards them. But most people would accept, in our opinion rightly, the view to which we have already referred above, namely, that we can have moral obligations that do not correspond to anybody else's rights, such as our moral obligation to go to the aid of somebody even if the person concerned may not be able to appeal to any right to our assistance.[23] Some of these moral obligations may be described as 'virtues'.

One can also enumerate all manner of characteristics of our natures or of our actions that most of us would regard as 'virtues' but that do not imply that somebody has any counterpart rights. These might include, for example, what O. O'Neill refers to as 'devotion as a virtue of family life . . . or of self-possession as a virtue for weathering misplaced hostility' or what she calls the 'Executive virtues [which] might include self-respect, self-control and decisiveness; courage and endurance, as well as numerous contemporary conceptions of autonomy; insight and self-knowledge . . .' (O. O'Neill, 1996: 149, 187ff).

But how far do the virtues that lie outside the domain of a rights-based morality impose obligations on us? For, to put it crudely, it may be nice to be virtuous but not morally obligatory. We may admire the virtuous person but not feel that somebody lacking in the same virtues is, in some way, failing to carry out his obligations. For example some people may believe that for people—usually other people—at a certain stage in their lives and in certain situations, celibacy is an admirable virtue. But it is difficult to see why, in all such circumstances, it would also be an obligation. And in this case it may sometimes be difficult to see who has the counterpart rights. Similarly, we may admire somebody's courage in climbing a difficult mountain, or publicly proclaiming an unpopular view, or making donations to charity, without feeling that he is under *obligation* to show any of these virtues.

But it is not enough to say that while rights, and their counterpart obligations, do not exhaust the whole of morality, all that is required to complete

---

[23] This is, of course, open to dispute, especially when, in some countries, it is a criminal offence not to go to the aid of people in need of it in certain circumstances.

the account of morality is to leave scope for virtues, which can be added on without necessarily imposing obligations on us. There may be what are known as 'imperfect obligations', namely, moral obligations that do not imply counterpart rights. For example, as indicated above, many people take the view that we have moral obligations towards animals or babies even though they cannot be said to have the same rights, in the normal sense of the term, as ordinary human beings. Treating them decently and with compassion is not merely one of the innumerable 'virtues' that should be tacked on to rights in order to arrive at a satisfactory conception of morality. It is more than that. It is what O. O'Neill describes as a 'required virtue'.[24]

How one should draw the boundary line between required virtues and other virtues raises complex questions that we do not need to discuss here. For present purposes it must suffice to say that, in our view, the fact that future generations *will* have interests is a sufficient reason for us to take those interests into account in policies that we adopt now, including policies affecting the environment. We could say either (1) that we *ought* to take the interests of future generations into account because this would constitute supererogatory virtue and it is a good thing to be virtuous, or (2) that we *ought* to do so because it is a 'required virtue', that is, one that constitutes a moral *obligation*. But whichever position we adopt does not seem to make any difference to the identification of which particular policies should be pursued in order to take account of the interests that future generations will have. It is the substance of our obligations to future generations that is important for our argument, not the way they should be classified in the context of philosophical discourse.

5. The Practical Advantages of the Obligations Approach

Many people confronted with the argument that future generations do not have rights but that, nevertheless, we are under a moral obligation to take account of the interests that they will have, question whether this is, in Hazlitt's famous phrase, a distinction without a difference. Like Baier (1981: 181), they may ask, What does it matter? But in our view it does makes a major difference.

For rights are invariably regarded as having some 'trumping' power over mere 'interests'. They constitute a constraint on how far decisions should be based on a comparison of interests alone. If X's interest in letting Y die is

---

[24] A detailed enumeration of what these might include and why some virtues are 'required' as distinct from being merely supererogatory is set out in O. O'Neill (1996: Ch. 5).

greater than *Y*'s interest in staying alive—as in the sort of situations discussed in connection with the euthanasia issue—taking purely an interest perspective would mean that it would be right to hasten *Y*'s death. But this would be violating *Y*'s fundamental right to life. If *A*'s interest in demolishing a group of old cottages in order to construct far superior accommodation for lots of families were greater than the interest of the owner of one of the cottages to go on living in it, a mere comparison of interests would require that the cottages be demolished. But this would be violating the widely accepted right of the owner of the cottage in question to go on living in his property unless he is persuaded to leave it voluntarily, for example by suitable financial inducements.

If, therefore, we deny future generations any rights, this means that they cannot have claims on the present generation that have the special status of the kind that one normally attaches to rights. Thus the interests of the present generation, particularly of the poorest people alive today, should not be sacrificed on the grounds that future generations have certain rights to inherit, say, the existing number of species of beetles. More generally, one should not lightly ask members of the present generation to sacrifice such rights as we believe they may have, or the important interests that they certainly have to pursue their conception of the good life, on account of some supposed right of future generations. If people do have rights they are members of the present generation (de-Shalit 1995: 117). In any case, as David Miller (1999: 153) has pointed out, if future generations were to be granted rights to environmental assets in particular, the present generation cannot be denied similar rights. Merrills (1996: 33) put it very forcefully:

Instead of treating future generations as shadowy rights-holders in order to give our current preoccupations an air of disinterested respectability, we would therefore be better occupied reviewing the claims to rights of those currently alive, together with their various moral responsibilities, which may, of course, include responsibilities to future generations.

The second reason why it is important to switch from a rights perspective to a less constrained *interests* perspective is that it substantially changes the relative importance that we ought to attach to our various obligations to future generations—although, as we repeat at various points, it does not make sense to rank objectives defined very broadly. For example, it would not make sense to say that every single violation of human rights, however trivial, ought to be remedied before taking action to prevent any environmental damage, however serious, or vice versa. Nevertheless, it does make sense to say that, on the whole, the specific individual applications of certain broadly defined objectives are more important than the specific applications of certain other objectives. And it is in this sense that we argue in later chapters that we ought to attach more importance to non-environmental objectives than would be the case if we were to insist that future generations have rights to inherit the present state of the environment. For, to jump the gun somewhat, we shall argue in later chapters that the safest predictions that can be made about future interests and threats to them imply that, on the whole, the extension and protection of basic human rights are likely to be far more enduring and serious contributions to human welfare than environmental preservation would be.

Even if one remained unconvinced by the theoretical arguments, there are practical advantages in concentrating on our obligations rather than on rights. The 'obligations' point of view focuses our attention on the question of *whose* obligations we are talking about. Indeed, the obligations approach is usually much more relevant to practical policy as well as to individual behaviour. It applies, for example, to the alleged 'rights' of animals or children, where, as pointed out above, the vocabulary of moral obligation or natural duty is perfectly adequate for purposes of specifying the way we should treat them, as well as being more practically oriented. It is true that in many such cases some of us have a special relationships with the people or animals concerned that imposes an additional moral obligation to be concerned with their welfare and protection. But this is not always the case.

Thus, although it may be more effective in political discourse to talk about rights rather than obligations, there is a danger that it is too easy to do so without specifying who has the counterpart obligations. And if one is genuinely concerned with policies and action, rather than just with fine rhetoric and noble gestures, there is not much point in talking about 'rights' unless the counterpart obligations of those people or institutions are clearly identified and spelt out. In some cases, of course, the obligation is on everybody. This is the case with basic human, or 'universal', rights, such as the right to life or the maximum liberty consistent with equal liberty to others, and other rights set out in the Universal Declaration of Human Rights adopted by the United Nations, and similar international conventions.[25] In other cases there may be specific rights that imply specific obligations on identifiable people or institutions. For example, it does make sense to talk about the moral right of all women to equal treatment in working pay and conditions, since it is clear that it is employers who should implement this right and that governments have a duty to ensure that this right is respected.[26]

However, it is often more difficult to defend the notion of rights of the kind often known as 'welfare' rights, which are often alleged rights to specific

---

[25] See an excellent survey of the issue of 'rights' in political philosophy in Plant (1991: Chs 3 and 7).

[26] The relationship between rights and the identification of whoever has the counterpart obligations is, of course, clearer in the case of most legal rights, such as the rights of women in some cases to ante-natal care, but we are not concerned here with legal rights.

goods and services (Parfit 1984: 365). And as regards future generations, even if they could be said to have 'rights' today, they clearly cannot do anything about it now, so it is more productive to concentrate attention on the obligations of the present generation. Only human beings alive today can have the capacity for action to discharge these obligations and to create the necessary institutions for doing so. So it is more productive to put the spotlight on the humans who have the obligations in order to identify in more detail what these obligations consist of and what sort of policies, in what domains, are required in order to honour them. For example, insofar as we have obligations to future generations, including those concerning the environment, collective action would be required to build and operate the appropriate institutions and to disseminate the appropriate attitudes that will be needed in order to honour these obligations. 'Although the rhetoric of rights has become the most widely used way of talking about justice in the last fifty years, it is the discourse of obligations that addresses the practical question *who ought to do what for whom?*' (O. O'Neill 1997: 132).

6. Conclusion

We have argued that future generations cannot be said to have rights, in spite of learned, if minority, opinions to the contrary. But rights do not exhaust the whole of morality. And insofar as our policies affect any other sentient beings, whether present or future, we ought to accord them 'moral standing' and take account of their interests. Thus, we have a moral obligation to take account of the interests of future generations in our policies, including those policies that affect the environment. From some points of view it may seem that it makes very little practical difference whether we think in terms of the rights of future generations or in terms of our obligations to them. However, we argue that, apart from the theoretical dangers of grounding our obligations to future generations on the seemingly indefensible view that they can have rights, there are also practical advantages in concentrating on obligations. It forces us to focus on who exactly has these obligations.

Furthermore, denial of the rights of future generations is a crucial step in our argument, set out in the next chapter, that the interests of future generations cannot be protected within the framework of any theory of international justice. The next chapter also critically examines two attempts, by John Rawls and Brian Barry, to defend a theory of intergenerational justice.

3

Justice Between Generations

1. Introduction

In Chapter 2 we argued that it would be unwise to base the case for our being under moral obligation to take account of the interests of future generations on the notion that they have 'rights'. The reason given for this is that future generations—or, strictly speaking, the individuals who will constitute future generations—cannot be said to 'have' any rights, since they cannot have, in the present tense, anything at all. And any coherent theory of justice attributes rights to those whose interests are to be protected within the framework of that theory. Insofar, therefore, that unborn people cannot be said to have any rights then their interests cannot be protected within the framework of that theory. Any attempt to construct a theory of justice encompassing groups, such as future generations, to which one could not attribute rights must, therefore, run into serious difficulties, if not be doomed to failure.

However, given that 'rights' and justice do not exhaust the whole of morality, this may not matter. For it does not preclude our having a moral obligation to take account of the interests that future generations will have and of the impact that our policies may have on them.[1] One might well ask, at the outset, therefore, as does Brian Barry (1978: 205), whether there is really any need for a theory of intergenerational justice and whether, instead, one could not be satisfied with defining our obligations towards future generations on the basis of common humanity. Barry's view is that such a theory is possible and also that it is necessary. For the reasons set out above, our view is that it is neither.

Probably the most extensive attempt to construct a theory of intergenerational justice has been presented by John Rawls (1972). But even he believed that the problem of justice between generations subjected ethical theory to 'severe if not impossible tests' (Rawls 1972: 284). But this did not deter him

---

[1] While this conclusion—namely, that the impossibility of appealing to intergenerational justice does not rule out our having obligations to future generations—is similar to that reached by Alan Holland (1999: 67), the route by which the conclusion is reached is entirely different. Holland rejects intergenerational justice on the ground that it is not a feasible guide in practice, whereas we are rejecting intergenerational justice on more fundamental theoretical grounds.

from attempting to formulate a theory of 'just savings' which was designed to distribute justly among generations the rate at which they would save for the benefit of succeeding generations. In later sections of this chapter we shall critically examine both Rawls's and Barry's attempts to overcome the difficulties of formulating a theory of intergenerational justice. Before doing so, however, we shall briefly discuss, in the next section of this chapter, one or two well-known difficulties.

2. Familiar Problems of Intergenerational Justice

We must begin by deciding how widely we want to draw the net around theories of justice. We shall first follow Barry (1999: 94) in accepting that 'the questions about intergenerational justice that are liable to create distinctive moral problems are very likely to be issues of justice in the narrow sense: cases where there is (or is believed to be) an intergenerational conflict of interest'. For example, it would clearly be absurd to say that it was unjust that somebody living in some century was not given the same opportunity as somebody living in another century to apply for exactly the same position of power and responsibility.

On the other hand, how far we should require that the theory of justice in question should be one that is circumscribed by the conditions set out by Hume and referred to by Rawls as the 'circumstances of justice' is much more debatable. The main argument of this chapter—namely, the rights-justice relationship combined with the impossibility of attributing rights to unborn people—appears to rule out any theory of intergenerational justice. But even if our argument is rejected, acceptance of the Humean conditions would appear to exclude any theory of intergenerational justice.

For the Humean circumstances of justice are described by Rawls as the 'normal conditions under which human cooperation is both possible and necessary . . . Thus many individuals *coexist together at the same time* on a definite geographical territory' (Rawls 1972: 126; emphasis added). The objective circumstances of the Humean concept of justice also include rough equality of power between the parties to the cooperation. For otherwise cooperation would be minimal or non-existent; the stronger would simply dominate the weaker.

This is related to a further Humean condition, namely, that people pursue their own interests. If, for example, conditions of inequality of power prevail but, nevertheless, the weaker are treated with decency and respect without any consideration of the advantages that the stronger will derive from their benevolent behaviour, this does not mean that the situation is more 'just'. It merely means that the stronger people are behaving with decency and compassion according to some highly commendable instincts or sense of moral duty. Thus on Hume's conditions of justice if peoples' behaviour towards future generations is motivated by considerations such as love for their children, this may be morally admirable but is nothing to do with justice. If, for example, we bequeath assets to our children, or future generations in general, because we are motivated by ties of affection or benevolence, we are not doing so on account of respect for some principles of justice.

On this conception of justice, principles of justice constitute that part of morality that enables people with conflicting ends to coexist, under conditions of some scarcity, in peace and harmony. It is not a way of removing their conflicting interests. It is a set of principles that will enable people to agree on the allocation of rights to whatever desirable assets or opportunities might be the source of conflict and be the subject of dispute. This enables people to settle this kind of potential dispute peacefully, if not amicably. It enables them to reconcile their conflicting interests and different conceptions of the 'good' without violence or infringement of basic rights to life and liberty or other threats to their peace and security.

It is difficult to see how intergenerational justice could be brought within the scope of these Humean conditions. Abstracting from the case of overlapping generations, it is obvious that one cannot talk sensibly about the relative degrees of power that different generations have over each other. Future generations cannot harm or benefit us, so there can be no question of our having to make any sort of concession or sacrifice in order to ensure their cooperation in any common endeavour. As Rawls (1972: 291) puts it, 'We can do something for posterity but it can do nothing for us. This situation is unalterable, and so the question of justice does not arise'.

Barry (1978: 239) accepts that the Humean 'circumstances of justice' would leave no room for justice between generations, but this is one of his reasons for rejecting them. He would prefer to broaden the scope of a theory of justice so that it would not exclude the notion of injustice in relationships between parties of unequal power. For example, the treaties signed between Western settlers and indigenous peoples in many parts of the world may well have been the best that the weaker parties could accept under the circumstances and to which, therefore, they may have been obliged to enter, but they should still be regarded as 'unjust' (Barry 1989). Barry's rejection of the Humean circumstances of justice does at least appear to give him a sporting chance of constructing an intergenerational theory of justice, and we shall discuss his solution below, following a discussion of Rawls's attempt to construct a theory of intergenerational justice.

Rawls's position on the implications of the 'Humean circumstances' for intergenerational justice is more ambivalent. The manner in which he tried to devise some rules of 'just savings' between generations in spite of the Humean circumstances, however, already relied much more on his concept of justice as fairness than on justice as a contract of mutual advantage between participating agents.

The rest of this chapter argues that no solution is possible, that two major attempts—by Rawls and Barry—to find one do not succeed, but that this is no great obstacle to identifying the priorities among our moral obligations to future generations.

3. The Rights-Justice Relationship

There are, of course, very many theories of justice. But a central feature of most, and possibly all, serious theories of justice is the attribution of moral 'rights'. Theories of justice differ with respect to the criteria by which these rights are allocated, or how far they can be allocated to groups of individuals, or institutions, rather than just to individuals. But the attribution of 'rights' is a crucial element in any theory of justice.

For example, Rawls's classic exposition of what a theory of justice consists of begins with several references to this relationship between justice and rights, as when, for example, he refers to 'the rights secured by justice' (Rawls 1972: 4), or to the conception of justice that motivates people to try to affirm 'a characteristic set of principles for assigning basic rights and duties', and so on (Rawls 1972: 5), or 'For us the primary subject of justice is the way in which the major social institutions distribute fundamental rights and duties' (Rawls 1972: 7), and so on.[2]

And even if explicit attribution of rights is not made, theories of justice implicitly attribute them according to some criteria or other. For example, in a well-known article Gregory Vlastos (1984: 44) gave a list of 'well-known maxims of distributive justice' such as 'To each according to his *need*' or 'To each according to his *worth*' and so on. Indeed, Nozick (1974: 164) has pointed out that the different theories of distributive justice can be seen as differences in the word (or expression) that is inserted at the end of statements such as 'to each according to his . . .'.

It is obvious that all such principles of justice imply certain rights. Consider, for example, the first principle, 'To each according to his needs'. Once the 'needs' in question have been defined and agreed, anybody who could demonstrate that he or she had the requisite needs would have a moral

---

[2] In similar vein, Vlastos (1984: 60–1) writes, 'Whenever the question of regard, or disregard, for substantially affected rights does not arise, the question of justice or injustice does not arise', or 'Again, whenever one is in no position to govern one's action by regard for rights, the question of justice or injustice does not arise', or 'A major feature of my definition of "just" is that it makes the answer to "is x just?" (where x is any action, decision, etc.) strictly dependent on the answer to another question: "what are the rights of those who are substantially affected by x?" '.

'right' to be accorded the corresponding amount of whatever was supposed to be given according to that need—freedom, income, medical care, or whatever. Thus instead of specifying theories of justice in the form of the maxims indicated above, one could have equally have specified them in the form 'Everybody has a right to what he needs', or 'Everybody has a right to what he merits', and so on. The same applies to any of the other maxims on Vlastos's list, or, indeed, to any other coherent principle of distributive justice. Consider, for example, a contractarian theory of justice. There are various forms of such theories—'actual', 'hypothetical', 'ideal' contracts, and so on— but, with minor adjustments that are irrelevant to the argument here, they can all be represented in one of the maxims on Vlastos's list, namely 'To everybody according to the *agreement* he has made' (Vlastos 1984: 44). This can then be converted into a proposition about rights in the same way as the other maxims specified above.

In short, a defining feature of any coherent and morally acceptable candidate for a theory of justice is that it attributes rights, and hence counterpart duties. But if, as has been argued in the last chapter, future generations do not have rights, any attempt to protect their interests within the framework of a theory of justice is doomed to fail. In sections 4 and 5 we shall examine the Rawlsian attempt and this will be followed by a discussion of the difficulties which we think are encountered in Barry's attempt. In concentrating on these two attempts to construct a theory of justice between generations we do not wish to imply that other attempts are not valuable contributions to what is obviously a very difficult and novel problem.[3]

4. Rawls on Justice Between Generations

Although Rawls more or less nails his flag to the mast of the Humean circumstances of justice—which means, as pointed out above, that justice does not apply between generations—he does propose a theory of what would be a 'just' rate of saving that each generation should make in the interests of succeeding generations, and he also presents it as if it emerges from some sort of contract between participating agents.

Indeed, at first sight it might seem that Rawls's famous device of the 'original position' could be just what one needs in order to overcome some of the obstacles to an intergenerational contractarian theory of justice mentioned above in connection with the Humean circumstances of justice.

---

[3] An excellent survey of various theories of intergenerational justice, including his own version of a communitarian theory, is provided by Avner de-Shalit (1995). As well as Rawls's theory, other notable contributions to the debate discussed in some detail by de-Shalit are those of David Gauthier and Jane English.

As is well-known, a central element in Rawlsian theory was to conceive of a hypothetical contract as being drawn up *not* by people who knew what their particular situation in life happened to be, but by people in what he called the 'original position', behind a 'veil of ignorance'. In such a situation they would not know to what particular status in life they would subsequently be called. Hence, they would not try to press for rules of justice that favoured this or that particular class of person. 'No one knows his situation in society nor his natural assets, and therefore no one is in a position to tailor principles to his advantage' (Rawls, 1972: 139).

This device suggests the image of a group of people drawing up rules for playing some game without knowing in advance what particular abilities or disabilities they will have when the game begins—for example, whether one will be fleet of foot, or very heavy, or possess good hand-eye coordination, or be quick thinking, or good at mental arithmetic, or whatever. But since they agreed on the rules in question none of them could have cause to complain that the rules were 'unfair' if, when the game commenced, some of them discovered that the rules did not favour the particular skills that they possessed.

Now different generations do not co-exist, so they neither can nor need fear each other, or agree with each other over the rules governing their relationship that would be necessary in order that they can live harmoniously together. Nevertheless, they might have conflicting interests, notably over the rate at which earlier generations should save or economize in their use of scarce resources in the interests of later generations. And Rawls's device of the 'original position' might make it possible to deduce what rules would be reached by notional representatives of different generations placed behind a 'veil of ignorance' and so not knowing to what generation they will, as it were, eventually belong. The rules they will draw up will thus be 'fair' and 'impartial' in the sense that they will not confer any 'unfair' advantage on any particular generation.

But Rawls himself seems to be somewhat ambivalent about how far his original position device does, in fact, overcome the particular obstacles to a theory of intergenerational justice. At some points Rawls seems to think that it is possible to overcome them. For example, he says,

The persons in the original position have no information as to which generation they belong. These . . . restrictions on knowledge are appropriate in part because questions of social justice arise between generations as well as within them, for example, the question of the appropriate rate of capital saving and of the conservation of natural resources and the environment of nature . . . They must choose principles the consequences of which they are prepared to live with whatever generation they turn out to belong to. (Rawls 1972: 137)

Similarly, he writes later, 'The parties [in the original position] do not know to which generation they belong . . .' and that 'since no one knows to which generation he belongs, the question [of finding a just savings principle] is viewed from the standpoint of each' (Rawls 1972: 287–8).

However, there are difficulties in using the original position in order to arrive at principles of intergenerational justice. The first difficulty is rather technical, and might appear to be nit-picking. But it typifies the sort of peculiar technical problems to which intergenerational justice gives rise. This is that, on some views, the faster the earlier generations are allowed to use up all the Earth's resources, the shorter the time span of the human race—that is, the fewer later generations there will be. Since the rules drawn up, therefore, could reduce the number of generations that are represented in the original position, it cannot constitute a position in which all potential generations are represented.

It is difficult to see, therefore, how one should interpret Rawls's statement that 'All generations are virtually represented in the original position . . . ' (Rawls 1972: 278).[4] If it refers to all the generations that will *actually* come into existence, then rules must already have been drawn up determining how many generations would come into existence. If, instead, it does not refer to all generations that will actually come into existence, it is not clear what other possible restriction on the number of generations would make sense. In order that the rules drawn up by the imaginary participants in the original position have morally binding force for those generations who actually do come into existence, it has to be assumed that the imaginary participants are genuinely representative of those who actually come into existence. But in that case it is difficult to see how they could be allowed, in the thought experiment, to draw up rules that prevent some of them coming into existence, for example by allowing resources to be used up very rapidly. So rules of this kind, or having this effect, cannot be part of the original contract if the contract is still to have morally binding force.[5]

In spite of this rather technical, but possibly decisive, obstacle, Rawls persists with an attempt to lay down some rules, reached in some contractarian framework, concerning the way any generation should take account of the interests of future generations. He does not, as is sometimes alleged,

---

[4] This objection to the use of the 'original position' device in the context of intergenerational justice was made in Beckerman (1983: 15). Brian Barry (1989: 194–5) made the same point clearly: '. . . if we know who the people at the gathering are, the choice of principles must already have somehow been made . . . there may be different numbers of generations under alternative arrangements'. He made a similar point in Barry (1978: 280–1). In both cases his particular objection was being raised in the context of a far more wide-ranging critique of Rawls's position as regards intergenerational justice, most of which we agree with but which we do not reproduce here.

[5] In his survey of various theories of intergenerational justice, de-Shalit rightly points out that the same objection applies to the contractarian solution to the problem of intergenerational justice proposed by Richards. Jane English has attempted to rescue the Rawlsian 'difference principle' in the intergenerational context but, as de-Shalit (1995: 109–10) points out, her solution needs to make motivational assumptions which would mean abandoning the Humean circumstances of justice which Rawls begins by accepting.

attempt to apply his famous 'difference principle', namely, the principle that would be agreed in the original position to the effect that, at any point in time, the only inequalities that are allowed to exist in society are those that will improve the position of the worst off members of society. Rawls (1972: 291) himself points out that the application of the difference principle between generations would lead to quite unacceptable results. For the first generation would presumably be the poorest generation, not being endowed with any starting capital; and if it cut its own consumption in order to invest for the future it would become even poorer. Hence, application of the 'difference principle' between generations would rule out economic growth from the accumulation of capital.[6] But we find that the main proposal he makes in his section on justice between generations, namely his 'just savings' rule, and, in particular, his attempt to fit it into the framework of the original position, is fraught with insuperable difficulties, which we shall discuss in the next section.

5. Rawls's 'Just Savings' Principle

Rawls's main contribution to his section on justice between generations was his famous 'just savings' rule, which is a rule that governs how much each generation should save for the benefit of its successors. Rawls stated,

Each [generation] passes on to the next a fair equivalent in real capital as defined by a just savings principle. (It should be kept in mind here that capital is not only factories and machines, and so on, but also the knowledge and culture, as well as the techniques and skills, that make possible just institutions and the fair value of liberty) . . . The just savings principle can be regarded as an understanding between generations to carry their fair share of the burden of realizing and preserving a just society. (1972: 288–9)

But it is not clear how this just savings principle is derived. Now, as indicated at various points throughout this book, one should not expect any theory of justice, or any ethical theory, to provide precise rules, let alone precise numerical rules, to cover every conceivable practical contingency. But it ought to provide a rough guide to the principles that have to be borne in mind. Unfortunately, Rawls's original (1972) proposed 'just savings' principle does not seem to do even that. For he proposed three methods, without demonstrating why they should lead to mutually consistent results. First, the parties to the original contract represent notional heads of families and seek to come to some sort of mutual agreement on a compromise between what they would like to inherit from their forefathers and what they would be will-

---

[6] See also Brian Barry (1989: 189–202).

ing to save in order to bequeath something to their descendants (Rawls 1972: 128, 289).

But at another point the contracting parties assign '. . . an appropriate rate of accumulation to each level of advance' which depends on the state of society. And it seems to depend on it in two ways. First, 'when people are poor and saving is difficult, a lower rate of saving should be required' (Rawls 1972: 287), which gives us a second formula. In addition, for some unspecified reason savings are apparently related to the need to move towards just institutions; and when these have been achieved no more saving is needed other than what is required to maintain capital intact. But presumably this would mean that less saving is required as society advanced over time, when it would presumably also become richer. This gives us a third formula; so we seem to have three different formulae for determining the appropriate rate of saving for each generation, which are most unlikely to give the same results.[7]

Partly, perhaps, on account of the problems inherent in his original proposals concerning just savings, Rawls revised them in 1993. He abandoned the rather complicated device he used in 1972, in which the parties to the original agreement in the original position '. . . are regarded as representing family lines, say, with ties of sentiment between successive generations'. In its place he proposes that '. . . the parties can be required to agree to a savings principle subject to the further condition that they must want all *previous* generations to have followed it' (Rawls 1993a: 274).[8] In the absence of reasons to the contrary, one must assume that Rawls's latest just savings principle is based on the same self-interest that motivated participants in the original position in his 1972 *TOJ* (e.g. p. 142). Participants in the original position would not like to run the risk of being born into a generation that was impoverished on account of the failure of preceding generations to save as much as they ought to have done [Wissenburg, 1999:176]. The motivational assumption has been dropped.

Rawls's revised just savings principle also resembles a Kantian 'categorical imperative', one well-known version of which is the moral injunction to 'Act only on the maxim through which you can at the same time will that it be a universal law'. Kant, however, would have denied that rational self-interest is the basis of his rule rather than the unavoidable recognition by rational people of an objective moral law. Nevertheless, although there may be a

---

[7] Some of the objections to Rawls's original solution to his just savings rule are succinctly discussed by de-Shalit (1995: 104ff), particularly the objection that his emphasis on the family ties motivation opens up a host of possibilities to other units of loyalty.

[8] We are indebted to Marcel Wissenburg (1999) for drawing our attention to this revision of Rawls's view of the determination of 'just savings'. Rawls states (1993a: 20) that he is indebted to Thomas Nagel and Derek Parfit for having suggested this revision of his just saving rule back in 1972, and that the same idea was proposed independently by Jane English in 1977.

major difference in the underlying motivations by which it is reached, the rule at which the participants in the original position arrive is effectively the same. Rawls's just savings rule would thus share with any attempt to derive a just savings rule that was a form of Kantian categorical imperative a severe limitation on its guidance in real world situations and its power to tell us how to trade-off conflicting moral imperatives. Neither approach tells us enough about what principle any generation could adopt that would 'bite'. It is not demanding too much of any theory of justice to expect that it can provide some rough standard against which the justice, or lack of it, of any institution at any point of time and in any place can be judged. One must not ask for a precise formula, but one must be able to form some idea as to whether any particular procedure is manifestly unjust or not. One can say, for example, that a society in which people are subject to arbitrary arrest, imprisonment, and death violates principles of justice to which almost every rational person would have subscribed before knowing her own particular circumstances. Similarly, the vast majority of rational people would probably also agree that a society is unjust if some people in it are destitute because they are clearly deprived of the freedom and opportunity to use such capacities that they possess.

But although there are many instances where the Kantian test can exclude extreme cases, it still leaves a wide range of intermediate situations on which little agreement could be expected even among rational people. This can apply even in personal decisions, such as striking a balance between how much one thinks one should give to a person in need and how much one thinks one would expect other people to be morally obliged to give to one if one was in need oneself (Nagel 1991: 50). And the difficulty of defining a useful rule somewhere between extremes is far greater when, as is the case here, we need to find a rule that will receive common consent among whole 'generations'.

Even for an individual generation there seem to be insuperable difficulties in assessing how far the actual saving rate is too stingy or too generous. These illustrate the general underlying difficulty of passing from principles of justice that are designed to regulate relations between individuals, to principles of justice that attempt to regulate relations between groups, whether they be nations or generations. This is not a matter of splitting hairs over the definition of a generation, that is, whether we distinguish between the 'older generation' and the 'younger generation', or allow for overlapping generations and so on. For the sake of argument, we shall interpret Rawls's rule as referring to the savings made by more or less all the people living at any moment of time, acknowledging that this will change from minute to minute as some people die and others are born.

Nor is it a matter of the dangers inherent in treating collectivities, such as nations or generations, as if they were individuals, although it is true that a 'generation' cannot have a single consciousness of acting unfairly or otherwise in the same way that an individual can. For the sake of argument we assume throughout that it is legitimate to conceive of all, or most, individuals comprising any generation or any other collective entity as being able to form a view concerning the fairness or otherwise of the behaviour of the entity of which they are members.

The difficulty to which we allude is a different one. It is that it is not possible either in principle or in practice for the individual members of any generation to do more than identify some extreme saving rates as being unjust. The most that individuals could do would be to pass judgement on extreme cases. For example, individual members of the present generation might reject the principle that it should save nothing, let alone have negative savings by running down the world stock of capital, both natural and man-made, since it would not have wanted previous generations to have done so. For this would have meant that we would still be living in Stone-Age conditions—but one prominent environmental philosopher, Baird Callicott (1995: 54) admires the symbiosis between humans and nature that existed in the Stone Age.

At the other extreme we might reject the principle that the present generation as a whole should cut its consumption drastically below the feasible level in order to save a much higher proportion of its total output for purposes of accumulation. For it would not have wanted previous generations, who would usually have been much poorer, to have accepted an even greater burden of saving and accumulation than the one that they actually did. Nor would it be prepared to accept the inevitable sacrifice that this would undoubtedly impose on the vast numbers of very poor people in the world today.

But between these two extremes it is difficult to see what more useful principle any generation would wish to impose on its own saving that would still satisfy the Rawlsian constraint of also wanting previous generations to have followed the same principle. This means that it will usually be impossible for any individual to know whether his 'generation' is saving the 'just' amount.

It is not surprising, in view of the difficulties set out above, that, in the end, Rawls (1972: 286) writes that 'How the burden of capital accumulation and of raising the standard of civilization and culture is to be shared between generations seems to admit of no definite answer'. As he says himself, his 'difference principle' does not apply. His procedural device of the 'original position' is not really coherent as applied to different generations, although Rawls seems to be ambivalent about how far this is the case. And his 'just savings' principle not only does not tell us enough to know what exactly it is, but whatever it is it would seem unable to provide a standard by which the saving rate of any generation can be assessed as being 'just'. And if we simply ask what people behind the veil of ignorance would probably accept as a savings principle, it would probably turn out to be that everybody should be free to save what he liked and that no constraint on this part of personal liberty should be imposed in the interests of some other unspecified objective.

However, although Rawls does not claim to have solved the problem of intergenerational justice he goes on to say that 'It does not follow, however, that certain bounds which impose significant ethical constraints cannot be formulated' (Rawls 1972: 286). And in one very important respect Rawls made an essential contribution to the form that these constraints should take. This is his emphasis on the role of 'natural duties' to contribute towards the development of 'just institutions'. As explained in Chapter 7, these constitute the core of our own view of the relative importance we should attach to our various obligations to future generations. But before coming to this and to other suggested guides to our obligations to future generations, we must also examine a contribution to intergenerational justice recently proposed by a leading authority on theories of justice, who also happens to have tried to present a coherent theory of intergenerational justice.

6. Brian Barry's Approach

Insofar as the Humean conditions for justice imply the exclusion of any scope for intergenerational justice, there are two possibilities. One is to escape the grip of these conditions by some device, such as the Rawlsian 'original position', which purports to deduce what different generations would agree about the 'just savings' rate in some 'ideal' contract drawn up in hypothetical circumstances in which the parties to the contract did not know to which generation they would belong. As we have seen, this escape route seems to run into various obstacles and, in the end, in spite of gestures made in the direction of the original position, Rawls's final suggestion concerning 'just savings' is a version of the Kantian categorical imperative that does not, in fact, seem to provide any useful guidance at all as far as any generation's saving rate is concerned.

The other way of avoiding the conclusion that the Humean conditions do not leave any room for intergenerational justice is simply to deny that Hume's conditions correctly define the scope of justice. As indicated above, Brian Barry rejects the Humean condition of rough equality of power on the grounds that this would exclude, for example, our assessing as 'unjust' the unfavourable treaties imposed on indigenous inhabitants by the more powerful Western settlers in North America. In other words, he broadens the scope of the theory of justice so that it can apply to different generations between whom, clearly, the Humean condition of rough equality of power could not exist.

But while broadening the scope of the theory of justice in order to accommodate intergenerational justice in this respect, Barry narrows it in another respect in order, again, to accommodate intergenerational justice. And he does so in a way that seems inconsistent with his reason for broadening it. For he proposes limiting the scope of intergenerational justice to be only forward looking—that is, so that one can talk about our behaving unjustly towards future generations while questions of justice over the past are ruled out of order. He writes,

... it must be conceded that the expression 'intergenerational justice' is potentially misleading ... It is simply a sort of shorthand for 'justice between the present generation and future generations'. Because of time's arrow, we cannot do anything to make people in the past better off than they actually were, so it is absurd to say that our relation to them could be either just or unjust. (Barry 1999: 107)

But the possibility of rectifying an injustice has nothing to do with judging whether or not there has been an injustice—as Barry accepts when he urges that we should be prepared to judge as 'unjust' the treaties reached between the indigenous people of North America and Western settlers that reflected the vulnerability of the former. Furthermore, if it is logical for us to judge whether our policies affecting future generations are 'just' or not then it would logical for future generations to pass judgement on whether our policies affecting them had been just or not. In that case it must also be logical for us to pass judgement on the justice of any policies pursued by our ancestors that affected us. If it is true to say, in year t, that X is just, then it must be true to say, a hundred years later, that, in year t, X was just.

Obviously what Barry really objects to, therefore, is to the notion of our behaving unjustly towards past generations, with which, of course, one cannot disagree. But if he believes that it is logical to talk about our behaving justly towards future generations then he would have to accept that past generations can be said to have behaved unjustly towards us. In this way his argument would still be consistent. But although this position is logically consistent, is it right?

The reason for thinking it is wrong takes us back to the rights-justice relationship and to the significance of the notion of having rights. As we have argued in the last chapter, at the time the dodo was made extinct we did not exist. Hence, we did not then have any rights. Hence, the inhabitants of the Mauritius could not have violated our rights in allowing the dodo to become extinct. Hence, their behaviour was not a transgression of the principles of justice as we conceive them, namely, principles that govern the rights and duties of members of any particular society. Of course, we may deplore the failure of the Mauritians to do more to protect the dodo on our behalf, and we may believe that they failed to honour their moral obligations to take account of the interests that we would have. But that is a different matter.

Another way of looking at this is that, as we pointed out in the last chapter, rights can only exist if they can, *in principle*, be fulfilled. In the case of physical objects one cannot have a right to something that cannot be provided. Hence, we cannot now have a right to see a live dodo. The corollary of this, though not an independent argument, is that the most commonly accepted interpretation of a 'right' to something is that one has a justified claim to it. But if we have a right to see a live dodo against whom do we have a claim?

In other words, as we have argued at more length in the last chapter, the chief reason why it seems strange to talk about our rights to something that was destroyed generations ago is that one can only have rights that can, in principle, be realized. Having a right to some object also means that somebody has an obligation to provide it. Hence, while it may make sense, though not necessarily be true, to say that our ancestors behaved *immorally* in depriving us of many things that we would like to have inherited, it does not make sense to say that they had violated our rights and, by doing so, had behaved unjustly towards us. In the first place, we did not then exist, so that we did not then have any rights. And now that we do exist we cannot say that we have a right to see a live dodo or that the inhabitants of the Mauritius three centuries ago behaved 'unjustly' towards us by violating our right to do so. Hence, for both reasons it is difficult to accept Barry's view that we can behave unjustly towards future generations by depriving them of the right to anything that will no longer exist. It may be immoral of us not to prevent the extinction of tigers, and we would greatly deplore such a development. But future generations cannot have any 'right' to see them.

Having successively broadened, then narrowed, the scope of the concept of 'justice' to facilitate its incorporation into his own conception of intergenerational justice, Barry then follows the perfectly reasonable procedure of beginning with some fundamental principles of justice between contemporaries and then seeing how far they can be applied intergenerationally. One of these is the premise of the 'fundamental equality of human beings', which is a normal axiomatic starting point in developing theories of morality in general or justice in particular. But Barry (1999: 96) also says that 'It is precisely because this premise does not make moral standing depend on the time at which people live that principles of justice valid for contemporaries are prima facie valid for intergenerational justice too'.

This, however, is a rather different matter, and is open to the objection, discussed in the previous chapter, to the notion of attributing 'rights' to unborn people. For the clause '. . . the time at which people live . . .' begs the question of whether or not they are living at all. Nothing in the fundamental equality condition implies that there can be any sort of equality between people who live and people who are not yet born. In the most important characteristic of all, namely, being alive, they are fundamentally unequal.

However, if we ignore this point and go further along the road followed by Barry, we come up against other difficulties. He believes that only two of his four fundamental principles of justice apply intergenerationally. One of these is the principle of 'responsibility', which he develops thus: 'A legitimate origin of different outcomes for different people is that they have made different voluntary choices . . . The obverse of the principle is that bad outcomes for which somebody is not responsible provide a *prima facie* for compensation' (Barry 1999: 98). Later he adds that 'People in the future can scarcely be held responsible for the physical conditions they inherit, so it would seem that it is unjust if people are worse off in this respect than we are'. Now it may well be that Barry did not intend this to be interpreted literally, since it would, for example, leave out entirely the question of 'bad luck'.[9] If future generations are worse off for no fault of ours—for example, changes in solar radiation that may have dramatic effects on the climate—Barry might not claim that they are victims of injustice. Barry probably meant that we would be acting unjustly if we followed policies that made future generations worse off than they would otherwise be. But even this is questionable. For any serious theory of justice would presumably ascribe interests and rights to people alive today, and these should not be violated in the interests of avoiding *any* damage to the interests of future generations, however small the latter may be and however great the former.

Even at any point of time few egalitarians, in whose ranks one should include Barry, would go so far as to say that it would be 'unjust' to take something away from any group in any society, however well off, in order to improve the welfare of some other contemporary group, however badly off. To adopt such a position would mean opposing any egalitarian policy involving a redistribution from richer to poorer. But if it may sometimes be just to make some group in society worse off against their will in the interests of helping people who are worse off, why would it always be unjust to follow policies that *might* conceivably make future generations worse off even if it is in order to avoid imposing certain burdens on some of the people alive today?

Furthermore, when redistributing from richer to poorer within any contemporary society one can usually, though not always, know who is going to be affected, and in what way. One has a fairly good idea who are the richer members of society and who are the poorer. But the predictions that Barry makes about the inevitable harmful effects of current environmental practices and population policies on the relative welfare of future generations are very

---

[9] There are, of course, theories of justice that maintain that it is 'unfair' and hence 'unjust' for people to be worse off through no fault of their own, even if no blame can be attached to anybody else. We discuss this in more detail in the next chapter, particularly in connection with Temkin's views on what constitutes 'unjust' inequalities.

speculative and, if the arguments of Chapter 6 are valid, are likely to be as decisively falsified as have similar apocalyptic predictions over the ages.

Exactly the same point arises in connection with the other principle of justice that Barry believes can apply intergenerationally. This is the principle of 'vital interests'. Barry believes that we should take account of the impact of our actions on the vital interests of future generations and that they have the same priority as the vital interests of people alive today. We agree but, again, we believe that it follows from simple considerations of benevolence or virtue. It does not help to try to bring such aspects of our behaviour under the umbrella of any theory of intergenerational justice, and attempts to do so probably merely confuse the issue. Avoiding policies that threaten the vital interests of future generations may appear to be an unambitious programme, but it is far more defensible than are the claims made on behalf of future generations as matters of 'right' or 'justice', such as that we should never allow their welfare to decline at any stage, or deprive them of any environmental facilities. Our humanitarian requirement to avoid policies that threaten future generations with poverty are on a par with the humanitarian considerations that require us to relieve poverty today without the need for any formal egalitarian theory or theory of justice.

7. Conclusion

In this chapter we have argued that the problem of intergenerational justice seems to raise probably insuperable obstacles. These stem basically from the logic of futurity. In the last chapter it was argued that future generations cannot be said to have rights. But, as pointed out in this chapter, most serious conceptions of a theory of justice imply the attribution of rights to the persons whose interests are to be protected within the framework of that theory. Hence, the interests of future generations cannot be brought within any theory of justice since they cannot be said to have any rights.

Nevertheless, while Rawls recognized the logical difficulty of constructing any theory of intergenerational justice, he did attempt to construct a theory of 'just savings', which is, to all intents and purposes, the main, and possibly sole, ingredient of any theory of intergenerational justice. But in his famous *A Theory of Justice* (1972) he seemed to have three criteria of a 'just savings' rate for any generation, none of which seems to be necessarily consistent with the others. And 20 years later he seemed to more or less abandon his earlier approach, and his proposed new solution resembles a form of Kantian 'categorical imperative' which, we have argued, cannot be expected to provide much guidance to the particular problem of how members of any given generation should evaluate the 'justice' or otherwise of their generation's rate of saving.

The other major contemporary serious contribution to the problem of intergenerational justice is that proposed by Brian Barry, who has addressed this problem at various times over the last two or three decades. But we find that he, too, in the end finishes up appealing more to some principles of virtuous behaviour that lie outside the scope of most conceptions of justice, so that the use of the language of justice, and hence of rights, is more likely to lead us into error in identifying which of our moral obligations to future generations should be regarded as being most important.

As Rawls pointed out, the probably insuperable obstacles to the development of any coherent theory of intergenerational justice do not absolve us from the need to impose some ethical constraints on our policies affecting future generations. In particular, as we argue in more detail in Chapter 7, the vital interests of future generations with which we should be concerned are far more in the sphere of political and social rights than in the sphere of the welfare we derive from the physical environment. And taking action to promote, and ensure the extension into the future, of basic human rights today does not imply any conflict of interests between generations. Hence, there is probably no need for any theory of intergenerational justice anyway. Human rights and just societies may be scarce in the world today but are not 'scarce resources' like some minerals are alleged to be and that need to be shared out over generations. Indeed, these constraints on our policies affecting future generations correspond closely to the Rawlsian view that priority should be accorded to the development of just institutions.

We set out our view of what constitutes our main obligations to future generations in more detail in Chapter 7. But before coming to that we need to consider other possible guides to our moral obligations to future generations that are widely touted and espoused, notably 'sustainable development' and its closely related concept of intergenerational egalitarianism. These two possibilities are examined in the next two chapters.

4

Intergenerational Equity

1. Intergenerational Egalitarianism

The moral claim of 'sustainable development', which is a very widely adopted objective today, is usually alleged to rest largely on its appeal to intergenerational 'equity'. Concern with equity is, in fact, often contrasted with the standard economist's concern with simply maximizing the future stream of utility over some relevant time period. For example, one of the leading authorities on 'green' political philosophy writes that the objective of sustainable development '. . . contrasts with the directive of ordinary expected-utility maximization to go for the highest total payoff without regard to its distribution interpersonally or intertemporally' (Goodin 1983: 1).[1] Or, as another authority on the concept of sustainability bluntly puts it, 'Sustainability is primarily an issue of intergenerational equity' (Norgaard 1992: 1).

Now 'equity' is not the same as 'equality', since egalitarian principles are not the only possible kind of principles of equity. Nevertheless, most, if not all, theories of equity within generations contain, as a crucial ingredient, some appeal to the desirability of equality of something or other.[2] For example, both Rawls (1972) and Sen (1982b; 1992) emphasize that equality of opportunity to pursue one's life goals is an essential feature of a just society. Others, such as Dworkin (1981), would appeal to a suitably defined equality of resources as essential for distributive justice.

Furthermore, most definitions of intergenerational 'equity' include some reference to the desirability of equality between generations of some variable, such as wellbeing, opportunity, or resources. For example, Goodin (1983: 13) states that 'considerations of intergenerational equity would demand . . . that each generation be guaranteed roughly equal benefits and insist that one generation may justly enjoy certain benefits only if those advantages can be sustained for subsequent generations as well'.

---

[1] The same contrast is noted by Alan Holland (1999), who, however, thinks that both objectives are equally over-ambitious.

[2] It is for this reason that scattered throughout the vast literature on justice and equity are learned discussions of the relationship in the original Greek language between the words 'justice' and 'equality'.

In what follows we shall not be concerned with issues such as how far everybody is equally entitled to vote, or own property, or stand for electoral office, and so on, since these do not concern equality in the distribution of the stock of certain goods. Principles such as 'everybody has an equal right to vote' or 'everybody has an equal right to stand for elective office' imply that everybody has the right in question irrespective of how many people there are. In fact, as Raz and others have pointed out, in such principles, which are 'entitlement' principles, the qualifying adjective 'equal' is often superfluous.[3]

We exclude these forms of equality for two reasons. First, the impetus behind the concern with intergenerational equality is a fear that the present generation might deprive future generations of its due share of some finite resource. In other words, what is really at stake in the discussion about inter-generational equity and 'sustainable development' are not the 'entitlement' principles but what Raz suggests is the characteristic form of egalitarian principle, namely, 'If there are x people each person is entitled to $1/x$ of all the G that is available'.[4]

Our second reason for by-passing the issue of equality of entitlement to certain privileges or positions is that it does not raise issues of conflicting interest between distant generations. As indicated in the previous chapter, intergenerational justice is really about distributive justice, and this limits our interest in equality to the equality in the distribution of resources.

We should also make clear at the outset that we are not concerned here with what it is that ought to be equally distributed. While most of the equality debate during the last two or three decades has been addressed to this issue, and various candidates for the appropriate equilisand have been proposed—for example, welfare, incomes, resources, opportunities, and so on—there has been relatively little discussion of why one should want equality of any of these things, or of anything else, anyway.[5]

2. Instrumental or Intrinsic Values

We want to consider separately two distinct types of arguments in favour of intergenerational equality, namely, arguments that purport to demonstrate its 'instrumental' or 'extrinsic' value and those that purport to demonstrate its 'intrinsic' value.[6] Intrinsic values are values that an entity possesses on

---

[3] For example, Raz (1986: Ch. 8). In an important discussion of the concept of equality Parfit (1991: 3) excludes these forms of equality on the grounds that 'Though these kinds of equality are of great importance, they are not my subject. I am concerned with people's being *equally well off*'.

[4] This corresponds closely to Raz's (1986: 222) version of this principle.

[5] A recent addition to the usual list of suspects is Cohen's (1993) suggested 'midfare'. One of us has (Beckerman 1997*a*) proposed another candidate as the focal variable, namely 'wilfare', though not in an egalitarian context.

[6] 'Intrinsic' values are also sometimes known as "inherent" values'.

account of being valued for its own sake rather than for its contribution to some other value. In environmental discourse nature is commonly alleged to possess intrinsic value. So we must begin by explaining briefly how we shall interpret and use these two terms.

First, we shall use the terms 'intrinsic value' and 'instrumental value' simply as referring to a two-fold classification of values into those that are instrumental—that is, required in order to promote some other value—and those, the intrinsic values, that that are valued for their own sake. Of course, some objects may be bearers of both kinds of value. One may value plants for their intrinsic aesthetic value but also for their medicinal properties.

Obviously, if there are any instrumental values there must, in the end, be at least one intrinsic value that is valued for its own sake. Otherwise, for what would the instrumental values be instrumental?

There is, of course, no generally accepted distinction between instrumental and intrinsic values and hence no generally accepted definition of either term.[7] But there is no need here to attempt to survey the main candidates. Furthermore, for reasons set out later, if there is any case to be made out for intergenerational justice it must rest on the intrinsic value of equality, so it is this concept to which we shall attach most importance.[8] Equally important for our purposes is the widespread but very controversial view that intrinsic values are those that do not depend on the existence of any valuer, that is, they possess some form of *objective* value. The philosopher Tom Regan puts this clearly in saying 'The presence of inherent value in a natural object is independent of any awareness, interest, or appreciation of it by any conscious being'.[9]

Our view, which is the *subjective* value view, and which we discuss in more detail in Chapter 8 in connection with the valuation of the environment, is that 'value'—that is, the value of some G—is a relational concept referring to the status that some G has in the eyes of some valuer, X. This does not mean that X must value G solely on account of the utility he or anybody else derives from it. He may value benefits derived by other people, or value things that are of no value to anybody else.[10] Nor does the fact that somebody values G

---

[7] According to Scanlon (1998: 87), 'The things that philosophers have generally listed as intrinsically valuable fall into a few categories: certain states of consciousness; personal relationships; intellectual, artistic, and moral excellence; knowledge; and human life itself'. Other philosophers will prefer different lists, though usually with a lot of overlap with Scanlon's list: for example, Nagel (1979: 14).

[8] For an excellent recent survey of the different interpretations of *intrinsic* values and of their role in environmental ethics see J. O'Neill (1993: Ch. 2).

[9] Quoted in Sylvan and Bennett (1994: 100) as having been endorsed by Arne Naess, the father figure of the deep ecology movement, who gives the first principle of the movement as follows: 'The well-being and flourishing of human and non-human Life on earth have value in themselves (synonyms: intrinsic value, inherent value)' (Naess and Sessions 1984). The original statement is in Regan (1982: 199).

[10] One such example suggested to me by G. C. Cohen would be an 'unseeable-by-anyone sunset on Pluto'.

imply that *G* is, or ought to be, valuable to anybody else. People value different things, some of which are regarded by others as despicable.

3. Can Intergenerational Equality Have Instrumental Value?

In public discourse probably the most common grounds put forward for equality in general are instrumental grounds. It is widely believed, for example, that equality is good on account of its alleged beneficial effects, such as reducing crime or social friction, and so on.[11] Similarly, one common argument in defence of equality of variables such as income, or status, or opportunity, is that it might promote a greater sense of social cohesion, or greater productive efficiency, and so on, all of which may promote welfare.

But it is difficult to transpose such instrumental advantages of equality to different *non-overlapping* generations. It seems unlikely, for example, that greater equality of incomes—or of anything else, for that matter—between *non-overlapping* generations would promote intergenerational harmony. In the same way, the type of benefit of greater equality in certain aspects of life that are eloquently set out by Tawney—reduction in envy, a greater sense of social solidarity and sense of community, and so on, brought about by greater equality '. . . not equality of capacity or attainment, but of circumstances, institutions, and manner of life' (Tawney 1964: 48) is not expected to apply between generations. Another common instrumental argument for greater equality is that great disparities of wealth or income eventually enable the rich to exercise undue power over the poor, leading, perhaps, to unacceptable inequalities of liberty. Clearly this, too, would not be feasible intergenerationally.

Even within any generation Raz (1986: 234) is surely right in saying, in connection with the view that greater equality would reduce envy and hostility between groups, that '. . . to the extent that some of these attitudes are deeply rooted in the human psyche, and social conditions only channel their expression, egalitarian devices are a wild good chase after the unachievable'. Those who advocate equality on grounds of its instrumental value in reducing envy may be merely providing moral authority for the envy that they are seeking to eliminate.

---

[11] For example, even the philosopher Hare's (1977) summary of the arguments for egalitarianism is essentially a simple utilitarian argument in terms of the extent to which greater equality would be instrumental in maximizing total utility. It is true that the utilitarian argument for greater equality could apply intergenerationally, up to a point, but if the maximization of welfare over time required transfers from later to earlier generations, as it is likely to do if our arguments in Chapter 7 are correct, this is hardly a practical possibility.

Incidentally, one implication of appealing to the way that some people's welfare depends partly on how well off they are by comparison with other people is that faster economic growth, leading to greater intergenerational inequality, would be desirable. For the most plausible 'relational' assumption we can make is that any given generation will get additional welfare from feeling that it is better off than the preceding generation and from the prospect that the next generation will be better off still. In that case it is obvious that total welfare, over time, will be greater the faster is the growth in the non-relational component of each generation's welfare. And this will also imply greater inequality over time in both the non-relational component of welfare and total welfare.[12] In other words, there does seem to be some conflict between aspirations for future growth and the demands of intergenerational equality. In the next section we shall examine this possible conflict in more detail.

4. Intergenerational Equality or Rising Human Welfare?

The Nature of the Conflict

One objection to intergenerational equality that immediately springs to mind is that most people would probably hope that future generations are better off than we are. Similarly, most people would probably feel rather pleased that we are far better off than were people in, say, the Middle Ages. Is there a conflict then between the objective of intergenerational equality and approval of the growth, over time, in human welfare?

In order to examine this question we need to spell out a bit more the concept of egalitarianism that seems to be at stake. If it is true that intergenerational equality can have no instrumental value, for reasons such as those set out above, then it can only be defended on the grounds that it has intrinsic value. What is meant by the intrinsic value of equality? While one prominent defender of the view that equality has intrinsic value, Larry Temkin, explicitly disclaims any proprietary rights in how such terms are to be used, there is much to be said for his suggestion that one should begin by restricting the term 'egalitarian' to '. . . anyone who attaches *some* value to equality *itself*. That is, an egalitarian is anyone who cares *at all* about equality *over and above the extent it promotes other ideals*' (Temkin 1993: 7; emphasis in the original).[13]

---

[12] For the benefit of the very suspicious-minded a trivial mathematical proof of this obvious conclusion is contained in Beckerman (1997a).

[13] Thus, if a utilitarian believed that greater, rather than less, inequality would maximize total utility—as it could easily do under certain plausible assumptions, such as a favourable effect on work

It is not claimed that the intrinsic value of equality confers on it some 'trumping' power over other objectives. Equality may be traded off against other objectives or ideals, such as freedom, or greater prosperity in general, or improvements in many specific valued aspects of human welfare. One situation may be better than another in one respect, namely, greater equality, but worse than another, *all things considered*, if it involves too great a sacrifice of other objectives. For example, consider two situations, in one of which half the population are blind and in the other everybody is blind. An egalitarian does not have to believe that the second situation is better than the first on account of its greater equality. For she may believe that the second situation is worse, *all things considered*.[14]

A further crucial aspect of pure egalitarianism is its conception of what sort of inequalities should be regarded as morally undesirable. For there are all sorts of inequalities that have no moral significance whatsoever. According to Temkin, 'I believe the egalitarian's core belief is that it is unfair or unjust for some to be worse off than others *through no fault of their own*. It is *undeserved* or *nonvoluntary* inequalities that are morally objectionable' (Temkin 1995: 78–9, fn.12).

Given these characteristics of the concept of the intrinsic value of equality, we can now return to the apparent conflict between intergenerational equality and the growth, over time, in human welfare.

Intergenerational Equality and the Future Growth of Welfare

One particularly important attempt has been made to show that, in fact, the conflict between the growth of welfare over time and intergenerational equality is more apparent than real.[15] This is the discussion of the conflict by Temkin (1995: 78–9, fn. 12), who writes, 'Some worry that . . . egalitarianism has the counterintuitive implication that it is better not to want one's descendants to be better of than one's own generation, all other moral factors considered'. He than goes on to say that, given the conception of egalitarianism according to which the inequalities that are unjust are those that are undeserved or nonvoluntary, then 'if we *want* our children or descendants to fare better than us, and voluntarily take steps to bring this about, there need

incentives, or differences between people with respect to their efficiency in transforming goods into utility—then she would have to be an anti-egalitarian. The same would apply to many other forms of instrumental egalitarianism.

[14] We abstract here from the question of the moral significance of the means by which one moves from one situation to another.

[15] We shall not consider here the question of how far there is such a conflict between future human development and equality among different groups in society at any moment of time, for example by reducing the savings rate or incentives to the growth of productivity. For a sophisticated discussion of this problem, which concludes that much depends on what one takes to be the equilisand, see Roemer (forthcoming).

be no objection to the resulting inequality'.[16] In other words, if we take measures, such as save and invest, that will help make future generations richer than us there is no need for the egalitarian to complain, since we are *voluntarily* worse off than future generations will be.

This is all very well. But suppose we were expected to be poorer than future generations for reasons that were outside our control. Suppose, for example, that advances in climate change prediction showed that some inevitable, or highly probable, natural changes in the climate, dwarfing any man-made effects, would lead to a more equable and stable climate than the one experienced today. Very cold regions would become warmer, rainfall would increase in arid areas, hot areas would enjoy milder climates, and so on. Future generations could then be expected to be much more prosperous than people alive today and hence have greater opportunities to pursue their conceptions of the good life than are open to people today. This means that, through no fault of their own, people alive today would be poorer relative to future generations than they would otherwise be.

Would such an inequality have to be deplored? It is true that we would not have voluntarily taken steps to make future generations better off as far as the climate is concerned. Nevertheless, such a prospect appears to satisfy the condition for regarding it to be unjust that is laid down in the above conception of pure egalitarianism, namely, we are worse off than future generations will be through no fault of our own. Hence it does appear to conflict with approval of future increase in welfare. For on the Temkin view, which regards natural inequalities as unjust, we would be morally obliged to take some action, however small after all things are considered, to reduce our poverty compared with future generations by, say, investing less or using up more of the Earth's supposedly scarce resources.

We might not be morally obliged to go very far in the direction of raising our own levels of consumption at the expense of future living standards. For we may still believe that rising standards of living in the future will be better *all things considered*. Nevertheless, if we do believe that intergenerational equality has *some* intrinsic value, we ought to be ready to constrain somewhat the extent to which we would pursue policies designed to raise future levels of welfare at our expense. How far we trade-off equality against future increases in welfare should also depend on how much richer or poorer we can expect future generations to be. But this is a more factual issue to which we turn in Chapter 6.

The above very broad concept of justice as encompassing undeserved inequality, even where it is the result of good or bad luck, is one to which

---

[16] Temkin's discussion of this conflict of objectives is particularly useful here since he also explicitly abstracts from the issue of what it is exactly that egalitarians are concerned with and uses 'welfare' as the focal variable for expositional convenience (Temkin forthcoming).

only a minority of philosophers subscribe. Such 'contingencies of nature' are not regarded as unjust in, for example, either the Rawlsian or the Nozickian theories of justice. To take Nozick's well-known example, if there are ten Robinson Crusoes on isolated islands that happen to enjoy different natural advantages it is difficult to disagree with his conclusion that, after they discover each others' differential luck, the differences do not give rise to claims in 'justice' (Nozick 1974: 185). The arguments we have advanced in the preceding two chapters still imply that there might be moral obligations on the richest Robinson Crusoe to help out the poorest, but that is a matter of benevolence, not a requirement of 'justice'. In the above climate change example, we would have been just unlucky not to have been born later when the climate is expected to be better. We may also be unlucky not to be born before cures for all sorts of currently widespread diseases and illnesses have been discovered. But most people would regard inequalities arising out of bad luck—that is, 'natural inequalities'—to be just bad luck and not examples of injustice. Thus, on Temkin's own conception of pure egalitarianism, it would be unjust if the current generation were worse off than the future generations on account of the latter's undeserved good fortune, so that there does appear to be some conflict between his conception of egalitarianism and unintended future increases in welfare. And the same conflict of objectives seems to apply when considering our response to the rise in human welfare over the past course of history.

Inequality Between the Present and Past Generations

If one believed in the intrinsic value of equality one would have to claim that, in one respect, namely the degree of inequality, the state of the world over the past thousand years is morally inferior to what it would have been had we made much less progress over this period. As Parfit (1991: 7) puts it, the intrinsic value of equality view, according to which inequality is bad even if it refers to unrelated communities, implies that '. . . it is bad if Inca peasants, or Stone Age hunter-gatherers, were worse off than we are now'. Of course, we may still decide that, *all things considered*, we regard the increase in inequality caused by the rise in incomes as having been worthwhile insofar as it may have promoted other objectives. In the developed world, at least, numerous diseases that were once rampant have been brought under control or eliminated, security of the minimum conditions of survival—food, clothing, and shelter—has been attained, opportunities to lead interesting and varied lives have been immeasurable expanded, working conditions have been transformed for the better, and the average expectation of life has increased dramatically. Nevertheless, if it is believed that equality has some intrinsic value, some trade-off of these other objectives in the interests of greater equality ought to meet approval.

Anybody who did subscribe to this view would presumably want to reduce the inequality by reducing current levels of welfare, provided this did not involve too much sacrifice of other objectives. After all, it is not at all impossible to move a little way towards intergenerational equality retroactively. We can do nothing to raise past levels of welfare. But a small cut in present standards of living would help reduce inequality over the past up to and including the present generation. So if one attaches *some* intrinsic value to intergenerational equality one ought to be ready to sacrifice a certain amount of *some* other value, such as current welfare, however small and however difficult to specify precisely, in the interests of reducing the intergenerational inequality to which the relative prosperity of current society contributes. If not, then the claim that intergenerational equality has some intrinsic value begins to look a little like humbug.[17]

But suppose we did accept some cut in current welfare levels in order to reduce inequality between us and past generations. This would increase the inequality between us and future generations. Indeed, it would affect the measure of inequality over the whole history of the human race—say, until the human race blows itself up or destroys itself in some way or other. What policy should the present generation adopt to deal with this? Here, to simplify the argument, we shall divide generations into three groups: the past, the present, and the future. We shall also measure inequality over the whole history of the human race by the size of the difference between the average welfare of all three groups and the welfare of the extremes of low and high welfare—that is, the amount of dispersion around the mean. Two possible policies that the current generation could adopt seem to be relevant.

First, insofar as current levels of welfare are reduced in order to reduce inequality between us and the past, the average welfare over the whole of human history will have been reduced. This means that if nothing is done to reduce future levels of welfare as well, the variation around the average—that is, the difference between the average and the extremes—will have been increased. Hence greater equality over the whole of human history can be achieved only if steps are also taken to cut the welfare of future generations as well. Advocates of intergenerational equality should, therefore, support some such cut in present as well as future levels of welfare, however small.

A second policy is one that is probably more in line with most environmentalist thinking and with the proclaimed objectives of 'sustainable development'. This consists of reducing our own levels of welfare—for example, by

---

[17] We are adopting here Frankfurt's concept of 'humbug', which refers to pronouncements made by people who are concerned less with the truth of their assertions or with persuading other people of their truth than with conveying the impression that they are people of noble characters, who have deep thoughts and great sensitivity, and other virtues that they expect to appeal to others, in this case compassionate concern with the well-being of future generations (Frankfurt 1988: esp. 121).

consuming fewer resources—in order to avoid having any harmful impact on
the welfare levels of future generations, but leaving the welfare of future
generations unchanged or even further increased. Given the reduction in the
intergenerational average level of welfare resulting from the cut in our own
welfare, such a policy would only increase overall dispersion around the average and hence increase intergenerational inequality.

In other words, the egalitarians should want to promote some cut in
welfare of both present and future generations, and environmentalists should
be prepared to accept some increase in intergenerational inequality. It is
doubtful whether supporters of either camp are fully aware of the implications of their positions. And, worse still, many people are in both camps
simultaneously, which makes their positions even more tenuous, if not positively treasonable.

Furthermore, so far we have been talking about the current generation's
level of welfare as if the current generation comprised a fairly homogeneous group of people, all enjoying levels of welfare that did not depart too
much from the average. But the fact is that the living standards of most
people in the Third World are far below those of the developed world, and
possibly billions of people in the Third World may be living at barely
subsistence levels. If one is egalitarian, therefore, there is little to be said
for making any sacrifice in the interests of future generations before trying
to do more for those people alive today and who are living in poverty and
destitution. It is true that this is far easier said than done. We do not mini-
mize the enormous practical obstacles to making significant progress in
reducing world-wide poverty today, and the limitations on the extent to
which the rest of the world can help. Nevertheless, various attractive
suggestions have been made that pinpoint likely changes in aid strategies,
backed up by an increase in the present paltry levels of official aid to developing countries, that could make a big impact (Sachs 2000). But this raises
issues in development economics into which we do not wish to enter.
Here, we are simply trying to draw attention to the objections that can be
made, *in principle,* on egalitarian grounds, to the objective of intergenerational equality.

5. The Intrinsic Value of Equality

We have argued above that there appears to be a conflict between, on the one
hand, intergenerational egalitarianism and, on the other hand, the growth of
welfare over time. But the existence of such a conflict does not tell us how far
either of the objectives—equality or human development—needs to be sacrificed in the interests of the other. Or perhaps neither needs to be sacrificed at

all. If there is no moral force at all in one or other, there would be no conflict. So we have to ask: what is the strength of moral force in each objective?

Let us begin by asking what moral force there is in the objective of human development, that is, of improving the well-being of distant generations. One could perhaps simply adopt the value judgment that, *other things being equal*, it is morally good to improve somebody's well-being. Of course, other things may not be equal, so that *all things considered* it may not be desirable to improve somebody's well-being. For example, it may be that some sacrifice is necessary in order to increase the well-being of future generations. Or we may have good reason to believe that some people are evil, so that by raising their well-being relative to others we would violate the norms of justice that are necessary for the best functioning of society which, in turn, is better for the well-being of the people in that society. Thus the objective of human development over time does not have any 'trumping power'. But it does have some moral force which, apparently, conflicts with the objective of intergenerational equality.

So what moral force does intergenerational equality have? We have already argued that intergenerational equality cannot have instrumental value. So the question we have to ask is: what is the *intrinsic* moral force of egalitarianism? In an important contribution to the equality debate titled 'What's the Good of Equality?', John Broome (1989: 251) asks, 'If we are to accommodate the value of equality properly . . . the first step should be to decide just what, if anything, is valuable about equality in the first place. Too much work on inequality consists of trying out various axioms . . . to see where they lead, without giving much attention to what could justify them'.

He then goes on to present his own theory of what is good about equality, which is a theory based on the concept of 'fairness'. He considers the case where 'there are several candidates to receive some indivisible commodity, but not enough is available to go round them all'.[18] He distinguishes between two classes of prima facie reasons why a person should get a commodity, namely, claims and other reasons. He then presents a theory of what would be a fair way of dealing with conflicting claims, which is based on his concept of fairness, where 'fairness is *only* concerned with claims, and not with other reasons' (1991b: 94). When claims conflict Broome proposes that what fairness requires is that they should be *satisfied in proportion to their strength*, though 'proportion' is not to be interpreted 'too precisely'.[19]

Consider the old example—not Broome's example, but similar—of a lifeboat that is overloaded and doomed to sink unless two people are thrown overboard to save everybody else. On Broome's interpretation, insofar as

[18] By 'commodity' here Broome is referring to any 'good thing', but the term 'commodity' here happens to fit the text of the above argument very conveniently.

[19] Broome (1991b: 95) explains that this should be taken to mean that stronger claims should be satisfied more than weaker claims, but even the latter should be satisfied to some extent.

every one had an equal claim to the 'good' of staying alive, fairness would require that equal claims be equally satisfied. In this situation it would not be possible to satisfy everybody's equal claim, so the fair procedure, according to Broome, would be to hold a lottery. Indeed, in a famous law case in the USA to which Broome refers, a sailor called Holmes was prosecuted for murder for his part in throwing people overboard from a lifeboat. The judge said that a lottery should have been held.[20] Broome points out that the reason why a lottery makes sense in such situations is precisely the appeal of 'fairness', that is, the view that claims should be met in proportion to their strength. Hence, in cases where claims are equal and not all of them can be met a lottery is the only 'fair' way of choosing between them.

Like Temkin and others, however, he recognizes that 'In some circumstances, no doubt, it will be very important to be fair, and in others fairness may be outweighed by expediency' (Broome 1991b: 96). In the lifeboat story, for example, if no allowance were made for other objectives the egalitarian solution would be to simply throw the whole lot overboard and be done with it. But Broome and other egalitarians would reject this on the grounds that it would involve too great a sacrifice of the objective of total welfare, or what Broome refers to as the 'aggregative' consideration.

Thus, Broome's theory of fairness, like any theory of fairness—or justice or any ethical system for that matter—cannot be expected to provide precise guidance in all specific situations. But for present purposes the crucial feature of Broome's whole discussion of fairness is that it is couched in terms of his view that 'the overall goodness of a distribution (e.g. of some G) is entirely determined by the good of the people. I call this the "principle of personal good"'. In other words the moral force behind the view that somebody ought to get an equal amount of some good, G, to which he has a claim that is as strong as that of the other people concerned, whether it is more income or more of the good 'staying alive' or whatever, is that it is good for that person, not that it is good in some impersonal abstract sense.

Grounding one's view of equality on the principle of personal good, that is, that a good distribution is one that is good for people, is, in fact, very important in the discussion of the intrinsic value of equality. For this principle happens to lie at the root of what is the most powerful objection to the notion that egalitarianism has intrinsic value. This is the well-known objection to egalitarianism that Parfit (1991) called 'The Levelling-Down Objection'.[21] This is the objection that equality cannot be good *per se* since, if it were, it would make sense to promote it even if this was to be done by reducing the welfare, or the 'G', of those who happen to have most of it without raising the G of the worse off—that is, we exclude cases where reducing the

[20] See Broome (1984).
[21] For lucid commentaries on this problem see Crisp (1998) and Temkin (1993: 256ff).

inequality of G gives some satisfaction to those who had less of it. And most of us would believe that this would not make sense. If we achieved greater equality of incomes, for example, simply by taking some away from the rich even though none of it would go to the poor—it would all get lost through reduced incentives, bureaucratic procedures, and so on—few people would support such a move on the grounds of its intrinsic value.[22]

Why do we believe that levelling down without improving the welfare of the worse off has no moral force? The reason is that most of us would subscribe to what is known among philosophers as the 'Person-Affecting Claim', to use the terminology of Parfit, who first demonstrated fully the power and implications of this claim, or what Temkin has called, more conveniently, 'The Slogan'. Temkin (1993: 248) defines the Slogan as follows: *'One situation cannot be worse (or better) than another if there is no one for whom it is worse (or better)'*. Thus increasing equality by reducing the welfare of the better off without raising the welfare of anybody else simply violates the Slogan. If reducing the G of the better off does not improve anybody's G, then the new situation cannot be better than the old one. As Crisp (1998) neatly puts it 'Even if there is a kind of goodness that is not good for any being, why should we care about it?'.

Now, as Temkin (1993: 256) has pointed out, the Slogan is more ambiguous than might appear at first sight and raises problems of its own. But it has great appeal and provides the basis for the Levelling Down Objection. It has nothing to do with what we take to be G. Whether it is utility, or welfare, or resources, or opportunities for any of these things or for anything else, the notion that we should equalize G by reducing the amount of G of those who have most of it without increasing the G of anybody else does not seem appealing. Roughly speaking, in common parlance, achieving greater equality—of anything—by taking away some of it from those who have a lot of it without anybody being better off is pointless.

Without wishing to go into the question of what makes people 'better off', it does seem difficult to accept that some policy, such as redistribution, is 'good' if nobody is better off and some people are worse off.[23] To rescue egalitarianism from the Levelling-Down Objection, therefore, it seems necessary to abandon the Slogan. Needless to say, its validity has been the subject of considerable intense and sophisticated scrutiny, which it would be out of place and unnecessary, as well as beyond our competence, to discuss here in any detail. We would like to make only one point about it here, concerning

---

[22] Those that did would probably be motivated largely by envy, which has no moral force, or by instrumental considerations, such as greater sense of social solidarity, which we have seen to play no role in intergenerational egalitarianism.

[23] We are also abstracting from cases where our decisions will affect the identity of the people concerned, that is, the well-known—to philosophers—'Non-Identity problem', a most important problem that has been brought to our attention in seminal works by Narveson (1967) and Parfit (1983; 1984).

one of the important criticisms of the Slogan discussed by Temkin, which, whether or not one is persuaded by it, does raise a fundamental and difficult question.

This is the consistency of the Slogan with other apparently compelling ideals. Temkin invites us to consider the conflict between the Slogan and the claims of 'proportional justice', that is, the view that people should be rewarded or punished according to their merits and worthiness of their behaviour.[24] Consider, for example, a situation *A*, in the after-life, in which saints are rewarded by enjoying a high level of well-being, but the sinners are punished by experiencing only a low or negative level of well-being (Temkin 1993: 260–1). Compare this with situation *B*, in which the saints are just as well off as in A, but the sinners are even better off—by hypothesis the saints, even if they had been capable of such base emotions, are not made to feel worse off just because the sinners have finished up even better off than they are. It might appear that, since there is *no* respect in which the situation was worse for anybody, the Slogan precludes our judging that situation *B* is worse than *A*.[25] But Temkin is probably right in saying that most people would find this hard to swallow. 'They believe there would be *something* morally bad about the evilest mass murderers faring better than most benign saints, even if there was *no* one for whom it was worse' (Temkin 1993: 260).

Thus it seems that insofar as the Slogan conflicts with some other intrinsic value, such as proportional justice in this example, we are faced with a dilemma. We must either stick to the Slogan and persist in maintaining, however reluctantly, that situation *B* cannot be said to be worse than situation *A*, or we must concede that situation *B* is really worse after all, which means we must reject the Slogan. But the fact that there seems to be a conflict between the two principles—between the Slogan and proportional justice in this example—does not tell us which one has to be rejected. It may well be that, even if we adhere to the principle of proportional justice in situations where it does not conflict with the Slogan, we would not, if we were rational, apply it in the particular example in question.

We ought to recognize that the only reason we believe in the principle of proportional justice, in general, is that we believe that, *however indirectly*, it ensures that, in the real world, respect for the principle is better for people, and that violation of the principle is worse for people. But in Temkin's example it

---

[24] Aristotle (1976: 178) says that 'Everyone agrees that justice in distribution must be in accordance with merit in some sense, but they do not all mean the same kind of merit'.

[25] If we followed what is known as the Pareto principle, or its close relation known as 'welfarism', we would even have to judge that, since *B* was better for some, namely, the sinners, and not worse for anybody, it was better than situation *A*. But this would be going beyond the Slogan, which is merely a necessary condition for any situation being better or worse than another, not a sufficient condition. That is to say, in the example in question, all that the Slogan tells us is that since nobody is worse off in situation *A* we cannot judge situation *A* to be worse. It does not tell us that, since the sinners are better off in *A*, we have to judge it to be better.

is assumed that nobody can become worse off as a result of the sinners being better off in the next world. Even if the rumour got around among people alive today that sinners did better in the next world, people would not believe it. Or perhaps they would. After all, hundreds of millions of them believe other equally unverifiable stories about the next world. So we would have to accept that our intuitive dislike of situation *B* is a sort of habit or a psychological emotional shadow of our fundamental intuitive adherence to proportional justice, which is really only based on it being good for people, that is, on the Slogan. If, therefore, we were to stick to the proportional justice value in the example given, in spite of its conflict with the Slogan, then we would simply not be behaving in a logically consistent manner. We would be allowing our rationale for adhering to proportional justice in the real world to distort our reaction to an other-world situation in which it does not apply. In that case our rejection of the Slogan would not be based on reason, but on emotion, or a failure to recognize that the reason why we are so attached to proportional justice simply does not apply in the special circumstances of the Temkin example.

In other words, if we are consistent, we ought to stick to the Slogan and deny that situation *B* can be worse than *A*. If we accept the Slogan and the assumption that nobody is worse off as a result of the sinners being better off in the next world, then we ought not to object to sinners being better off in a situation where this can do no harm to anybody unless we are motivated by considerations of revenge, for which it would be very difficult to provide any moral force.

One can, of course, think of many other possible conflicts between the Slogan and various commonly held 'intrinsic' values. For example, suppose it happened to be true, as most dictators proclaim, that freedom is bad for people all things considered. In that case, if one accepted the Slogan, one could no longer believe that freedom was valuable unless one believed that it had some intrinsic value over and above its goodness for people. Much would depend on what one believes constitutes being 'bad' or 'good' for people. Various candidates have long been discussed in the philosophical literature, such as mental state theories, preference satisfaction theories, objective list theories, and so on, and it would be inappropriate for us to try to adjudicate between them. All that is relevant here is to make the point that many widely accepted top-level 'intrinsic' values and conceptions of the 'good' may appear to conflict with the Slogan yet, at the same time, the Slogan appears to have considerable force. Something has to go. Which?

There is no clear-cut answer to this question. Temkin (1993: 282) points out, in defence of equality, that it is just as difficult to prove that inequality is intrinsically bad as to prove that injustice, or lack of freedom, is bad. This may well be true, but the argument cuts both ways. Indeed, it rather gives the game away. For it suggests that it is just as difficult to prove that proportional justice and freedom are intrinsically good as it is to prove that equality is intrinsically good. In other words, it is just as difficult to prove that any of these ideals is intrinsically good.

It is, of course, easy to give practical examples of the way that more justice or freedom can actually be good for people, or, for that matter, bad for them. The same could be done for more equality. In other words, it is easy to show how more justice or freedom or equality can affect the lives of people in various ways. But it is far from easy to show how any of these values is good or bad when they do not affect anybody. And the fact that it may be just as difficult to prove that X is good as to prove that Y is good does not imply that Y must be good. It is more likely that neither of them is good. Similarly, the fact that it may be just as difficult to show how ideals like justice, or freedom, have intrinsic value even when they do no good for anybody as it is to show that equality has intrinsic value even when it does no good for anybody does not imply that equality has intrinsic value. It could merely mean that none of them, including equality, has intrinsic value. In other words, it could merely mean that there is only one top-level intrinsic value, namely, 'good for people', and that there are no strictly impersonal intrinsic values that are not good for people, however indirectly.

This might be an unattractive and uncomfortable position to adopt, but that is a different matter. For example, Temkin (1993: 260) points out that one important theory of 'the good', namely, the theory that only the quality of conscious mental states is intrinsically valuable, would, if true, 'undermine virtually every ideal'. This may well be the case. But this is hardly an argument against the theory. Once again we are confronted with a conflict between two principles: in this instance the mental state theory of the good and some other ideals that claim to be good independent of their effect on peoples' mental states. And once again, the fact that there is a conflict does not tell us which side ought to prevail unless independent reasons are given for choosing one rather than the other. In the case of equality, for example, we need to be given convincing positive reasons to believe that greater equality is good even if it is good for nobody. There may well be cogent reasons for this belief but we have not yet met any.

More generally, 'ideals' that are not anchored in what is good for people should always be treated with great suspicion. Ideals are essential for the health of decent societies and, in practice, conflicts between them are inevitable, even in the judgement of any given individual. This is because being 'good for people' is inevitably a vague concept and can often refer to different, and often incomparable, ways of being good for them, so we cannot appeal to any clear guidance as to which among various competing ways of being good for them should have priority. This is the essence of 'plural values'. But this does not mean that any of the different values or ideals can depart from the criterion of being good for people. Over the course of history too many people have been sacrificed on the altar of great ideals—nation, race, religion, class, some ideology or other—which have been exploited by ruthless leaders who regarded their harmful effects on millions of people as, at most, a price that had to be paid for some 'greater good' of the promotion of some abstract and impersonal ideal.

Meanwhile it must suffice here to say that *if the Slogan is accepted* it seems that one is obliged to accept the Levelling Down Objection to the intrinsic value of equality. Given the Slogan, the Levelling Down Objection shows that the intrinsic merit of equality is zero, nought, nothing, period. It cannot even be traded off against other objectives since it simply has no trade-off value at all. Achieving some increase in equality by making some people worse off without making some other people better off simply would not constitute a move from one situation to another that is morally better, *in any respect.* Hence, in any conflict between, on the one hand, the intrinsic value of equal-ity and, on the other hand, the growth of welfare over time, whether over the past or the future, there would be no need to sacrifice any growth of welfare.

6. How Many People Really Believe in the Intrinsic Value of Equality Anyway?

In fact, we doubt whether many people really believe in the intrinsic value of equality. A survey of the reasons given by people for valuing equality showed that the proposed benefit that attracted most assent was the instrumental benefit of reducing social conflict between people.[26] It is also highly likely that those who value equality do so largely as a means of raising the welfare of those who are relatively badly off. This is why nearly all discussions of equality are in terms of the equality of some 'good', such as income, or wealth, or status, or resources, or opportunities, and so on. One rarely comes across any discussion of the desirability of equalizing the distribution of bads, such as poverty, sickness, pain, and so on, on the grounds that equality is intrinsically desirable. Yet making happy people miserable would usually be a far easier means of increasing equality than would be a policy of increasing the equality of happiness by making miserable people happier.

Indeed, if one examines the way people behave it appears that the belief that equality is an intrinsic good is probably not really shared even by many of those who are under the impression that they do share it. Consider, for example, the behaviour of people who strike for higher pay on egalitarian grounds. In the days when strikes were far more common than they are now, a common justification put forward for strikes, for example by the crews on

---

[26] Results of a survey to which reference is made in Miller (1991/92).

some cross-Channel ferry line, or the employees on some airline, or in some educational institution, was that employees doing exactly the same job in some other shipping company, or airline, and so on, were being paid more than they were and that this violated egalitarian principles. But one hardly ever heard the employees in the other companies, where they were getting higher pay, asking for lower pay in the interests of egalitarianism, let alone threatening to strike unless their pay was reduced. It is tempting to conclude, therefore, that egalitarianism was not the motive for the strikes in the former, and very common, cases, as much as a perfectly reasonable desire to increase one's own pay (Beckerman 1979).[27]

In short, most people, egalitarians included, do not seem to be much concerned with equality per se. But many people are genuinely concerned with equality as a means of reducing some 'bad'. They want equal incomes to reduce the 'bad' of poverty, or equal welfare to reduce the bad of misery, or equal health care to reduce the bad of physical suffering, and so on. They are sufficiently humanitarian to be distressed by the sight of, or knowledge of, the various manifestations of poverty, suffering, sickness, and so on. In any given society it is natural to resent the coexistence of such conditions with the affluence enjoyed by other sections of the population. And in a given society at any point in time total resources are more or less fixed, so that the only way one can reduce, say, the poverty of some is to take something away from others. This naturally leads to the intuitive feeling that what is ethically indefensible is the inequality per se. But in fact what really offends us is not so much the inequality as its assumed consequences in the particular society in which we live, namely, the poverty and suffering that exist.[28]

As Harry Frankfurt (1997: 5–6) has put it:

The egalitarian condemnation of inequality as inherently bad loses much of its force, I believe, when we recognize that those who are doing considerably worse than others may nonetheless be doing rather well . . . Inequality is, after all, a purely *formal* characteristic; and from this formal characteristic of the relationship between two items, nothing whatever follows as to the desirability or the value of either. Surely what is of genuine moral concern is whether people have good lives, and not how their lives compare with the lives of others.

In similar vein, Raz (1986: 240) writes that 'wherever one turns it is revealed that what makes us care about various inequalities is not the inequality but the concern identified by the underlying principle. It is the hunger of the hungry, the need of the needy, the suffering of the ill, and so on'.

Is it true then that, if it were not for its contribution to reducing the

---

[27] Jerry Cohen has pointed out to us, however, that it could also be argued that human frailty is such that although people do subscribe to the intrinsic value of equality they only perceive its merits when they are the victims of inequality.
[28] Martin Feldstein (1999) gives a striking presentation of this view from an economist's perspective.

poverty of the poor, or the hunger of the hungry, few people would not attach any importance to the concept of 'equality'? What about equality in the distribution of 'bads'? Suppose, for example, one had to chose between imposing 100 units of pain on one person and two units, of equal intensity, on 100 people. Most of us would prefer the latter even though the total pain suffered would be 200 units.[29] However, this does not prove that, at heart, we are egalitarians even where greater equality does not raise anybody's welfare, let alone that we ought to be. For a preference for spreading the pain in the manner suggested is probably just another facet of simple compassion. It would correspond to a form of what most philosophers call 'the Priority View', that is, that we should give priority to the worse off.[30]

Even Nagel's argument in favour of the intrinsic value of equality is essentially an argument in favour of giving priority to those in greater need. He argues that 'egalitarianism . . . establishes an order of priority among needs and gives preference to the most urgent' (Nagel 1979: 116–17). He defends this on the grounds that, as a matter of basic principle, society ought to choose the option that is least unacceptable to the person to whom it is most unacceptable. And, he argues, 'A radically egalitarian policy of giving absolute priority to the worst off, regardless of numbers, would result from always choosing the least unacceptable alternative, in this sense' (1979: 123).

But, as Crisp (2000) has pointed out, a crude version of the Priority View is open to certain objections. Suppose, for example, that, in the process of transferring, say, money or income or resources in general from a better off group to a worse off group, a lot is lost in the process. This might be the result of reductions in work incentives, or the bureaucratic processes and costs involved in making the transfer. It is what Okun (1975) once famously called 'the leaky bucket' effect. And suppose that we divide the population into two homogeneous groups, one of which is less well off than the other but is, mercifully, relatively very small. On account of the leaky bucket effect it may well be that in order to give a very small amount to the very small worse off group we would have to take a lot away from the better off group. How much are we prepared to go in making such a transfer? Much would depend, presumably, on the size of the leak but also on how badly off the worst off are, how many of them there are, and how much good one can do for them by comparison with the harm that we do to the other group which might not be all that much better off. Thus, as Crisp has shown, we might prefer an

---

[29] We owe this particular example, as well as much else, to Larry Temkin.

[30] The Priority View is the term that Parfit used in Parfit (1991). As pointed out in Chapter 2, it is what Temkin (1993: 247) called 'extended humanitarianism', which he said could be not so much what egalitarians actually do care about but what it might seem, mistakenly in his opinion, they *ought* to care about. In his 1978 Presidential Address to Section F (Economics) of the British Association for the Advancement of Science, Beckerman (1979) urged that humanitarianism replace egalitarianism as a central objective of distributive policy, but this was not in connection with future generations.

amended version of the Prioritarian view, namely, what he calls 'the Threshold Priority' view. According to this view, we give priority to people below a certain threshold of welfare, or to people who might be subject to considerable pain, but above some rough threshold we would not care much about the distribution of welfare or of pain.

Thus, suppose, in the earlier example, that the 100 units of pain to be inflicted on one person consisted merely of depriving him of the satisfaction of his desire to eat an ice-cream and the two units of pain to be inflicted on each of 100 other people consisted of not letting them have one lick each of the ice cream.[31] In such case we would probably not care one way or the other, since the pain of depriving one person of the ice cream would probably not put him below our compassion threshold.

This Threshold Priority view relieves us of any obligation to worry about the welfare of some group whose welfare could still be high even if it is below that of some other group. And this has considerable bearing on how much sacrifice the present generation should make for future generations if the latter can be expected to be far richer than we are, which, as we argue in Chapter 6, is highly likely. Furthermore, this view helps remind us again that the whole discussion so far has been in terms of whole generations, as if they were homogeneous, when, in fact, there are enormous disparities between the welfare levels of most people in the advanced countries and the widespread destitution in many parts of the Third World. There is certainly no moral obligation to impose sacrifices on the billions of people in dire poverty today, who would undoubtedly suffer further from any deliberately contrived cut in current levels of economic activity and growth in the interests of some environmentalist objective.

7. Resource Conservation and 'Fairness' between Generations

Most of the above may seem to be too abstract and really rather irrelevant to the current fashionable concern with intergenerational equality as a means of preventing the present generation using up an 'unfair' amount of the Earth's resources.[32] And some people may believe that even if we cannot really know how large potential supplies are of natural resources or what the cumulative

---

[31] It is assumed that they would get twice as much utility per lick than would one person eating the whole ice cream.

[32] The formulation of egalitarianism along the lines suggested by Raz—that is, 'If there are x people each person is entitled to $1/x$ of all the G that is available'—immediately reveals, of course, the *practical* impossibility of applying intergenerational egalitarianism even in one wanted to do so, since it would be necessary to know how much G will become available over the indefinite future and how many people there will be. And we cannot know either of these magnitudes.

size of the world population will be from now until the human race becomes extinct, we do know enough about certain resources and likely population levels over the foreseeable future to be legitimately concerned with the problem of using up more than our 'fair' share of such resources.

Consequently, many people believe that even if we abandon any attempt to defend a strictly egalitarian approach to our obligations to future generations we should at least accept that resources are 'finite' so that it would be 'unfair' if we took advantage of the fact that we happened to have been born first to use up more than our 'fair' share of them. It is rather like coming across an oasis in the middle of a desert. Suppose there is more water in it than we need for making a cup of tea. There might be enough to take a bath or a swim. But we know that, from time to time, other people will probably come across the oasis and want to find some water left in it that they can drink. It would seem that using up more water than necessary would be taking 'unfair' advantage of the fact that we happened to be there first.

There are many different concepts of 'fairness' and different ways of interpreting the implications of 'impartiality'. One conception of 'fairness' that might apply to the 'finite resource' question is Broome's (1991b) concept, which we have described above—though this does not mean that he would apply his concept of 'fairness' to relations between generations. The relevance of this concept of fairness to the problem of finite resources would be that if, for example, people have equal claims to a minimum supply of some good, fairness would require that they are given equal amounts of it, though 'other reasons' might require that, when *all things are considered*, the amount of the good in question could be shared out unequally. But, as we indicated earlier, there are problems with any such theory when one seeks to put it into practice on account of other considerations. In this particular instance it is very difficult to draw a clear dividing line between considerations that determine how far different peoples' 'claims' differ in strength and considerations that are 'other factors'.

To return to the lifeboat example, suppose that there is an old man in the boat who does not have many years left to live. One may well think that this weakens his claim to stay in the boat, in the same way that old people are often thought to have less claim to scarce medical resources than younger people who are expected to live much longer. By contrast, the woman in the boat with several small children back home may be thought to have a stronger claim. Or is this just another type of reason for overriding the 'fairness' criterion?

Thus, egalitarian distributive principles provide no easy answers on account of constraints on the information available and on the comparability of the various 'other factors' about which we may have information. We need to appeal to certain specific features of each case. And this difficulty seems insuperable in connection with the distribution of allegedly finite resources between generations. For even if future generations were to be granted equal 'claims' to allegedly finite resources, there is no useful sense in which one can identify what their 'equal' claims actually amount to. It may be possible to identify the equal claim, in the earlier example, to stay on board the lifeboat—though we have suggested that even this may not be so easy—or, to take a different example, the equal claim that all the inhabitants of a besieged city may have to a share in the available water and food supply. One knows how much food there is and how much water there is. But if we were to share out finite resources over time equally, on the grounds that everybody should have an equal share to the limited supply, we would be committing ourselves to the rule that 'the available supply of scarce resource, X, has to be shared out equally among all the people who will ever inhabit the Earth, including those who are alive today'.

But we have no idea what the potential supply of resources is. The vast increases over the past in the estimates of supplies of some key resources are shown in Chapter 6. And we have no idea how the demand for different resources will change over the ages in the light of changing technology, or the changes that may take place in the development of substitutes, the pattern of output, tastes for different types of goods and services, and their relative prices. Furthermore, we have no idea how many people will eventually inhabit the Earth anyway. Ought we assume that the human race will continue for ever, in which case our shares would be reduced to zero? Unfortunately, there would still be an inherent contradiction, for this would mean that we would all starve so that there would be no future generations to be worried about anyway (Streeten 1986).

Theoretically, this might mean that this is a prime example of a situation in which a lottery would be justified on the grounds that there is no other way of making a rational decision. But this would be too late anyway as far as past generations are concerned. And, as far as future generations are concerned, to all intents and purposes the lottery has already taken place and we may well have won it.[33] But what exactly is the prize? The best prize would be to be allowed to decide how we use our good fortune. So we have to ask how decent people should behave when they win this sort of lottery. The implication of the earlier chapters is that we ought to use our judgement of the likely course of events in order to ensure that we do not follow policies that will condemn future generations to poverty. As so often, beneficence plus informed judgement concerning the facts have to be our guides rather than any utopian appeals to some precise egalitarian formula. So we are back to square one, namely, that actual policy depends on some analysis of what are, in fact, the prospects for the supplies of resources.

[33] Except that we have not won the lottery for the most advanced technology. And future societies, including even those who will also turn out to have failed to win the lottery, may well find that having won only the 2,786th prize in it more than compensates them for not being in the same position as we are as regards the choice we have made today over our use of 'finite' resources.

In other words, 'fairness' does not imply any futile attempt to share out finite resources equally between generations. The present generation should, however, use its lucky primacy in time with humanitarian concern for future generations. It should respect the Lockean proviso not to waste resources. In his *Two Treatises of Government* John Locke (1965: 309, 328–9) wrote that an individual may fairly appropriate land for his own use, without belying the equal status of his fellows, provided that he (1) uses rather than wastes what he appropriates and (2) leaves 'enough and as good for others'. But Locke was not referring to the particular problems of future generations, who, insofar as the arguments we have advanced in Chapter 2 are accepted, do not have any 'rights'. In any case, the growth of standards of living over time in spite of continuous use of the Earth's resources, on account of investment in human capital, education and research, suggests that Locke would hardly have wanted his proviso to imply that no generation should use the Earth's resources at all.

In our oasis example, if we could see how to fix up a system that would provide an indefinite supply of water as long as we could drink enough water to keep alive for long enough to carry out the necessary works, we would not feel obliged to limit our own use of it. On the other hand, if we knew that other people who would be even more in need of water than we are would be arriving later and there was no way we could increase the water supply in time we should be very careful not to waste any of it. But if there was plenty of water and good reasons to believe that it would be replenished there is no reason why some of the people concerned should not use more than others, whether they are around at the same time or not. Some people may like to take baths more than others. Some people may need them more. Sometimes it is desirable to set them a good example.

No complex and highly contentious theory of justice is required in order to tell us what a humanitarian way is of dealing with the contingency of nature that takes the form of our generation having access to resources before posterity. The moral obligation not to deprive future generations of resources essential to their avoiding poverty is part of our natural duty to avoid inflicting unnecessary suffering on other people. The justification for any great sacrifice by the present generation is even less if account is taken of the actual prospects for material shortages afflicting future generations, as is shown in Chapter 6.

8. Conclusions

The strongest case for egalitarianism is on instrumental grounds, that is, as a means to reduce the poverty of the poor or the suffering of the sick and so on, *when the total of resources available is more or less fixed.* And it is almost certainly mainly in this spirit that most egalitarians are concerned with promoting greater equality at any point in time. For at any point in time an improvement in the position of deprived people in almost any dimension that is taken seriously in the equality debate—resources, welfare, opportunities, and so on—requires at least some equalization of the share of resources going to them. So it is natural to focus on egalitarianism as a means to improving the lot of deprived people.

It is thus natural for those who are accustomed to believing, rightly or wrongly, that equality has ethical value within any society to take the further step and assume that intergenerational equality is also ethically justified. But this step is open to various objections. First, we have argued that greater equality between generations cannot be defended on instrumental grounds, so that it would have to be defended on grounds of the intrinsic value of equality. We have then discussed at some length our basic objections to the intrinsic value of equality. We concluded that it should be replaced by a humanitarian concern to relieve obvious cases of poverty and suffering and hardship, and that above a certain threshold we ought to try rid ourselves of any other obsession with differences between people.

For, as we argue in Chapter 7, the most important bequest we could make to future generations would be a 'decent society' characterized by greater respect for basic human rights and the toleration of differences between people. By contrast, belief in the value of equality invites one to be critical of various kinds of differences between people. It is true that the sort of differences given most attention by egalitarians are undeserved differences in welfare, or some closely related variable. But one suspects that if the sources of 'unjustified' or 'unfair' differences between people to which most attention is normally given were all eliminated, some other undeserved inequality would become the target of complaint.

This attitude to inequalities should not be lightly encouraged. Concentration on the undesirability of certain differences between people, whether deserved or undeserved, is an attitude of mind that is inherently undesirable. There will always be differences between people of one kind or another that will not correspond to differences in merit or desert or any of the other usual criteria of so-called 'just' inequalities. Some people will be stronger than others, or have different colour skins, or be cleverer, or be of different ethnic group or religion, or have different degrees of musical or sporting talent, or just differently shaped noses. One of the main sources of conflict between humans—probably *the* main source of conflict—has been intolerance of various forms of difference between individuals or groups. To move towards a more 'decent society' of the kind discussed in Chapter 7, the essential requirement is that people accept differences between people as not detracting from their common humanity. Concern with comparative inequalities, however undeserved, rather than merely compassionate concern with suffering or sickness or hunger only encourages concern with the differences between people and to that extent is fundamentally undesirable.

A decent society would try to cultivate peoples' sensibilities and respect for diversity of cultures, beliefs, and individual personalities. A society in which its members enjoy basic human rights and are free of poverty but in which diversity is under suspicion could still be boring and uncreative and possibly also lacking in compassion. Such a society kills progress; and progress must be the goal of a decent society, by contrast with a yearning for some utopian equality. Thus, insofar as we seem to be faced with a conflict between human development, with all its risks, and intergenerational equality, there seems to be no contest.

Finally, even if one wants greater equality, presumably, like charity, it should begin at home, that is, with the present generation. So those who do believe in egalitarianism should at least make sure that it is not the present-day impoverished sections of the world population that bear any of the burden of the sacrifices that might have to be made in the interests of future generations. The problem of the equitable sharing out of the burden of environmental preservation, therefore, is one to which we return in the final four chapters of this book.

5

Sustainable Development

1. The Appeal of 'Sustainable Development'

We have argued in the previous chapters that there is little chance of being able to construct a logically coherent theory of justice between generations. In particular, we have criticized, in Chapter 4, one particular principle that is widely believed to provide some guide to our moral obligations towards future generations, namely, intergenerational equity. But probably the principle that is most widely believed to provide firm guidance as to how we should conceive of our obligations to future generations is the currently very fashionable and influential principle of 'sustainable development'.

To some extent the popularity of sustainable development owes much to the claim that it can fill some of the gaps in conventional economics to which we drew attention in Chapter 1. For sustainable development is claimed to provide a wider concept of what development should consist of than do conventional measures of economic growth. It would be less restricted to goods and services transacted in the market; it would give more importance to distributional aspects of economic development in general; and, in particular, it would avoid penalizing future generations in the interests of maximizing the welfare of the present generation.

In 1987 the popularity of the sustainable development concept was given a great boost by the publication of *Our Common Future*, the report of the World Commission on the Environment and Development, known as the 'Brundtland Report', after its chairperson, Mrs Brundtland, the then Prime Minister of Norway. This report firmly established the concept of sustainable development as a substitute for the orthodox economist's paradigm of maximizing the stream of welfare over some future time period. It was not surprising, therefore, that it soon acquired a very wide following. And it is undeniable that it may actually be useful as an important reminder of the environmental dimension to economic development.

But there is no evidence yet that the concept has been able to provide any additional operational guidelines for environmental policy in practice, let alone provide any valid insights into the formulation of our moral obligations to future generations.[1] In fact, we shall argue in this chapter that the opposite would seem to be the case. Nor does the concept of sustainable development help fill any of the three perceived limitations on traditional economics.

In the first place, although it is true that, in the past, development policy has tended to ignore environmental issues, particularly those having very long-run consequences, this is not because of any gap in economic theory. Indeed, the first full analysis of the 'externalities' that are at the root of environmental pollution was made by the great economist, Pigou, back in 1920, and most of the serious analysis of both the theory and the practice of environmental problems was being carried out by economists for decades before their discovery by environmentalists. If environmental issues have not been given much attention in development policy, this has been for the simple reason that, in most cases, there were more urgent priorities, as most developing countries themselves have often pointed out. When one is anxious about how to get a square meal the next day one is not likely to worry much about the effect of deforestation on the global uptake of carbon through the process of photosynthesis.

Second, the notion that economics is not seriously concerned with distributional issues could not be further from the truth. In fact, early pioneers of economics, such as Ricardo, were primarily concerned with the way that the national product—this term was not then used—was distributed among the main factors of production, land, labour, and capital. Pigou's classic work *The Economics of Welfare* included extensive analysis of the distribution of incomes between different groups in society, and many other major studies by economists were devoted solely to this issue. In some—in the works by the great Polish economist Michal Kalecki, for example—the distribution of income between wages and profits also plays a pivotal role in his model of the determination of the overall level of employment and output.

It is true that professional economists agree less about what determines the way that national income is shared out than about, say, what determines the pattern of output. But economists have still provided a massive amount of sophisticated and detailed analysis of the distribution of incomes among different groups in society, the measurement of inequality, and the way that income distribution varies over time, or between countries, or between different social groups, and so on. By comparison, the contribution of the concept of 'sustainable development' has simply become more confused as time goes by and bears little or no clear relationship to any of the statistical 'indicators' of sustainable development that, from time to time, are bandied about. Indeed, as two distinguished authorities in the field have said of sustainable

---

[1] Some advocates of 'sustainable development' do not think that its lack of operational value matters. For example, Henryk Skolimowski, a Professor of Ecological Philosophy, writes 'Who on earth would want to operationalise the idea of "Sustainable Development?" ' (Skolimowski 1995: 69).

development, 'It would be difficult to find another field of research endeavour in the social sciences that has displayed such intellectual regress' (Dasgupta and Mäler 1994: 12).

2. The 'Sustainable Development' Bandwagon

Notwithstanding its intellectual fragility, 'sustainable development' is now firmly entrenched in the minds of many institutions, individuals, and policy-makers. Apparently, some large corporations are now so concerned with the political correctness of sustainable development that they have incorporated programs into their computers that automatically insert the word 'sustainable' before the word 'development' in any document they produce. It has spawned a vast literature and has strengthened the arm of empire builders in many research institutes, universities, national and international bureaucracies, and statistical offices.[2]

But it is difficult to see what contribution can be made to dealing with obvious urgent environmental problems, whether in cities in rich countries or all over the place in poor countries, by projects such as, for example, a recent publicly financed ESRC project which '. . . sought to relate debates in environmental philosophy and sustainable development to the changing nature of commitment and "belonging" in modern society' and which involved 'exploration of the "social worlds" of several unstructured "lifestyle" networks', the results of which are alleged to have potentially radical implications for 'sustainable development', notably by demonstrating the need to '. . . reflect better attunement to the deeper dynamics of the web of cultural networks that are reproducing themselves in civil society' (ESRC: 1997: 6–7).

Nor is it easy to see the point of an official UK governmental publication titled *Indicators of Sustainable Development*, which reproduces lots of statistics that had been appearing elsewhere in different publications for many years already but which seem to bear no obvious relationship to any conceivable definition of 'sustainable development' . It shows, for example, that there has been an increase, over the last 30 years, in the amount of 'aggregates'—crushed rock, gravel, and so on—extracted in Britain. They are no doubt used for all those terrible motorways, school, houses, and hospitals that are being

---

[2] In 1992, at Rio de Janeiro, the United Nations held a Conference on Environment and Development (UNCED), in which almost all the countries in the world participated. They adopted a document of several hundred pages, known as 'Agenda 21', which set out, among other things, their agreement to monitor their own developments from the point of view of their 'sustainability' and to submit regular reports on these developments to a newly established Commission on Sustainable Development (CSD). Chapter 8 of this agreement states that 'Governments, in cooperation, where appropriate, with international organisations, should adopt a national strategy for sustainable development'. It goes on to say that countries should draw up sustainable development strategies the goals of which 'should be to ensure socially responsible economic development while protecting the resource base and the environment for the benefit of future generations'.

built all the time. So it is easy to understand the moral outrage of the eco-warriors who smashed up the Whatley quarry in Somerset a few years ago or of the spokesman for the Green pressure group 'Earth First' who threatened that 'We will be stepping up our action against the quarry firms'![3]

But perhaps their anxiety or indignation had been needlessly aroused by the sort of 'indicators' of sustainable development that are paraded in front of us. For the increasing volume of aggregates extracted from quarries for various building purposes may not really be a good 'indicator' that Britain, or the world as a whole, is not following a path of 'sustainable development'. In fact, over 2,000 years ago Pericles warned his countrymen that world resources could not sustain the increased demand on them that they were experiencing—all those temples, statues of Poseidon, hand-painted vases, and other consumer durables!—yet the human race has managed to hang on and even increase several hundred-fold or so (French 1964).

Many years ago a common criticism of much pre-war statistical business-cycle research in the USA was that it was 'measurement without theory'. It is true, as stated at the beginning of *Indicators of Sustainable Development*, that 'There is no universally accepted definition of what constitutes sustainable development' (UK Department of the Environment 1996: 5). But the same applies to concepts such as 'unemployment' or 'inflation' and so on, yet it is usually fairly obvious that there is a close connection between these concepts and the measures that are used. So before spending large amounts of public money rehashing a motley collection of statistical indicators, it would have been nice at least to attempt some explanation of the precise link between them and *some* definition of sustainable development.

3. The Search for a Definition

In the Brundtland Report sustainable development was defined as 'development that meets the needs of the present without compromising the ability of future generations to meet their own needs' (WCED 1987: 43). Over the years innumerable other definitions of sustainable development have been proposed. But there is a fairly clear trend in them. At the beginning, sustainability was interpreted as a requirement to preserve intact the environment as we find it today in all its forms. The Brundtland report, for example, stated: 'The loss of plant and animal species can greatly limit the options of future generations; so sustainable development requires the conservation of plant and animal species' (WCED 1987: 43).

---

[3] See *Construction News* (7 December 1995).

But, we might ask, how far does the Brundtland report's injunction to conserve plant and animal species really go? Are we supposed to preserve some of them or all of them? If the former, how many, and if the latter, at what price? Are we supposed to mount a large operation, at astronomic cost, to ensure the survival of every known and unknown species on the grounds that it may give pleasure to future generations, or may turn out, in a hundred years time, to have medicinal properties? About 98 per cent of all the species that have ever existed are believed to have become extinct, but most people do not suffer any great sense of loss as a result. How many people lose sleep because it is no longer possible to see a live Dinosaur?

Clearly such an absolutist concept of 'sustainable development' is morally unacceptable. Given the acute poverty and environmental degradation in which many of the world's population live, we could not justify using up vast resources in an attempt to preserve from extinction, say, every single one of the several million species of beetle that exist. The cost of such a task would be partly, if not wholly, resources which could otherwise have been devoted to more urgent environmental concerns, such as increasing access to clean drinking water or sanitation in the Third World.

When it soon became obvious that such a 'strong' concept of sustainable development was morally unacceptable, as well as totally impracticable, many environmentalists shifted their ground. There are, of course, innumerable definitions of 'sustainable development' and advocates of some of them often disagree with each other even more than they disagree with us.[4] But there has been a trend in the literature towards what has been described as 'weak' sustainability. This allows for some natural resources to be run down as long as adequate compensation is provided by increases in other resources, perhaps even in the form of manmade capital. But what constitutes adequate compensation? How many more schools or hospitals or houses or factories or machines are required to compensate for using up of some mineral resources or forests or clean atmosphere? The answer, it turned out, was that the acceptability of the substitution had to be judged by its contribution to sustaining human welfare.

This is clear from one of the definitions provided by David Pearce, a leading world authority on the concept of sustainable development. For example, in conjunction with Warford, he defined sustainable development as 'development that secures increases in the welfare of the current generation provided that welfare in the future does not decrease' (Pearce and Warford 1993: 49). Similarly, John Pezzey (1992: 11), in an authoritative and extensive survey, concluded that most definitions still 'understand sustainability to

---

[4] See the controversy between one of us and some critics, who disagreed with each other on major aspects of sustainable development, in Beckerman (1994; 1995*b*); Daly (1995); Jacobs (1995); and El Serafy (1996).

mean sustaining an improvement (or at least maintenance) in the quality of life, rather than just sustaining the existence of life'. He went on to adopt as a 'standard definition of sustainable development' one according to which welfare per head of population must never decline.[5] The same definition is adopted in the editorial introduction to a more recent extensive collection of articles on sustainable development, where it is stated that 'Consequently, non-negative change in economic welfare per capita becomes the inter-temporal equity objective' (Faucheux, Pearce, and Proops 1996). The same definition has been confirmed in other authoritative sources.[6]

One of the important features of all these definitions is that, in the end, they are couched in terms of maintaining 'wellbeing' or 'welfare', not some other concept such as the overall stock of natural capital, which is the key variable in some definitions of sustainable development. In other words, it allows for substitutability between different forms of natural capital and manmade capital, provided that, on balance, there is no decline in welfare. The central variable, welfare, that must not be allowed to decline is thus treated as some sort of 'catch-all' variable. But if the choice between preserving natural capital and adding to, or preserving, manmade capital depends on which makes the greater contribution to welfare, the whole point of replacing the orthodox economist's paradigm of welfare maximization by some allegedly wider concept that incorporates non-welfarist values is fatally undermined. In the attempt to rid the original 'strong' concept of sustainable development of its most obvious weaknesses the baby has been thrown out with the bath water.

But many environmentalists argue that it is impossible to make certain values commensurate with each other, and hence capable of being represented in some unique catch-all variable, such as 'welfare'. One of the usual environmentalist criticisms of cost-benefit analysis in environmental projects, in fact, is that the environment represents some incommensurate values that cannot be incorporated into the usual economist's paradigm of welfare maximization. This criticism is discussed at much greater length in Chapters 8 and 9 on environmental valuation, so need not detain us here.

But it should be remarked, *en passant*, that it reveals a dilemma in the attempt to differentiate sustainable development from conventional economic analysis. For either one genuinely subscribes to irreducible plural

---

[5] In a more recent paper, Pezzey (1997) has indicated that the variety of definitions of sustainable development has proliferated enormously since his 1992 survey and provides a useful classification of the three most common sustainability 'constraints' encountered now in the literature.

[6] See, for example, a recent study that emerged from the collaboration between the World Bank and the Centre for Social and Economic Research on the Global Environment (CSERGE), by Atkinson *et al.* (1997), which, in the Introduction, defines sustainable development as non-declining human wellbeing over time.

values or one doesn't. If one does not and one believes instead that everything can be subsumed into one top-level value, namely, welfare, then there can be no objection to the economist's model of maximizing the future stream of welfare—although it is usually referred to as 'utility'. If, by contrast, one subscribes to plural values of which the welfare that economists seek to maximize is only one, then one might want to allow it to decline in circumstances where this may be offset by increases in some other top-level intrinsic values. In that case the 'no decline in welfare' rule should be abandoned. This rule would appear to be totally indefensible anyway, for the reasons set out below, quite apart from its apparent conflict with the acceptance of plural values.

4. The Ban on Future Declines in Welfare

The second crucial feature of many concepts of sustainable development is that they rule out any decline in per capita welfare below the level enjoyed by the current generation.[7] But it is difficult to see why one should attach crucial normative significance to the current level of welfare. It cannot be argued that, by some extraordinary coincidence, the present average standard of living constitutes some minimum subsistence level below which future generations must not be allowed to fall. For past generations seem to have survived with far less.

The arbitrariness of the rule that welfare should not be allowed to fall below the present level becomes clear if we imagine sticking to this rule in the future. Imagine, for example, exhorting the public in the year 2050 to pursue policies that ensured that future per capita welfare levels did not fall below those prevailing in the year 2000. Thus, as Brian Barry (1999: 107) concludes, the only plausible interpretation of the rule that future welfare levels should not fall below those prevailing today is that the rule has to be adjusted over time: that is, each generation must ensure that successor generations did not fall below the level of welfare that they had reached, however high that may be. But in that case the rule is really being transposed into the rule that precludes any decline in welfare at any point of time.

So we have to examine the moral force of the general rule that excludes future declines in welfare for any period of time even if this may be a necessary price to be paid for higher levels of welfare before or after, and even if it is from a much higher level of welfare than that prevailing today. Such a rule

---

[7] This is implied by the rule that per capita welfare should never be allowed to decline but the rule that it should never fall below the current level of per capita welfare is also sometimes explicitly specified (for example, Howarth and Norgaard 1992: 473–4).

appears to be based on the claim that there is something special about effects on the state of mind caused by *changes* in the level of welfare that cannot be incorporated into welfare itself. This special effect on our states of mind we shall call Z.

This claim does not seem very plausible. Most subjective experiences and mental states differ from each other in one way or another, sometimes in ways that may be fundamentally incommensurate. But it is difficult to see why those arising from *decreases* in welfare should be singled out as being incommensurate with those that one derives from the *level* of one's welfare, let along totally outranking the satisfaction derived from any given *level* of welfare. And if one believes that the satisfaction—or dis-satisfaction—derived from a change in welfare is incommensurate with the satisfaction obtained from the level of welfare, then the whole exercise is futile anyway and the analysis of changes in welfare between generations should be abandoned. This would also mean, of course, abandoning most definitions of the concept of 'sustainable development'.

Furthermore, if we do accept that there is some mysterious desirable experience or state of mind, Z, that is adversely affected by *declines* in welfare but that does not constitute part of welfare, there seems no reason to treat *declines* in welfare differently from *increases* in welfare. In that case it is perfectly possible that the loss of the mysterious Z caused by some decline in welfare could be offset by the extra Z caused by the preceding, or following, increase in welfare. It is no doubt true that a very rich man may suffer some extra loss of welfare if he has had a bad year on the stock exchange and has had to sell his yacht. He would not miss the yacht so much if he had never had owned one before. But if he had not started out in life owning a yacht he would have got some extra satisfaction from acquiring one. So in this case the extra negative Z that we are invited to subtract from his total lifetime welfare as a result of losing the yacht should be offset by some extra positive Z he derived when he acquired it. In other words, if we are to attach a separate value to *changes* in welfare, they need not be only negative. We should also include any increases in welfare that preceded the decreases, or that may follow it.

The same need for symmetry applies to different generations. For if the feared decline in welfare of future generations that we are asked to avoid at all costs is from a higher level of welfare than the one we enjoy now, the intervening generations must have experienced more increases in welfare than declines in welfare. On balance, therefore, as well as being credited with more welfare for reaching higher levels, future generations should be credited with even more welfare because they reached the higher levels in the only possible way, namely, by experiencing more increases than decreases! So there would be even less reason to feel sorry for them.

5. A Nozickian Approach

But, it may be argued, this is too mechanistic an approach to the balancing of increases and decreases in welfare.[8] Even without appealing to the mysterious Z, it may well be that one should take account of the whole shape and direction of the time path of welfare—that is, whether it is rising or falling—quite apart from its total cumulative level. No less an authority than Robert Nozick (1989: 99ff.) has defended this position at some length without claiming that the value of the *decrease* in welfare is incommensurate with welfare itself, so he does not even rely on the mysterious variable, Z. Nozick actually presents his argument in terms of 'happiness', but this makes no difference to the argument here.
He writes:

... even if happiness were the only thing we cared about, we would not care solely about its total amount ... We would care also about how that happiness was distributed within a lifetime. Imagine graphing someone's total happiness through life; the amount of happiness is represented on the vertical axis, time on the horizontal one .. . If only the total amount of happiness mattered, we would be indifferent between a life of constantly increasing happiness and one of constant decrease, between an upward- and a downward-sloping curve, provided that the total amount of happiness, the total area under the curve, was the same in the two cases. Most of us, however, would prefer the upward-sloping line to the downward; we would prefer a life of increasing happiness to one of decrease. Part of the reason, but only a part, may be that since it makes us happy to look forward to greater happiness, doing so makes our current happiness score even higher. (Yet the person on the downward-sloping curve alternatively can have the current Proustian pleasure of remembering past happiness.) *Take the pleasure of anticipation into account, though, by building it into the curve whose height is therefore increased at certain places*; still most of us would not care merely about the area under *this* enhanced curve, but about the curve's direction also. (Which life would you prefer your children to have, one of decline or of advance?). (Nozick 1989: 100; emphasis added)

In the Annex to this chapter we present in diagrammatic form, with two minor modifications that do not, we believe, affect the argument, the situation described by Nozick. But the basic idea is very simple and can be described adequately in words. Compare two life paths. One is the life path of a woman who has five cars, a big yacht, two holiday villas in superb locations in each of which she keeps a handsome lover, and a lovely 15-speed bicycle. The other path is of a woman who has just one old bicycle and one lover, who is really rather unpleasant anyway. Nothing else in their lives offsets these differences so that, however much we may wish it were not true, the first woman is much happier and leads a far more satisfying life than does

---

[8] We are indebted to Robert Nozick himself for drawing our attention to his treatment of the question.

the second woman. Even worse, they know each other and the second woman is madly envious of the first, particularly of the bicycle. But then the first woman finds that the sharp rise in the price of petrol means that she really ought to give up one of the cars that uses a lot of petrol and also switch to a smaller yacht. The time path of her life style and, by assumption, her welfare slopes downwards. The second woman, however, finds a slightly better-paid job and is able to buy a better bicycle. The time path of her life style slopes upwards. Which time path would most people prefer? Presumably the former, since the total level of welfare over the whole of the first woman's life is far greater than that of the second woman, in spite of the fact that the former time path sloped downwards and the latter sloped upwards.

However, for Nozick this is clearly not the end of the matter, since he goes on to say that, even under the key assumptions of his model—that is, incorporating the anticipation and recollection effects—one may still prefer a life represented by the rising path to the life with the declining path even when the cumulative welfare—happiness—in the former life is less than under the latter. This may be because in the situation where we are evaluating alternative life profiles for, say, our children, we would evaluate 'the life as a whole from a point outside it' (Nozick 1989: 101 fn), and it would be we, not the children, who would prefer their lives to follow the rising welfare/happiness paths. And if we transpose this example to the intergenerational context, it would amount to this generation having a preference for a rising path for future generations even though, in terms of the above model, total welfare was no greater, and possibly even smaller, than under the falling path.

But in both cases—that is, of evaluating the life path of individuals, for example our children, or of future generations—it is *our* preferences that are being satisfied, not those of the subjects in question—our children or the future generations. This rather reduces the moral force of such preferences. Neither our children nor future generations may thank us for choosing a rising path rather than a falling path if cumulative welfare under the former were smaller than under the latter, particularly if they had very good memories of their pasts and gave little thought to their futures. It is true that both would normally prefer rising paths to falling paths, *other things being equal*. But if the falling path starts from a much higher level so that total welfare over the whole period is greater than that of the rising path, since this starts from a low level, there is little doubt that they would prefer the former, whatever we, as outside observers, may prefer.

Furthermore, Nozick (1989: 100) does accept that if the downward sloping path 'encompassed vastly greater area, the choice might be different'. In other words, there appears to be some trade-off between the direction of the time path of welfare and the total cumulative welfare. This is, of course, implicit in his acceptance of the commensurability of the two aspects of welfare—the level and the effect of the direction—which is needed in order to refer to them in the spatial terms that Nozick describes verbally. But we are given no clue as to what determines the trade off. Furthermore, in view of our earlier argument about the need to allow for increases in welfare to outweigh decreases, his argument could not be used by those advocates of sustainable development who would prohibit *any* declines in welfare even if necessary to provide for preceding or subsequent increases.[9]

6. 'Sustainable Development' versus Maximizing Future Welfare

If the arguments we have set out above are correct, it may appear strange that advocates of sustainable development should attach so much importance to the issue of rising or falling welfare instead of concentrating on the total cumulative welfare that individuals or generations can be expected to enjoy. The explanation is probably that, for most people, the preference given to upward-sloping welfare paths is really based on a simple and natural tendency to prefer going up to going down when we are dealing with some 'good', such as welfare, and when it is assumed *that we are starting from the same level*. For example, we derive psychological satisfaction from the prospect of our children's progress throughout their lives chiefly because we envisage them as starting from some given level of happiness.

For it is, of course, true that, *starting from any particular level*, if we want to maximize something 'good', like 'welfare', it is better for it to go up, or even remain stable, than to go down. But that is only because, and insofar as, we expect that this will lead to total welfare over the future being greater than it would otherwise be. So in the end all that one is really concerned with is the total welfare over some future time period, and the purely technical characteristic of 'going up' or 'going down' is irrelevant.

---

[9] A possible defence of Nozick's position, independently of the incommensurability of *changes* in welfare with *levels* of welfare, is that the effect of the changes cannot be allocated to any particular time. For example, it may be thought that an increasing welfare life path is a feature of the whole time path and its desirability cannot be allocated to any particular point in time as is done in the above model. But this means accepting the notion of a satisfaction, or 'good', or source of happiness or welfare, that does not ultimately accrue to somebody at any particular time. This would then raise the question: to whom would any particular time path of development properly have value? If excluding some feasible time path of welfare simply because it comprised a period of declining welfare meant excluding a path that gave a higher total level of welfare over the whole of the time period in question, then we must be depriving some later generations of the welfare that they would otherwise have obtained. What moral force can we claim for such a policy? Nozick's footnote to page 101 discusses some other complicated issues that arise in making the sort of comparison attempted above, but it would be beyond the scope of this book as well as of our own competence to embark on a discussion of them. But while we remain unconvinced, we are particularly indebted to John Broome for persuading us that it may not be possible to dispose of the argument in the simple manner set out in Fig. 5.2 in the Annex to this chapter.

This means that, faced with the choice between two technically feasible development paths over some given future time period, if one path includes a period of declining welfare and the other does not, but the former leads to higher total welfare over the whole period, then that is the one that should be chosen. If, instead, we reject it on—perhaps mistaken—egalitarian grounds we must have forgotten why we tend to prefer periods of rising rather than falling welfare and we are making a choice that is inconsistent with our underlying objective of maximizing welfare.

And it is perfectly feasible, even starting from the same level, for a path that did not contain any periods of declining welfare to lead not only to greater intergenerational inequality but also to lower total welfare than does a path containing a period of declining welfare but that would fulfill the usual economist's objective of maximizing social welfare over whatever time period is regarded as relevant.

Consider, for example, Fig. 5.1, in which there are two alternative feasible paths of development. One of them, path *SD*, contains no periods of declining welfare and so is a sustainable development path. The other path, *MSW*, is the path that maximizes feasible social welfare over the whole period. To follow this path it would be necessary for earlier generations to use up far more resources and achieve higher standards of living, and hence to have maintained higher levels of investment, which would benefit the following generations. Nevertheless, resources would decline, in the end, under *MSW*, although thanks to the higher rates of investment in man-made capital and human knowledge made by the earlier generations, total welfare did not fall very much from a peak.

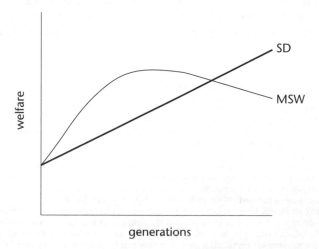

FIGURE 5.1. Sustainable development versus maximum social welfare

By assumption, *SD* represents both lower total welfare over the whole period and greater intergenerational inequality than does the path, *MSW*. It seems unlikely that any ethical principle to justify choosing *SD* would be easy to find. To reject *MSW*, which is what is required in the interests of sustainable development, is, therefore, quite unjustified. Indeed, the sustainable development requirement to exclude any future declines in welfare, at any price in terms of total cumulative welfare, seems to be so senseless that one is forced to conclude that its exclusion is just an attempt to differentiate the product from the conventional economist's paradigm of simply maximizing welfare over whatever period of time is thought to be relevant.

7. Maximizing Future Welfare and Intergenerational Equity

The third way in which the sustainable development concept is often alleged to be superior to the standard economist's maximization model is its claim, referred to at the beginning of Chapter 4 above, to attach more importance to the distribution of welfare over time. It is true that the most elementary economist's standard model is usually the behaviour of some individual. A favourite example is Robinson Crusoe, before the arrival of Man Friday, having to decide how to allocate his time optimally between hunting and fishing for food and building a boat that would eventually increase the productivity of his fishing expeditions. In such cases—that is, where optimization is being assessed from the viewpoint of one individual—it is easy to see that it may be worthwhile accepting a period of declining income, say, in the interests of greater total income over one's whole lifetime. For example, one may choose to embark on a period of lengthy and expensive professional training and education or to gain some important, but lowly paid, work experience, in the expectation of a greater lifetime income. In this case the person who accepts the sacrifice of a decline in income and welfare earlier on in life is the same person as the person who would be compensated by gaining the extra income and welfare in later life.

As between generations this does not apply. A generation making a sacrifice of a decline in welfare would not be compensated by any resulting gains in welfare accruing to later generations. And the case for sustainable development rests largely on its claim to take account of intergenerational equity by contrast with what is alleged to be the standard economist's procedure of maximizing total welfare over some time period.

But we have argued, in Chapter 4, that the case for intergenerational egalitarianism is particularly weak. Furthermore, it is not even consistent with any common definition of sustainable development. One of the apparently many inconsistencies in the sustainable development concept is that the 'no decline in welfare' rule does not ensure greater intergenerational equality of welfare at all. In fact, the opposite is the case. Paradoxically, it is trivially obvious that nothing could lead to more intergenerational inequality than a continuous increase in welfare. And the faster it increases the greater the inequality. Of course, as pointed out in the last chapter, faster development may be regarded as better *all things considered*. But it would be worse *in one respect*, namely, in respect of unjust inequality, provided that earlier generations are poorer than later generations involuntarily and through no fault of their own. To achieve an optimum compromise, therefore, between sustainable development and intergenerational equality from now into the future would imply imposing some restraint on any further rise in welfare. It is doubtful if advocates of sustainable development realize that they are subscribing to this strange objective.

Furthermore, when it comes down to seeking guidance for making an optimum trade-off between total welfare and equality, it is to conventional economic tools of analysis that one has to turn. For example, some standard cost-benefit techniques incorporate in the estimates of total benefits of a project an allowance for the way in which the costs and benefits are shared out among different income groups (for example, Little and Mirrlees 1974). Similarly, as regards the distribution of utility over time, standard discounting is based on the implicit assumption that, as people become richer, the additional utility obtained by a given increment of consumption declines. Estimates of welfare that allow for varying degrees of inequality of income distribution can easily be made within existing models, such as the Atkinson concept of an 'equally distributed equivalent income'. In other words, conventional economic tools enable one to take account of inequality in the distribution of incomes, whether between groups at any point of time or between generations over time, in a manner that can give precision to one's degree of inequality aversion—which is more than can be said for vague hand-waving in the direction of 'equity' under the banner of 'sustainable development' (Atkinson 1970; Beckerman 1980).

8. Should 'Sustainability' be a Constraint?

We have argued above that the concept of sustainable development suffers from three weaknesses.

1. The concentration on 'welfare' or 'well-being' as the central variable in the concept of sustainable development appears to be inconsistent with its familiar claim to represent 'plural values' that go beyond the standard economist's objective of welfare maximization.

2. Its insistence on some 'no decline in welfare' rule is full of logical flaws.
3. Its claim to be more intergenerationally equitable than the standard economist's paradigm of maximizing welfare over time is untenable.

But sustainable development is also sometimes presented as being less an overriding guide to development policy than a 'constraint' on the objective of welfare maximization. Mimicry of the economist's use of the concept of a 'constraint' is the latest twist in the evolution of the concept of sustainable development. It represents a further step in the retreat, under fire, from the original presentation of 'sustainable development' as a great breakthrough in our thinking on the subject. First there is the retreat from strong sustainability to weak sustainability, and then from weak sustainability as an objective of policy to weak sustainability as just a constraint. The idea is that welfare should be maximized, but subject to the constraint that the path of development being followed be sustainable. However, this position is no more tenable than the other positions and is based on a misunderstanding of the concept of a 'constraint'.

Economic theory is dominated by the notion of how to make optimal choices when faced with constraints of one kind or another. For example, firms are seen as seeking to maximize profits *subject to constraints*, such as the prices they can charge for the goods they sell or the wages they need pay employees. Or households are assumed to be trying to maximize utility *subject to constraints* in terms of their incomes and the prices of goods they buy, and so on. If, for example, the firm could relax the wage constraint and pay lower wages it could make higher profits. If a household could relax its income constraint by earning more, or by borrowing, it could increase welfare.

But only if there is a conflict between the 'constraint' and what it is that one is trying to maximize does it make sense to use the term 'constraint'. For a constraint is something that, if relaxed, enables us to obtain more of whatever it is we are trying to maximize. Where there is no conflict, however, there is no scope for a 'constraint'.

Sustainable development could constitute a constraint on welfare maximization, therefore, only if it conflicted with it. The 'strong' sustainability criterion of policy could logically constitute such a constraint, since it is obvious that higher welfare might have to be sacrificed in order to preserve the environment in all its entirety in its present state—assuming that this was feasible, which it isn't. But 'strong sustainability' has been more or less abandoned on account of its moral unacceptability. And 'weak' sustainability obviously cannot conflict with welfare maximization since the criterion of whether a substitution of manmade capital for natural capital is acceptable is whether it makes an adequate contribution to welfare.

For sustainability to constitute a constraint on welfare maximization, therefore, some other source of conflict between sustainability and welfare maximization had to be found. We have discussed at some length one that has been given much prominence, namely, distributional considerations, particularly the intergenerational distribution of welfare. But, as we have indicated, there is a long tradition in economics to the effect that income distribution is an integral part of welfare, and conventional economic techniques already exist for incorporating distributional considerations into a comparison of alternative levels of total welfare, whether at any point of time or over time.

The advocates of sustainable development as a constraint, therefore, face a dilemma. Either they stick to 'strong' sustainability, which is a logical candidate for a constraint, but which requires them to subscribe to a morally repugnant and totally impracticable objective; or they switch to some welfare-based concept of sustainability, in which case they are advocating a concept that appears to be redundant and unable to qualify as a logical constraint on welfare maximization.

9. Conclusions

It is widely believed that the concept of 'sustainable development' fills the gaps that appear to exist in conventional ethical theory or economic theory as far as our obligations to future generations is concerned. As such it is often represented as a 'radical' departure in ethics, a form of 'New (green) Ethics', like 'New (not-red) Labour'. But a radical change in direction is pointless unless it is the result of some newer and deeper insights into the problems faced. And on closer inspection, sustainable development seems to be full of confusions and logical errors. There seems little point, therefore, in trying to find some clear definition of what it is supposed to mean, let alone any clear structure of argument in which one could see how the conclusions follow from the premises. As a popular slogan it may do some good if it provides a rallying point for pressures in society to remedy some of the obvious defects in the market mechanism which prevent environmental protection from being given due weight. But if it becomes a rallying cry for extremist elements who mislead the public and bully politicians into giving priority to the environment over meeting other more urgent human needs, it can only do harm and discourage serious scientific research into many environmental problems.

None of the above conclusions means that we are not left with serious environmental problems when attempting to decide what is an *optimal* policy. The world is faced with real environmental problems and, left to itself, the environment will not be managed in a socially optimal manner. There are too many market imperfections. But in many cases—particularly with global environmental issues, such as the preservation of certain endangered species or the prevention of excessive production of greenhouse gases—it is not easy to devise economic incentives that can be accepted and implemented internationally in order to secure socially optimal cooperative action. These are serious issues, many of them requiring extensive scientific research as well as economic research into, for example, the economic evaluation of environmental assets, or the costs of pollution reduction, or the relative efficacy of alternative schemes to achieve socially optimal levels of environmental protection.

Serious research into these and related environmental problems is being carried out in various institutions all over the world. If it is occasionally necessary to talk in terms of 'sustainable development' in order to obtain the funds for this research, all well and good. But it would be a pity if the cost of this was that a lot of time, effort, and funds were also to be devoted to dubious research projects simply because they wave the flag of 'sustainable development' to which everybody is expected to show immediate support and unquestioning loyalty.

Annex

In Fig. 5.2, as in Fig. 5.1, the minor and irrelevant modifications that we make to Nozick's exposition of the problem are (1) that successive generations replace successive stages in the lifetime of a single person, and (2), as indicated above, the term 'welfare' replaces 'happiness', solely in order to preserve continuity with the preceding argument of this chapter, not to indicate any intentional difference in their meanings.

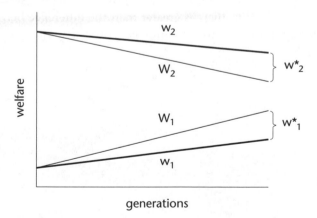

FIGURE 5.2. Alternative paths of social welfare including effects of changes in welfare

We shall also assume, as does Nozick, that all the welfare—happiness—that we would derive from anticipating a future increase in welfare, not necessarily our own, would be incorporated into the 'instantaneous' welfare at the moment of time when the anticipation is experienced. Conversely, the loss of welfare resulting from an expectation of decreasing welfare would be subtracted from the welfare experienced at the time the expectation is held. Cumulative welfare over the whole period, under these assumptions, therefore, will incorporate these expectational additions or subtractions.

Let the welfare, W, of any unit—in this case a generation—be composed of two elements, w and w^*. w is a vector of all variables, such as income, status, family life, and so on, that determine the unit's welfare other than its relationship to the w of other units, and w^* is the effect on its total welfare of the relationship between its own w and that of other units. The Σ sign indicates the summation over the time period in question of the 'instantaneous' welfare experienced at any moment in time. Since, in this model, the units are generations, we can make the extremely plausible psychological assumptions that each generation's w^* is positively related to

(1) the excess of its own w over that of the previous generation's, since it will not feel guilty about having failed to transfer wealth to earlier generations, and will be pleased that, for example, the incidence of infant mortality has decreased, literacy has risen, and so on; and
(2) the expected excess of the next generation's w over its own, since it will be proud of being able to hand on a better world to the descendants.

Consider now the two life paths shown in Fig. 5.2. In one scenario w_1 is rising, so that w^*_1 is positive and hence W_1 rises even more. In the other w_2 is falling, so w^*_2 is negative, and W_2 must fall even more. But clearly this does not imply that the ΣW_1, which is identically equal to $\Sigma w_1 + \Sigma w^*_1$, is greater than ΣW_2. It only implies this if the arithmetic sum of the two Σw^*—remember that one of them is negative—is greater than the difference between the two Σw. Obviously this is not logically implied by the assumptions.

6

How Much Richer Will Future Generations Be?

1. Introduction

The conclusion reached in earlier chapters is that, as far as material well-being is concerned, our main obligation to future generations is not to aim at some sort of intergenerational equality or to be constrained by any notions of the 'rights' of future generations to inherit any particular environmental assets, but to avoid pursuing policies that might condemn future generations to poverty. This would be in accord with our conclusion, in Chapter 4, that, as a basic ethical principle, egalitarianism should be replaced by the 'Threshold Prioritarian' principle. That is to say, we should be concerned, as a matter of compassion rather than as a matter of comparing the *relative* positions of different people, to give priority to people whose welfare is below some threshold.

How far this requires us to give priority to poor people alive today over future generations is more a factual than a theoretical question. In our view, all that the theory can tell us is that we should avoid policies that might condemn future generations to poverty. Apart from that, our priorities should be influenced by the predictions that can be made about the future course of economic development. For presumably almost any theory of distributive justice should take account of the extent to which some generations are likely to be better off or worse off than others. In the next section of this chapter, therefore, we shall briefly survey the prospects for economic growth over the course of the twenty-first century and the evidence for the view that sustained economic growth at recent rates is impossible on account of the limits imposed by the exhaustion of so-called 'finite resources'.

2. How Much Richer are Future Generations Likely to Be?

All long-range predictions of economic growth rates are hazardous. How many people, for example, would have predicted in the 1980s that the Japan-

ese economy was soon to enter into a period of prolonged economic stagnation? But if we are predicting over very long periods we can abstract from
possible short to medium-term forces, such as the catching-up on war-time
dislocation that characterized the 1950s in many Western countries, or the
recuperation from the oil shocks that characterized the 1970s, or eccentric
bursts of dogmatic monetarism that characterized the 1980s, or the speculative excesses and financial profligacy in some parts of the world that marked
the later 1990s. In the very long run these forces can be seen to be relatively
transient. To predict growth rates over the twenty-first century we can fall
back on an appraisal of what are the really fundamental underlying determi-
nants of economic growth in the modern world. In our view such an appraisal
leads to the conclusion that the world per capita growth rate of national
income, in 'real' terms—that is, adjusted for inflation—over the next 100
years is likely to be somewhere between 1 and 2 per cent a year, but could be
much higher.

Our reasons for this are as follows. The average growth rate of real income
per head in the world over the last 40 years, which cover periods of exceptional growth and exceptional stagnation, has been 2.1 per cent a year. And
there are two reasons to believe that the future growth rate is likely to be at
least as high as this. First, in the very long run the main source of growth in
incomes per head is technological and scientific progress, and, above all, the
rate at which the resulting inventions and innovations are diffused. This is a
function of variables all of which are tending to increase, some at a phenom-
enal rate. In particular, the number of highly educated people in the world,
especially those having technological and scientific qualifications, is increasing so rapidly that it far surpasses the corresponding number of people having
similar qualifications only two or three decades ago, and is likely to go on
expanding rapidly. The main source of current high levels of income and
output in the modern world is not so much physical capital or material
resources as human capital, that is, knowledge, training, skills, and attitudes.
And there is no physical limitation on the growth of this human capital.

Second, the rate of international diffusion of innovation and technical
progress, which many studies have shown to be decisive in determining
growth rates, will continue to accelerate.[1] As Gore Vidal put it, 'Thanks to
modern technology . . . history now comes equipped with its fast-forward
button'.[2] This is partly on account of the 'information revolution' and partly
on account of the increasing 'globalization' of economic activity. This does,
of course, bring with it certain problems, but it also means that technical
progress and innovations will spread more quickly than in the past, as already

[1] See a magisterial and optimistic study of the prospects for future growth in the light of a
detailed analysis of the past in Easterlin (1996).

[2] Quoted in Streeten (1996: 777) from G. Vidal, *Saving History* (Cambridge, MA: Harvard University Press, 1992).

seems to be the case. This will be intensified by one of the more favourable aspects of the policy revolution of the 1980s, namely, the widespread conversion to freer and more competitive markets, including the labour market, than had been the case previously. Some countries, particularly those in the ex-Soviet bloc, are having great difficulty adjusting to a new competitive environment, and it may be decades before their economies really move into the modern world. But, in the longer-run, they will no doubt do so. This could unleash vast potential growth rates in many major countries, such as India and those of Latin America—and even Africa—where, in fact, some signs of this are already visible.

These two underlying forces for *long-run* growth suggest that the average annual long-run growth of output per head over the twenty-first century should be above that of the last 40 years. Since this has been 2.1 per cent, our projection of between 1 and 2 per cent a year seems on the cautious side and may be giving excessive weight to the slowing-down during the last decade or so. But to simplify the argument we shall assume a single figure of 1.5 per cent as the annual average growth rate of real incomes per head over the next 100 years. The power of compound interest being what it is, this means that world average real incomes per head in the year 2100 would be 4.43 times as high as they are now!

And it should not be thought that the above guess at the annual average growth rate of gross world product (GWP) over the next 100 years is a fanciful figure. A recent draft report of the UN Intergovernmental Panel on Climate Change (IPCC) adopted, for purposes of estimating possible levels of energy use and carbon emissions, four possible 'storylines'—to use their terminology describing possible scenarios of rates of growth of population and incomes. These put per capita GWP in about 100 years' time at between 4.3 and 20 times as high as it is today! In other words, our guesstimate is at the bottom of the range adopted by the IPCC. It is thus a conservative and modest estimate.

And the IPCC scenarios are by no means fanciful. As one of the contributors to their work points out, even on the assumption that world incomes will rise about tenfold over the course of the century, namely to about $300 trillion at present prices, this would be consistent with per capita incomes in the rich countries rising at only 1 per cent a year and those of the developing countries rising at only 3 per cent a year (D. Anderson 1998a: Table 1, 8).[3] The former figure is well below its rate in the twentieth century and almost inconceivably low in the light of the long-run influences on modern economic growth set out above. And given the scope for 'catching up' among developing countries, the latter figure corresponds to their having reached, by 2100,

---

[3] Anderson's introductory note points out that the scenarios in question are still the subject of discussion in the relevant IPCC group and should not be interpreted as representing any final agreed consensus.

merely the average income level enjoyed in the rich countries today. Given the international transmission of technical knowledge and productive techniques it is equally virtually inconceivable that, taken as a whole, they will have failed to achieve this.

3. GNP and Welfare

Of course, as all professional economists have always been aware, national income per head is not the whole of welfare. The great British economist Pigou stated about 70 years ago that 'there is no guarantee that the effects produced on the part of welfare that can be brought into relation with the measuring-rod of money may not be cancelled by effects of a contrary kind brought about in other parts, or aspects, of welfare' (Pigou 1932: 12). The late Arthur Okun (1971: 129) put the matter very clearly:

It is hard to understand how anyone could seriously believe that GNP could be converted into a meaningful indicator of total social welfare. Obviously, any number of things could make the Nation better off without raising its real GNP as measured today: we might start the list with peace, equality of opportunity, the elimination of injustice and violence, greater brotherhood among Americans of different racial and ethnic backgrounds, better understanding between parents and children and between husbands and wives, and we could go on endlessly.

At the same time, two points need to be made here. First, insofar as there is any conflict between generations over a 'fair' share out of resources, the non-economic components of welfare, such as peace and racial harmony, or better family cohesion, and so on, are not 'finite resources' that can be shared out equitably or inequitably between different generations. Second, while the correlation is far from perfect, it does happen to be the case that there is a strong correlation between changes in income and changes in many other important components of welfare, whether they are physical environmental indicators or other major ingredients of welfare such as educational achievements, longevity, or political freedoms. For example, the relationship between GNP per head and some other major components of 'the quality of life', such as life expectancy at birth, infant mortality, adult literacy, a civil rights index, and a political rights index, has also been well documented and established (for example, Dasgupta and Weale 1992; Crafts 1997). Of course, the relationship is far from perfect. In 1992 the USA ranked top in terms of GNP per head but only tenth in terms of a far wider index of the quality of life, whereas Sweden ranked twelfth in terms of GNP per head and second in terms of this more inclusive index.[4] Similarly, although the correlation

---

[4] The index of the quality of life referred to here is the 'amended Dasgupta and Weale' index.

between incomes and the 'Human Development Index' produced by the UN Development Programme is far from perfect, it is still strong (UNDP 1998: Table 1.2, 20).[5]

Slightly more straightforward strong positive statistical relationships between incomes per head and access to crucial environmental assets, namely, clean drinking water and sanitation, have been well known for many years (for example, Beckerman 1992a, b; World Bank 1992).[6] Similarly, the particular inter-relationship between economic growth on the one hand and improvements in health and education on the other have been documented in various sources. For example, as pointed out in the World Bank's (1993) report *Investing in Health*, a child born in 1950 in the developing world had a life expectancy of 40 years, whereas by 1990 this had risen to 63 years. This is the result of rising incomes, which have permitted increased education, improved access to clean drinking water and sanitation, and public health programmes (UNDP 1998: 20ff).

Of course, there is still an urgent need for further major progress. And rising prosperity is not the only means to improving health. As Drèze and Sen (1989) have shown in a famous study, at various times some countries, such as Costa Rica or Jamaica, managed to achieve rapid progress in health with only moderate increases in GNP per head, whereas other countries, such as Brazil, have experienced periods of fast growth with little improvement in overall health, and possibly even a deterioration for some sections of the population. Health in many parts of China also seems to have been very badly affected by the severe environmental degradation, particularly air pollution, that has accompanied rapid industrialization (Lardy 1999). Thus, as recent UNDP studies confirm, the link between economic prosperity and human development is far from automatic. But as the studies by Dréze and Sen and others show, there seems little doubt that, in the longer run, rising incomes have played a major role in raising standards of health which, together with some of the other components of the quality of life mentioned above, is certainly a dominant influence on human welfare.[7]

The original DW index comprised the items enumerated in the text above, but amended by Crafts to replace adult literacy by years of formal schooling and to replace GNP per head by GNP per hour worked. The details of the amendment and the resulting rankings of countries are given in Crafts (1997).

[5] The Human Development Index is based on life expectancy, educational attainment and an adjusted estimate of incomes (UNDP 1998: 15).

[6] This does not mean that there are no difficult conceptual problems to be faced in using estimates of access to clean drinking water or sanitation and that the data thereon are highly reliable.

[7] See also World Bank (1993).

4. The Climate Change Constraint

It may be argued that all this assumes no disastrous environmental developments that could upset the predicted growth of incomes. If climate change were to lead to catastrophic declines in world income then the above figures would be irrelevant. Society would be faced with a choice between, on the one hand, reductions in current incomes and growth rates, especially in poorer countries, in an attempt to reduce the burning of fossil fuels that are believed to be the chief cause of climate change, and, on the other hand, possibly much greater cuts in living standards for future generations. But while the evidence in favour of the 'consensus' scientific view that burning of fossil fuels is having a significant effect on the global climate seems to be increasing, there is still very little reason to believe that it is likely to have serious, let alone catastrophic, effects on average world living standards.

This is largely because it is still very difficult to predict the impact of climate change in individual regions of the world (RCEP 2000: 29). And predictions of regional climate impacts are vital if enough progress is to be made in predicting the economic effects, particularly on agriculture. For example, there is general agreement that global warming will lead to more rain—or snow—taking the world as a whole. If the additional rain were to come down in a country that was heavily dependent on agriculture but faced a water constraint, the economic effects could be beneficial. But if, as is more likely, 'Murphy's Law' prevails and it all comes down where we live—Oxford—or on the west coast of Ireland, it would not help at all. And even if a local climate change is bad for the economy in one part of the world, it could have offsetting effects elsewhere.

Consequently, although the possible adverse effects of global warming are well publicized, people are less aware of the various reasons why global warming might do very little damage *to the world as a whole*. These reasons are not hard to find. First, there will be longer growing seasons and less frost, so that agricultural output in vast areas of the globe can be increased, such as in North America and Russia. Second, the increased precipitation is likely to be beneficial for agriculture in the world as a whole. Third, increased carbon concentrations also increase food output by increasing photosynthesis.[8] Fourth, for the world as a whole there will be increased cloud cover, thereby retaining soil moisture, as has already been observed in the main crop-growing states of the USA.[9] Increased cloud cover also means that most of the warming will take place at night, not during the day.

---

[8] This is a well-known and understood process and is frequently being verified in various scientific studies (see for example Clark *et al.* 1997).

[9] Balling (1992: 111). See also Mendelsohn and Nordhaus (1996) for a particularly convincing demonstration that moderate global warming will, on balance, benefit U.S. agriculture, and for reasons that would apply to other vast areas of the globe.

Given that climate change can have favourable as well as unfavourable effects, and in view of the enormous obstacles to sound regional predictions in this area, it is not surprising that most experts are agnostic as to the likely net damage, if any, that would result from climate change. For example, in its recent report on climate change the Royal Commission on Environmental Pollution (RCEP 2000: 51) quotes Nordhaus, one of the most respected economists to have studied the economic impact of climate change in great depth, as saying that 'It must be emphasised that attempts to estimate the impacts of climate change continue to be highly speculative. Outside of agriculture and sea-level rise for a small number of countries, the number of scholarly studies of the economic impacts of climate change remains vanishingly small'. And, for the reasons given above, even the net impact on agriculture is highly uncertain taking the world as a whole.

In response to an article by one of us in *The Times* (Beckerman 1997*b*), a correspondent in that paper pointed out,[10] correctly, that Working Group III of the IPCC has stated that the various available estimates they had surveyed of the damage that would be done by climate change by the end of the twenty-first century in the absence of measures to prevent it would be between 1.5 per cent and 2 per cent of world output and income.[11] The members of the IPCC Working Group, which included many eminent economists, were no doubt correct in their assessment of what the literature on the subject suggested, on the whole, was the likely damage from global warming (IPCC 1996*b*: Table 6.6). But this does not imply that they regarded this estimate as something to be alarmed about, unlike the author of the letter in *The Times*.

Indeed, the absurdity of regarding damage on such a small scale as a global disaster can be seen various ways. It implies a reduction in the annual growth rate over the twenty-first century from our assumed rate of 1.5 per cent a year to 1.48 per cent a year. It still brings average incomes per head in the year 2100 to 4.34 times as high as they are today, instead of 4.43 times as high as they would be on our assumption. In other words, the cut in incomes per head in the year 2100 would be roughly equal to the average increase in real incomes that one can expect in a single year. So that it means that if world incomes are cut by about 2 per cent as a result of global warming, the people alive in 2100 would have to wait until 2101 before they could enjoy the income level that they would otherwise have been able to enjoy in 2100. They will just have to be patient.

Another recent example of the absurdity of some of the dire prophecies of

[10] *The Times* (15 December 1997), 21.
[11] This was about the same as that given in what is probably the most authoritative estimate of the damage that might be done by a doubling of carbon concentrations in the atmosphere, namely, Nordhaus (1994).

the effects of global warming is a recent study prepared for the North West Climate Group on the economic impact on the north-west of England of climate change. The study warns that labour productivity will fall in sweltering summers and that employers will have to give workers more breaks— presumably for tea—in rising temperatures, reducing output levels. According to one of the authors of the study, 'Most of the summers in the 1990s have been very hot and this has affected the performance of workers' (Jones 1998). But what about the poor workers further south, in, say, Lyon, which is roughly in the centre of France—in a north-south direction—and where the average summer temperature, like that in New York, is about 5° Celsius higher than in Britain: that is, about twice as much as the total warming expected over the course of the next century, during which time British firms will no doubt have managed to adapt?[12] In fact, the average summer temperature in the whole of France, as in Germany, is about 3° Celsius higher than in Britain. Yet labour productivity in both countries is higher than in Britain. Perhaps all that is needed is to replace tea breaks by wine or beer breaks.

There are, of course, many other dire prophecies of the impact of climate change, particularly in the context of steps taken by insurance companies to raise their premiums. But according to one of the IPCC's Working Groups, 'Some in the insurance industry perceive a current trend toward increased frequency and severity of extreme climate events. Examination of the meteorological data fails to support their perception in the context of a long-term change' (IPCC 1996a: 11; see also IPCC 1990: xxv). As the eminent scientist Bert Bolin, who was, until recently, the chairman of the IPCC, points out, 'Environmental activists, for example, seize eagerly on the occurrence of extreme events (hurricanes, floods, droughts, etc.) as signs of an ongoing change of climate. Even though extreme events may be harbingers of change, there is still as yet little scientific evidence to prove this, nor can we as yet ascribe such changes to human interference' (Bolin 1997: 107).

The British Prime Minister, Mr Tony Blair, is not an environmental activist but he seems to have been misled by some of them in his entourage to attach great importance to the idea that global warming will increase storms. This is the only piece of evidence he gives in an article on climate change in which he wrote that 'it is clear that, unchecked, climate change . . . will impose enormous human and business costs . . . Global warming could lead to an increase in stormy weather . . . To give some idea of that threat, the great storm of 1987 cost our economy about £3 billion at today's prices. That is nothing compared with what could happen if we allow global warming to go unchecked' (Blair 1997). In similar vein, the British Minister for the Environment, Michael

---

[12] *The World Weather Guide*, annual.

Meacher (1997), wrote that 'The north (that is, the developed countries) is right to be concerned about worsening degradation that seriously threatens the viability of the planet', and he referred in particular to 'global warming, which will generate hurricanes, droughts, floods and severe crop losses across the world'.

In fact, it is far from certain that there is any upward trend in the frequency of storms. Some authorities deny any evidence of such a trend over the last few decades and add that existing climate models do not predict that global warming would lead to an increase, on balance, in the global incidence of storms (for example, Bolin 1997). And other scientists report evidence of a downward trend in the frequency of storms (Henderson-Sellers *et al*. 1997; Landsea *et al*. 1996; Schiesser *et al*. 1997). But it may well be that such conclusions will have to be revised in the light of the most up-to-date evidence. Of course, the damage done by a storm of any given intensity is likely to be greater today than 50, or even ten, years earlier. But this is simply because there are more buildings around to be damaged and their prices are much higher. Naturally, the steadily rising value of storm damage these days is used by insurance companies as an excuse to jack up their premiums on the grounds that it is a legitimate response forced on them by climate change. But, in fact, it has nothing to do with climate change and is simply the result of increased urbanization and buildings and continuous inflation.

There is equally little substance to the claim that climate change will greatly add to the spread of insect-spread diseases, such as dengue fever and malaria, which are widespread in many poor tropical countries. Any likely increase in this type of disease on account of warmer climates would be negligible by comparison with the high incidence of these diseases in countries where it is clearly the result of poverty and all its accompanying features: lack of drainage, clean water and sanitation, and public health systems. In a recent article in *The Lancet*, Paul Reiter, the Chief Scientist of the Dengue Fever branch of the Centers for Disease Control, writes, 'The distortion of science to make predictions of unlikely public health disasters diverts attention from the true reasons for the recrudescence of vector-borne diseases. These include large-scale resettlement of people, rampant urbanisation without adequate infrastructure . . . and the deterioration of vector-control operations and other public-health practices' (Reiter 1998: 839). In developed countries deaths from such diseases account for only about 1 per cent of all deaths, although these diseases were widespread in such countries in the past before they attained their present levels of affluence. For example, malaria and cholera were major health problems in the USA in the nineteenth century; and malaria was widespread in southern Europe until the mid-twentieth century, when good health practices and the use of insecticides and drainage programmes wiped out large mosquito-breeding areas.

In fact, even ignoring the contribution of economic growth, a warmer climate is likely to reduce mortality and disease in developed countries. A recent authoritative study of German mortality statistics over the last 50 years showed that colder weather is a more significant killer than hotter weather (Lerchl 1998). Similar results were found in a British study, coming to the conclusion that, other things equal, a rise in average annual temperature of 3°C would reduce annual mortality in Britain by 17,500 (Bentham 1997). Of course, all such estimates are subject to a large margin of error. Nevertheless, they establish the point that, contrary to the impression given in much alarmist literature, a moderate rise in temperature, far from increasing disease and mortality is likely to decrease it.

And in the developing countries the main cause of disease and mortality is poverty, so economic growth is likely to be very beneficial on balance. For example, a recent report by the UN World Health Organisation (WHO) emphasizes that it is poverty that is by far the major cause of infectious and parasitic diseases, not climate. In fact, the WHO (1998) Annual Report states in the Executive Summary that 'As the new millenium approaches, the global population has never had a healthier outlook', and it goes on to say that the only significant growth threat to human health is HIV/AIDS, which also has no relationship to climate. The WHO report surveys the enormous increase in life expectancy and in the reduction of diseases and suffering over the course of the twentieth century, almost all of which can be traced to rising incomes, which confirms the results by Drèze and Sen referred to above. As the UN *Human Development Report 1991* put it, 'Developing countries do not need lectures on the global commons. They need the resources to finance environmentally sound development' (UNDP 1991: 79).

Similarly, the American Council on Science and Health insists, in a recent survey of the alleged relationship between climate change and health, that 'The optimal approach to dealing with the prospect of climate change would (a) include improvement of health infrastructures (especially in developing countries) and (b) *exclude any measures that would impair economies and limit public health resources*' (1997: 6, emphasis added). The former includes intensive cost-effective control of insect vectors and improvement in clean drinking water and sanitation in developing countries. The latter implies that what developing countries need is a rapid growth of incomes and hence an increased use of energy, not measures to hamper their growth in a short-sighted attempt to restrain their growth of energy more than the steady technological advance in energy saving is producing anyway. The report adds that 'Regardless of whether human-induced climate change will occur, we need policies for coping with infectious diseases and severe weather impacts of natural origin' (1997: 7).

None of this means that climate change should not be taken seriously. For the above discussion has been addressed to the question of how much damage might be done by the sort of climate change that might take place during the course of the twenty-first century. But, in the first place, even such estimates are still subject to a high degree of uncertainty. Second, as the recent RCEP report has reminded us, given the very long lags in the climate change process and the persistence of carbon molecules in the atmosphere for up to 200 years, unless action is taken during the course of the next few decades to reduce the rate of carbon emissions, a degree of damage that could be easily accommodated by a much richer world if the global mean temperature rises by, say, 2°C by the end of this century, could become far more serious if the temperature were to go on increasing throughout the following century.

Of course, the uncertainties work in both directions. For example, it is quite possible—and many energy experts would think it is highly probable— that the world could emit very little carbon anyway by the middle of this century. Rapid advances are being made in technologies for obtaining energy from non-polluting sources, such as wind power and solar energy, especially when accompanied by more economic fuel cells. Given the prospects for scientific and technical progress, it could well be that energy technology will be totally transformed during the course of this century and all the fears about rising temperatures into the year 2200 and beyond could turn out to have been totally unfounded.

All these uncertainties mean that, while we do not wish to condone the undue deference that is widely given to the so-called 'precautionary princi- ple', there is everything to be said for an old-fashioned economic approach to the problem. This involves an acceptance of 'risk aversion' together with its implication that one should adopt a portfolio of policies, along the lines proposed by Bolin (1998), namely, a prudent strategy that would include adopting a 'portfolio' of policies, including mitigation, adaptation, and research aimed at improving our knowledge of the processes involved.

Some of the policies that could be intensified rapidly include 'no-regret' policies, that would not merely cost nothing but would actually add to current world output and incomes. For example, it is estimated that world subsidies for fossil fuels amount to about $230 billion per annum, and in developing and 'transition' economies alone energy subsidies amount to nearly $200 billion.[13] Subsidies mean that resources are used in activities that have less value to society than do the resources in question. Eliminating such subsidies, therefore, adds to overall incomes. Measures could also be taken to reduce market failures that prevent research and innovation designed to promote energy savings and the development of renewable energy from attaining their socially optimal level. There is also scope for various methods of preventing carbon from reaching the atmosphere, including further progress in carbon sequestration and a move towards zero-emission power plants (Ausubel 1999; RCEP 2000: Ch. 3).

---

[13] *The Financial Times* (30 August 1997), 6, and UNDP (1998: 10).

But, for reasons discussed more fully in Chapter 11, if effective action is to be taken in time to mitigate the current increase in carbon emissions more progress is required to prepare the ground for effective international arrangements to distribute among countries the 'pain' of restricting carbon emissions. Steps should be intensified to set up the machinery and rules that would be required to operate an international scheme, such as tradable carbon emission permits or quotas, that can provide rapid reductions in carbon emissions in a manner that is both economically efficient and equitable should further scientific research over the next few years strengthen the likelihood of more serious damage from climate change.[14]

Nevertheless, while we support such a mixed portfolio of policies, it seems highly likely that, even if no drastic action is taken to prevent global warming, the world will be incomparably richer by the end of the twenty-first century than it is now. Of course, global warming, like innumerable other changes that are constantly taking place in the world, will affect countries differently, some favourably and some unfavourably. The development of new products and new techniques of production, the discovery of new materials, changes in tastes, the growth of new industrial powers, political developments, and so on have always meant that the economic environment of individual countries changes relative to others. Such changes, on top of existing differences in economic circumstances, have always provided an incentive to major migrations of population.

But how the world should deal with vast international differences in income distribution has been a persistent problem that needs to be tackled irrespective of any effects of future climate change. And insofar as draconian measures to prevent climate change slowed down the growth rates of developing countries, the inequity of such a policy is clear both in its impact on poor people in the Third World today and in the prospects for their descendents. As the IPCC (1996b: 33) points out, 'If we take aggressive action to limit climate change they [future generations] may regret that we did not use the funds instead to push ahead development in Africa, to better protect the species against the next retrovirus, or to dispose of nuclear materials safely'. The future generations in these countries might also resent that the resources were not used to improve their general standards of living, education, health, housing, and so on.

---

[14] It does not seem that the world's leaders are prepared to give priority to instituting a mechanism that would rely mainly on a universal system of tradable emission permits, which would be the lowest-cost method of curtailing carbon emissions, let alone initiate any serious study of imaginative schemes to combine energy production with the sequestration of the related carbon emissions, such as that proposed by Peter Read (1994).

5. The Resources Constraint

Finally, one popularly perceived threat to the future growth of prosperity is the oft-alleged danger of using up so-called 'finite resources'. A full-scale exposition of the factual and theoretical reasons why one can discount this possibility would be beyond the scope of this book. Some of them have been set out in detail elsewhere (Beckerman 1995*a*: Ch. 4; Cooper 1994: Ch. 2; Schelling 1995). As one of us pointed out a long time ago, we have managed very well without any supplies at all of Beckermonium, the product named after his great grandfather who failed to discover it in the nineteenth century (Beckerman 1972; 1974).

The main reason why we will never run out of any resource, or even suffer seriously from any sudden reduction in its supply, is a very simple one. It is that whenever demand for any particular material begins to run up against supply limitations a wide variety of economic forces is set in motion to remedy the situation. These start with a rise in price, which, in turn leads to all sorts of secondary favourable feed-backs, notably a shift to substitutes, an increase in exploration, and technical progress that brings down the costs of exploration and refining and processing as well as the costs of the substitutes. In the end, the relative prices of some of the materials in question may still rise, which will cause demand for them to gradually contract towards more and more highly valued uses. If, for example, coal were ever to become a very scarce commodity its price would rise to the point where, like other scarce minerals such as diamonds, it was used only for jewelry or certain very special industrial purposes. We would never run out of it. And the process would take place very, very gradually, allowing time for economies to adapt. Key materials disappear overnight only in science fiction stories.

It was this total failure to allow for the way that markets work which led the Club of Rome in 1972 to issue its alarming prediction of the imminent exhaustion of many key minerals (Meadows *et al.* 1972). In the event, during the following 20 years the consumption of these materials more or less matched, or exceeded, the levels of 'known reserves' that existed in that year. Yet the known reserves at the end of the period finished up being about as big as or, in some cases, much bigger than they were at the outset (Beckerman 1995*a*: 53). Even for energy, where more serious students of the subject believed that there might be a gradual depletion of economically viable sources of supply, the outcome has been very different.

As an editorial in the *Financial Times* of 12/13 December 1998 put it,

Of all the prophecies of economic doom, that made by the Club of Rome in 1970 looks about the most foolish . . . The Club, established by a group of international experts and politicians, proclaimed in its report, *Limits to Growth*, that the world was running out of basic commodities and that prices would soar . . . Yesterday, the Bridge/CRB Futures Price Index reached a 21-year low . . . Non-oil commodities now cost about 70 per cent less in real terms than when the Club of Rome was issuing its warning.

One could go on and on enumerating the environmental scare stories that have captured the attention of the public during the last decade or so, but are forgotten as soon as the scientific refutations are produced, or subsequent developments sharply contradict the alarmists' predictions. A survey titled 'Environmental Scares' in *The Economist* (20 December 1997) reminds us of Paul Ehrlich's statement in the early 1970s that 'The battle to feed humanity is over. In the 1970s the world will undergo famines—hundreds of millions of people are going to starve to death'. Similarly, in 1974 Ehrlich forecast a 'nutritional disaster that seems likely to overtake humanity in the 1970s (or, at the latest, the 1980s) . . . before 1985 mankind will enter a genuine age of scarcity' in which 'the accessible supplies of many key minerals will be nearing depletion' (Ehrlich and Ehrlich 1974). The survey goes on to point out that

He was not alone. Lester Brown of the Worldwatch Institute began predicting in 1973 that population would soon outstrip food production, and he still does so every time there is a temporary increase in wheat prices. In 1994, after 21 years of being wrong, he said 'After 40 years of record food production gains, output per person has reversed with unanticipated abruptness'. Two bumper harvests followed and the price of wheat fell to record lows. Yet Mr Brown's pessimism remains as impregnable to facts as his views are popular with newspapers.

The same survey gives other predictions that have been falsified equally dramatically, but this never seems to shake the faith of their authors or the extent to which their predictions continue to be taken seriously by the media and by public figures who ought to know better.

6. The Energy Constraint

In fact, the falsification of predictions of rapidly approaching shortages has a very distinguished pedigree. For example, the great economist W. S. Jevons (1865) predicted shortages of coal supplies in a very sophisticated piece of applied economics which would still compare favourably with most contemporary applied economics. But the falsification of his and other similar early predictions did not deter later authoritative bodies from making equally mistaken predictions. Ninety years after Jevons's book, the 1955 UN Atoms for Peace Conference made estimates of both 'proven' and 'ultimately recoverable' reserves of fossil fuels, which are now seen to be one quarter and one twelfth, respectively, of current estimates (D. Anderson 1998*b*: 438). One could list innumerable equally falsified predictions in later years. Here is a selection.

Countries with expanding industry, rapid population growth . . . will be especially hard hit by economic energy scarcities from now on. (Amory Lovins 1974, quoted in Mills 1999: 8–9)

The supply of oil will fail to meet increasing demand before the year 2000, most probably between 1985 and 1995, even if energy prices are 50 per cent above current levels in real terms. (MIT Workshop on Alternative Energy Strategies 1977)

The diagnosis of the U.S. energy crisis is quite simple: demand for energy is increasing, while supplies of oil and natural gas are diminishing. Unless the U.S. makes a timely adjustment before world oil become very scarce and very expensive in the 1980s, the nation's economic security and the American way of life will be gravely endangered. (Executive Office of the President, *National Energy Program*, Washington DC [1977])

The oil-based societies of the industrial world cannot be sustained and cannot be replicated. The huge increases in oil prices since 1973 virtually guarantee that the Third World will never derive most of its energy from petroleum. (Worldwatch Institute 1979, quoted in Mills 1999: 8–9)

What seems certain, at least for the foreseeable future is that energy, once cheap and plentiful but now expensive and limited, will continue to rise in cost. (Union of Concerned Scientists 1980, quoted in Mills 1999: 8–9)

Conservative estimates project a price of $80 a barrel (in 1985) even if peace is restored to the Persian Gulf and an uncertain stability maintained. ('Energy: A Special Report in the Public Interest', *National Geographic*, 19 [1981])

The falsification of past predictions of energy shortages is the result of three major forces, stimulated in most cases by the economic feed-back mechanism outlined above. First, estimates of recoverable energy resources continually increase. Second, continuous technical progress is being made in the efficiency with which conventional energy is used. Third, there is also substantial progress and innovation in the exploitation of renewable sources of energy.

As regards the first factor, namely, supplies of conventional fossil fuels, current expert opinion is that 'In sum, the availability of fossil fuel resources can be measured in units of hundreds—perhaps thousands—of years. The availability of renewable energy resources (including geothermal resources), even if used on an immensely expanded scale has no known time limit' (D. Anderson 1998a: 30). The number of years' consumption at 1994 rates that are covered by total resources, including those not yet identified but that are likely to be insofar as prices provide the necessary incentive, varies from 240 years for oil to 1,570 years for coal. Combining oil, natural gas, and coal in units of oil equivalent,

The total reserves of fossil fuels are currently thought to be around 5000 Gtoe [gigatons of oil equivalent] or about 700 times the current annual rate of world consumption. Even this, however, is an underestimate. Excluded . . . are 'additional occurrences' of fossil fuel reserves known likely to exist but whose scale can only be guessed at. It is thought they amount to at least 24,000 Gtoe, of which four-fifths are natural gas hydrates. Thus estimates of the ratio of total resources to today's rate of consumption are now around 4,000 years. (D. Anderson 1998*b*: 437)

As for technical progress in the use of renewable energy, it should be born in mind that the total energy received from the sun is about 10,000 times total world energy consumption; and if only a very small fraction of this can be harnessed in an economically viable manner the whole energy problem disappears. And, indeed, technical progress in the harnessing of solar energy has been substantial. Already photovoltaic systems and solar-thermal power stations, such as those now operating in California, manage to convert about 10 per cent of the incident solar energy into electricity, and, with further developments in the pipeline, are expected to convert about 20 per cent of it. On conservative assumptions concerning the duration of sunlight and conversion efficiency, it can be shown that only about 0.25 per cent of the area now under crops and permanent pastures would be needed to meet all of the world's primary energy needs. Even if these needs rise, as they may well do, fourfold over the course of this century, this still means that only 1 per cent of this land area would be needed to supply the whole world demand for energy. Land is not one of the main constraints, therefore, which are costs and storage (D. Anderson 1998*b*: 440).

But given the pace of technical progress, especially in fuel cells that can store or produce electricity, there is every reason to believe that these constraints will continually to be loosened. And such rapid progress is now being reported in the development of fuel cells that produce electricity by one means or another that automobile companies, often in conjunction with major oil companies, are heavily involved in research and development on fuel cells for use in cars that they expect to be commercially viable within a decade or two.[15] Progress is also being made in developing economically viable wind power. Although there has been legitimate opposition to the spread of wind farms in countries where space is at a premium, it seems that the potential for economically viable wind power in North America, the former Soviet Union, Africa, and other parts of the world is such that it could meet 20 per cent or more of the world's electricity needs within the next few decades (Grubb and Meyer 1993).

Indeed, it is likely that the only constraint on the pace of research and development of ways of exploiting renewable forms of energy would be a defensive cut in the price of fossil fuels. In many local specialized uses renewable energy is already competitive with fossil fuel-based energy. But the prices of the latter could still be reduced substantially in many parts of the world, aided partly by technological progress in discovery, extraction, and processing, not to mention the large cushion of prices over extraction costs of oil in

---

[15] 'Fuel Cells Meet Big Business', *The Economist* (24 July 1999), 69–70.

many parts of the world that provide plenty of room for further cuts in prices. So the future is likely to be much more one of competition between renewable and non-renewables, leading to further long-term declines in energy prices, than one characterized by any shortages on account of an exhaustion of supplies of fossil fuels.

7. Conclusion

Future generations are likely to be much richer than is the current generation, and there is little reason to believe that the steady rise in real incomes will be significantly reduced by climate change or some constraint on the availability of resources. Thus, while, as is argued in this book, we do have a moral obligation to take account of the interests of future generations, this does not entail any need to sacrifice current standards of living in order to protect posterity from poverty. However, we do have a moral obligation to take account of the *possibility*, however, small, that climate change could seriously depress the living standards of future generations. This would be in line with our general theme to the effect that we do have an obligation to avoid policies that would condemn future generations to poverty. The problem is how much sacrifice should be imposed on the present generation in order to avoid a remote possibility that climate change could condemn future generations to poverty.

For giving priority to concern with poverty also means concern with the quite certain poverty that exists throughout the world today. Hence, we have to ensure that steps taken to reduce the very small risk of serious future environmental damage do not inflict certain present damage on the Third World countries that are incomparably poorer today than they are likely to be by the end of this century.

In other words, if one is really concerned with reducing intergenerational inequality of welfare it would be a mistake to give unqualified priority to people who will be alive in the future over those alive today when future people are very likely to be far better off materially than those alive today. For example, there is something paradoxical about the current willingness in environmental circles to impose constraints on the extent to which the present generation of Chinese can increase their carbon emissions, which would reduce their income levels, in order to add a few percentage points to the GNP of Chinese alive in, say, 100 years' time when their income levels are likely to be ten or 20 times as high as they are now. This would be inverted ancestor-worship that is not likely to appeal to the Chinese of any generation.

The implication of our view concerning the future growth of incomes in the world as a whole is that our main moral obligation to future generations is not in the field of material supplies or any other environmental area. It is in the field of institutions and social attitudes. This is because our main obligation to posterity is to bequeath a more just and decent society than the one in which most of the world's population currently live.

7

Our Obligations to Future Generations

The twentieth-century history of large-scale cruelty and killing is only too familiar: the mutual slaughter of the First World War, the terror-famine of the Ukraine, the Gulag, Auschwitz, Dresden, the Burma Railway, Hiroshima, Vietnam, the Chinese Cultural Revolution, Cambodia, Rwanda, the collapse of Yugoslavia. These names will conjure up others . . . We are a species both brutal and sickened by brutality. This conflict between our cruelty and our aspirations goes as far as we can see back in human history. However, it is not parochial to think of our own time as particularly important. The outbreaks of killing are now especially dangerous because technology makes them a threat to the survival of the whole species.

Jonathan Glover (1999: 2, 41)

1. Introduction

The outcome of the previous chapters has been that we cannot expect much guidance concerning our moral obligations to future generations from the ethical 'systems' to which appeal is most commonly made in this context. First, future generations cannot be said to have rights. Second, this means that their interests cannot be represented in any theory of intergenerational justice. Third, appeals to intergenerational equity embodied in some form of intergenerational equality are equally unconvincing, since egalitarianism is either basically flawed or, at best, inapplicable as between generations. And, finally, the currently fashionable concept of 'sustainable development' cannot fill the gaps, real and imaginary, in the way that conventional ethical or economic models handle the problem of how to maximize human welfare over time.

But, as we have stressed at various points, this does not mean that we have no moral obligations to future generations. These may reflect different motivations, even excluding those arising from the bonds of affection between overlapping generations which we are taking to lie outside the domain of moral constraints. For example, some of us may feel that we should be concerned with the welfare of distant generations on account of our common humanity. More specifically, certain communitarian political theories claim that there is some continuity across generations in the community of human beings (de-Shalit 1995). Others may justify concern for future generations on the grounds that it protects the sensibilities of our contemporaries or helps foster desirable humanitarian instincts in ourselves which will benefit contemporaries as well as future generations.

Another attractive approach is to adopt the practical procedural rule that, irrespective of their location in space or time, 'whenever agents base their action on the assumption of connection to other agents and subjects, they must include those others within the scope of their ethical consideration' (O. O'Neill 1996: 123). This procedure for establishing how widely around different categories of people—or animals—we should draw the boundary of those who have 'ethical standing' implies that many common boundaries, such as those that divide nations or generations, should be ignored.

Hence, our denial of 'rights' to future generations does not mean that we are under no moral obligation to be concerned with the consequences of our actions that may affect them. A clear and simple example suggested by Parfit (1984: 356–7) is as follows. 'Suppose that I leave some broken glass in the undergrowth of a wood. A hundred years later this glass wounds a child. My act harms this child. If I had safely buried the glass, this child would have walked through the wood unharmed. Does it make a moral difference that the child whom I harm does not now exist?' Parfit's answer is that it does not. And although he then goes on to build on this in developing a critique of the use of the discount rate in economic cost-benefit analysis, which we do not accept for reasons set out elsewhere (Beckerman 1995a: Ch.11), we share his conclusion, namely, that we have a moral obligation to take account of our actions affecting future people.

Of course, the particular example Parfit gives is a very simple one in that the only conflict of interest involved is the trivial cost of taking the trouble to bury the broken glass. Unfortunately, one can easily conceive of cases where avoiding action that would harm future generations would call for major sacrifices by the present generation. In such cases it is arguable that in the same way that—other things being roughly equal—we would tend to give priority to family over friends, to friends over strangers, and so on, we should give priority—other things being fairly equal—to the present generation over future generations. Human nature will always prevent us from being completely impartial, cosmopolitan beings, who will rank the interests of distant people or generations equally with those near and dear to us. But this does not mean that we should attach no weight at all to the interests of distant people or generations. And the main implication of our denial, in Chapter 2, of the 'rights' of future generations was only that their interests did not possess 'trumping value' over those of the present generations. Thus we can agree that the answer to Parfit's question 'Does it make a moral difference . . .?' is 'No', but only in the sense that future generations have 'moral standing' so that their interests have to be taken into account. It does not mean that their interests 'trump' those of people alive today.

The starting point, then, for assessing our moral obligations to distant generations has to be some prediction of what their most important interests are likely to be. This should be followed with some assessment of what effects our policies will have on their interests and how far they conflict with the interests of the present generation.[1] Of course one cannot draw up any 'lexicographic' ordering of priorities in general terms—that is, in the way that, in a dictionary, all words beginning with the letter 'b' come before all words beginning with the letter 'c'. Notwithstanding distinguished precedents to the contrary, it seems impossible to rank the relative importance of objectives such as relief of poverty, or environmental preservation, or the extension of human rights, when they are expressed in broad, general terms.[2] The concepts are incommensurate; each covers many dimensions; and in each dimension the degree of gravity may vary.

For example, abuses of human rights can range from horrific behaviour to minor restrictions on peoples' freedom of movement or freedom to dispose of their property. Poverty can range from mass starvation to isolated instances of temporary poverty in generally affluent communities as a result of some transient bad luck or other exceptional circumstances. Environmental problems can range from the elimination of atrocious urban air conditions that were found in major cities of the industrialized countries until relatively recently or the absence of clean drinking water today in most parts of the developing countries, at one extreme, to the reduction in noise levels from the occasional neighbourhood street party, at the other.

It would not make sense, therefore, to say that all cases of human rights violation should be eliminated before tackling any instance of poverty or environmental damage, however serious, or that that nothing should be done to relieve *any* poverty, however acute, or to prevent *any* environmental damage, however serious, until we have exhausted all possibilities of redressing violations of human rights, however trivial. There may often be cases in practice where, say, the urgent relief of dire poverty or the solution of some flagrant environmental problem may mean overruling somebody's rights. Much of the debate between various single-issue pressure groups, whether in favour of priority for the environment, or education, or poverty relief, or any other of innumerable perfectly worthy causes, tends to be misplaced on account of their failure to share the economist's preference for concentrating on marginal values and avoiding all-or-nothing solutions.

---

[1] To some extent this is a circular procedure. One's prejudices, intuitions, and predilections for certain priorities among obligations will naturally colour one's prediction of what one perceives to be the most salient and relevant features of the future evolution of human society. But there is no way of breaking out of the circle by appealing to some external objective formula for ranking the obligations.

[2] A well-known feature of Rawls's theory of justice is his 'serial' ranking—the term that he says he prefers to the clumsier term 'lexicographical'—of his first principle of justice, which is concerned with liberty, over his second principle, which is concerned with inequality. Some of the difficulties to which such a ranking of general principles leads are set out in Hart (1975: 245).

Furthermore, the objectives of relief of poverty, environmental protection, and the extension of human rights are often positively related. On the one hand, people who are dying of starvation or disease cannot be exercising their right to life or any other rights. And conversely, lack of basic human rights is often the cause of much poverty and of needless environmental destruction. So progress towards one objective will usually contribute towards progress towards the others.

Apart from the environment, poverty, and human rights there are, of course, many other acute contemporary problems, such as international conflicts, family breakdown, terrorism, drugs, crime, and so on. But in an attempt to concentrate on our obligations to future generations we need to focus on those threats to human welfare that can be most safely predicted into the long-term future. This book is *not* addressed to the question 'What are the most important problems of present day society?' In the following sections, therefore, we shall give our reasons why we believe that, subject to the above qualification about ranking aggregative objectives, in the very long run the most important and permanent interests of future generations will lie in the area covered by the general concept of human rights.

2. The Inevitability of Future Conflict

The safest prediction that can be made for the long-term future is that there will always be potential conflict between peoples for all sorts of different 'reasons' and that can all easily lead to horrific violations of basic human rights. At the same time one can predict with great confidence that people will always want life and security, and freedom from fear, discrimination, and humiliation. And the best guarantee that these permanent needs, that are the essence of what constitutes a human being, will be satisfied is a society that protects basic human rights and provides the maximum liberty compatible with similar liberty for others.

Except in some utopian scenarios, human wants will always expand more or less in line with what is available, so that, whatever we do now about the future availability of resources, and however much technical progress expands our potential for producing goods and services, there will always be conflicting interests in the way that potential output is shared out. Some people will want a larger share and others will be unwilling to provide it. Future generations may not have the institutions or traditions that ensure that, whatever level of output is available in the future, it is shared out peacefully, if not equitably.

Furthermore, conflicts of interest over material possessions are by no means the only causes of conflict, any more than are cultural differences.

There is no shortage of other causes. Even within any given culture or civilization there are conflicts of various kinds between interests, objectives, and values, which will divide members of any community. For example, in recent years most conflicts have been civil wars or internal conflicts between groups that share common cultures, such as in Cambodia, or Bosnia, or Rwanda, or Angola, where groups that appeared to be culturally homogeneous slaughter each other. The total cultural assimilation of most of the Jewish populations of Germany and Austria, for example, and their great contribution to their cultural environments did not save them from being almost completely exterminated. In many countries today, as Appiah (1997: 36) points out, 'It is not black culture that the racist disdains, but blacks. There is no conflict of visions between black and white cultures that is the source of racial discord . . . Culture is not the problem, and it is not the solution'.

In any case, as is clearly apparent in Jonathan Glover's (1999) recent brilliant but horrific analysis of inhumanity in the twentieth century, the human species does not need anything resembling a rational 'cause' for some groups to impose incalculable suffering on others. For whatever the social psychology of human malevolence may be, it does appear that there will always be a number of evil people who, given half a chance, can exploit the otherwise suppressed instincts in others in order to lead or incite them to acquiesce or participate in acts of barbarism.[3] The 'banality of evil' does not prevent evil people having a big advantage over the vast majority of the population in any struggle for power, namely, their willingness to stop at nothing in order to gain power. There is not much likelihood that the weaknesses inside most human beings will ever be eradicated.

Even if appeals to love one's neighbours and practice universal altruism were to have any effect they would not totally eliminate potential conflicts.[4] For people will always have very different conceptions of what is 'good', *including, therefore, what is good for other people.* People have been tortured in an attempt to save their souls from eternal damnation. Others have been inspired to suicidal acts in the belief that they would then enter into eternal Paradise. People have been subjected to great and pointless suffering in the often mistaken belief that it was for some greater communal or spiritual good.

Thus lack of tolerance combined with differences of opinion as to what constitutes 'the good life' will be a permanent a source of potential conflict. Isaiah Berlin (1997: 13–14) reminded us of Alexander Herzen's essay in which

he said that a new form of human sacrifice had arisen in his time—of living human beings on the altars of abstractions—nation, Church, party, class, progress, the forces of

---

[3] It is a commonplace that many human emotions, including hatred and love, cannot be analysed in terms of rational behaviour, and all sorts of hypotheses to explain these emotions have been advanced over the years. Even some recent socio-biological theories that trace these emotions back to their evolutionary functions are by no means entirely new (see Graham Wallas 1914: 169).

[4] This point is well developed by Nagel (1991: 164) and Barry (1995: 28).

history—these have all been invoked in his day and in ours . . . The one thing that we may be sure of is the reality of the sacrifice, the dying and the dead. But the ideal for the sake of which they die remains unrealised.[5]

3. Prospects for Poverty

During most of human history sheer poverty has also been a major—sometimes *the* major—cause of human suffering, degradation, and humiliation. And in many parts of the world this is still the case. The relief of poverty, therefore, must also be among the priorities for policy. But for reasons set out in the last chapter, we expect a continual growth in incomes per head. On the whole this will eventually trickle down to the poorest nations, though, as has been seen during the post-war years, mismanagement in some can often prevent this. Furthermore, what horrifies most of us about the past is not so much the acute poverty in which earlier societies lived on account of the low level of development or their poor environments, but the needless atrocities, persecution, humiliation, and suffering inflicted by some sections of the world population on others—as is still too often the case today.

Poverty, both absolute and relative, will no doubt always persist, even in democratic countries with flourishing economies. Some people will always fall through what might have appeared to be more or less 'foolproof' safety nets in the form of universal income maintenance programmes. Others will remain poor on account of being trapped in a vicious circle of poverty—family breakdown, parental neglect or abuse, crime, drugs, and vicious environments—that are feature of many cities in affluent and democratic countries. Of 17 prosperous industrial countries covered in a recent report, the country that came top in terms of per capita GNP—the United States—came bottom in terms of the Human Poverty Index (UNDP 1998: 28).[6] Even Sweden, which comes out best in terms of the Human Poverty Index, has a significant proportion of its population that is deprived in some dimensions, including income.

Leaving aside sociological causes of persistent pockets of poverty, the economic determinant of the extent of poverty is the way that incomes are distributed within a country. A major cause of maldistribution of incomes and of the resulting persistent poverty in some countries is the absence of democratic institutions and of respect for basic human rights. While it is futile to

---

[5] See also Judith Shklar (1989: 32 and *passim*).

[6] This is a special index devised to apply particularly to developed countries and which includes, in addition to the three different dimensions of deprivation in human life—education, longevity, and the standard of living—covered by the poverty index used for the developing countries, a fourth dimension, namely, 'social exclusion' (UNDP 1998: 25–7).

try to predict the way the income distribution within countries will change over time, at least there does not seem to be any *economic* reason to expect it to become markedly more unequal than it is today. In that case, other things being equal, a continual rise in income levels must lead to a substantial reduction in 'absolute poverty' even if 'relative poverty' might always persist.[7] In the last chapter we argued that the average standard of living in the future will be probably be incomparably higher than it is today and will never be constrained by resource limitations. In that case there appears to be no insuperable *material* obstacles to the alleviation of widespread poverty over the course of the present century in the same way that there are insuperable obstacles to the spread of universal peace and harmony and goodwill among all human beings. Human sensibilities do not keep pace with technical progress.

4. The Environment and Human Rights

In the same way that we do not believe that there is any insuperable long-term obstacle to the elimination of poverty, we do not believe that vital interests of future generations will be permanently threatened by environmental degradation. Our reasons for this have been summarized in the last chapter. It is true that, in the course of economic growth, there is usually some environmental damage, often very acute. In industrializing countries environmental deterioration goes back to the eighteenth and nineteenth centuries and persisted until half way through the twentieth century. But as they became more affluent two forces combined to ensure that measures were taken to deal with their most serious environmental problems. First, they could afford to devote more resources to environmental protection. Second, public preferences shifted in favour of more environmental concerns. The same sequence of events will no doubt be followed in countries currently in the course of development. The speed with which the necessary policies are introduced to cater for environmental concerns varies, of course, from country to country. Economic growth is not enough by itself, and the pace of environmental improvement depends on the pace with which policies are adopted. But variations in this are also closely linked to the political institutions of the countries in question.

---

[7] 'Relative poverty' is usually defined as being below some fraction—say, a half or a third—of average incomes, whereas 'absolute poverty' is defined in terms of criteria such as lack of access to minimum dietary needs, adequate clothing and shelter, and other conventional 'necessities' of life. It is sometimes believed that 'relative poverty' must always be with us as a matter of definition. But this is a mistake. There is no inexorable arithmetic reason why anybody should fall below some 'relative poverty' line, such as half of average per capita incomes.

Greater respect for basic human rights will not only help reduce poverty in many countries, it will also help protect the environment in many of them. If the existing international conventions and declarations of human rights, which usually include rights to association, political expression and participation, legal redress, and so on, were implemented everywhere, it would go a long way to enable weak groups in many countries to improve and protect their environments and hence their living conditions.[8] At present environmental interests, along with others, are too easily trampled on by despotic governments.

It is no accident, for example, that the countries of the ex-Soviet bloc experienced some of the worst environmental devastation that has ever been witnessed. And in more recent years there are many other examples of environmental protest being stifled by lack of basic human rights. For example, the much-publicized disregard of the environmental interests of the Ogoni tribe in Nigeria and the intolerable treatment of those who protested at this treatment could not have taken place in a decent and just society. It is striking that, until this case brought to light the environmental aspects of the situation, it did not get much international and media attention. In some circles it seems that basic human rights can be trampled on without much outcry as long as the environment is not harmed![9]

The relationship between democratic participation in environmental policy and protection of the environment is also born out in cross-country statistical studies. Although the measurement of political 'freedom' is an even more subjective matter than the measurement of environmental conditions, various studies using different measures seem to show that, on the whole, 'the observed levels of environmental quality will depend . . . also on citizens being able to express their preferences for environmental quality and on governments having an incentive to satisfy these preferences by changing policy. In short, they will depend on civil and political freedoms' (Barrett and Graddy 1997: 1)

One particular environmental benefit that would flow from greater respect for human rights is the voluntary reduction in the birth-rate in countries where this is highly desirable on environmental as well as on other grounds.

---

[8] See M. Anderson (1996: Ch.1, esp. 4–6).

[9] Other less spectacular examples of the relationship between human rights and environmental protection are, of course, less well known outside the countries concerned and a small circle of research workers in the field. One such example is the research carried out into the factors that have recently been bringing deforestation under control in the Philippines and Thailand. The progress made has been attributed to a growing expression of dissatisfaction with autocratic rule and the way that people concerned with the environment were able to have more influence on policy-makers as the countries became more democratic and pluralist. One of the chief authors of the research reported that 'The key lesson for other tropical countries is that while the spread of deforestation is linked with socio-economic development, controlling it may well depend on political development. So unless agricultural expansion is curbed by rising farm yields, deforestation may not be controlled until countries become sufficiently democratic and pluralist to allow internal pressure groups to affect government policy' (Grainger 1997).

Even in many countries where certain universal human rights such as free-dom of assembly or of political representation are respected, some basic women's rights are still violated. If they were no longer subject to discrimi-nation and their rights to equal education and to social and economic status were respected, this would significantly reduce the high birth rates that are a cause of poverty and environmental degradation in many parts of the world.

Thus there is no conflict between giving priority to the extension of human rights and concern with the environment. If anything, the two objec-tives are complementary. There are many cases in which 'poverty, fertility, and environmental degradation reinforce one another in an escalating spiral' (Dasgupta 1995: 1897). But there are serious dangers if the priorities are reversed. It is true that environmental degradation and deprivation often lead directly to the infringement of basic human rights to life, health, and employ-ment. In communities where few people have access to clean drinking water or elementary sanitation, mortality and sickness rates are inevitably very high (Beckerman 1992a, b). But an improved environment will obviously not remedy most other violations of basic human rights. Emphasis on the way that an improved environment permits the enjoyment of basic human rights 'sometimes serves as a moral comforter which temporarily cloaks the extremely difficult questions which must be faced'; moreover, 'For people vulnerable to torture or chronic hunger, the urgent problems of immediate survival are likely to displace concern for long-term ecological integrity' (M. Anderson 1996: 3).

Insofar as a decent society gives priority to institutions that ensure that people are treated with respect and compassion it is a useful antidote to the excessive concern with the natural world that characterizes some of the 'deep ecology' sections of the environmentalist movement. Most environmentalists are no doubt motivated chiefly by highly commendable compassion for animals, aesthetic appreciation of nature, and altruistic concern for future generations. But there is a danger that, to some people, a love of nature is the counterpart of a disregard, if not something worse, for human beings. And, unfortunately, some environmentalists distrust the priority that human rights activists accord to human beings relative to other species (M. Anderson 1996).

It is not entirely coincidental that the most detailed legislation for the protection of nature and animals in the history of humanity was introduced by the Nazi regime and Hitler personally in the 1930s (Ferry 1995: xxii, Ch. 5); or that the author of *The Impeachment of Man*, which was a ferocious defence of animal rights and ecology, was Savitri Devi—real name Maximini-ani Portas—who was a leading Nazi supporter before World War II and a lead-ing neo-Nazi propagandist after it; or that the project to draft the World Charter for Nature was originally proposed by the notorious despot President Mobutu (Bowman 1996: 18).

Indeed, even at a far less extreme level, some of the well-meaning mystical reverence for the environment and the appeal to a return to pre-modern conditions of life that is encountered in much deep-ecology literature seems to be an appeal to renounce the rational, scientific, and humanist tradition that has largely dominated human thought throughout the twentieth century or more.[10] Giving priority to decent standards of behaviour by human beings towards other human beings is thus a valuable antidote to the danger that excessive concern with the environment leads to opposition to scientific and technical progress. Because the progress of science constantly throws up new problems it is now open to attack from various quarters. These range from fundamentalist ecological groups to the Prince of Wales, who a few years ago stated that 'Science has tried to assume a monopoly—or rather a tyranny—over our understanding of the world around us. Religion and science have become separated, and science has attempted to take over the natural world from God . . . We are only now beginning to gauge the disastrous results of this outlook'.[11]

But, on the whole, there has been great progress in human health during the last half century—as in previous years. For example, global infant mortality has fallen from 148 per 1,000 live births in 1955 to 59 in 1995; and life expectancy at birth has risen from just 48 years to 65 years over the same period (WHO 1998: 1). It is true that there has been some religious revival in a few countries, but, while we have no evidence to prove it, it is likely that science also made some contribution to these and other favourable transformations in the lives of countless millions of people.

Of course, many people are naturally disappointed that economic growth, and the sort of society that it has produced, has by no means solved all our problems and has even created some new ones. Unfortunately, disillusion with the benefits of modern civilization is too easily channelled, by some groups, into an attack on rising standards of living, humanistic values, and a rational approach to the solution of our problems. Some of these groups either participate in or provide tacit support to violent and anti-democratic practices. Societies that have confidence in the ability of their own institutions to tackle their problems in a peaceful and democratic manner do not have to try to escape from them by conjuring up melodramatic apocalyptic environmental scenarios involving artificial conflicts between generations.

5. Bequeathing a Decent Society

By contrast with the long-term prospects for poverty and the environment, it seems virtually inconceivable, for the reasons set out above, that there will be

---

[10] See also J. O'Neill (1993: 148ff.) for a discussion of the unjustified attack on science in much deep ecology literature, in spite of its occasional appeals to a scientific basis for some of its claims.
[11] 'The Sacred in Modern Life', speech to the Investcorp Dinner, London (10 July 1996).

any decline in the need for continued vigilance in defence of basic human rights. Our most important obligation to future generations, therefore, is to bequeath to them a more 'decent society'. The chief characteristics of a 'decent society' would be a respect for basic human rights and for personal autonomy and identity that rules out any form of institutional humiliation of people, a tolerance for differences in conceptions of the good life, and democratic institutions and traditions that enable people to sort out their inevitable conflicts peacefully, free of fear of oppression and persecution.[12]

It is not necessary here to discuss the difficult philosophical problems concerning the grounds for believing that there are basic human rights.[13] For purposes of the present argument we shall accept the desirability of guaranteeing respect for the basic human rights specified, together with others, in various international conventions, such as the Universal Declaration of Human Rights, the International Covenant on Civil and Political Rights, and the European Convention on Human Rights. These comprise rights to life, liberty and security of the person, protection against slavery or torture and cruel and inhuman punishment, equality before the law and access to legal remedies for rights violations, right to own property, freedom of thought, conscience and religion, freedom of speech, freedom for peaceful assembly, association and political participation, and so on.[14] It is true that countries with very different cultural traditions may differ about what constitute fundamental human rights, although, as Sen (2000: 31–8) has recently argued, the differences are not as great as are widely believed and exaggeration of the differences can be an obstacle to the pursuit of rational policies in defence of human rights.

The international conventions also include certain economic and social rights which are often known as 'welfare rights', such as rights to social security or to paid holidays. These 'rights' raise special problems which lie outside the type of basic human rights with which we are concerned here. It is true that a 'decent society' will also be sensitive to the welfare of its members and non-members. This will include the elimination of poverty. Impoverished people are not only deprived of their dignity but are also unable to take advantage of the other privileges and rights that a decent society should make available. Minimum levels of nutrition, shelter, and so on are essential to peoples' survival and to the exercise of their basic human right to autonomy.

---

[12] Probably the best recent discussion of the characteristics of a 'decent society' is A. Margalit, who points out (1996: 272–3) that a Rawlsian 'just' society must be a 'decent society', for one of the conditions of Rawls's just society is that there is a just distribution of primary goods, of which the most important is self-respect.

[13] There are many excellent relatively recent surveys and discussions of this topic, such as in Gewirth (1996); O. O'Neill (1996: Ch. 5); Plant (1991: 257–84); Raz (1986: Chs. 7 and 8); and Waldron (1984).

[14] Among numerous surveys of human rights legislation, one of the most authoritative is Robertson and Merrills (1996).

But there seems little point in pious articles in international conventions that prescribe 'welfare rights' going well beyond this to poor countries that simply cannot afford them.[15]

It is also often forgotten that the protection of almost all basic human rights imposes some costs.[16] Some of the basic human rights such as those that protect the security of the individual or the protection of property can be extremely costly in terms of police forces and judicial systems. Even the cost of the network of civil courts for dealing with cases involving an infringement of the right to work in an environment free of sexual harassment is, apparently, enormous.[17] So since resources are limited everywhere society has to make political choices concerning which 'rights' are to be protected and enforced. This is one of the reasons why one must eschew an absolutist approach to the protection of rights.

Quite apart from the costs of protecting many rights, there may be conflicts between the 'rights' of different groups or individuals. This is often apparent in environmental conflicts. For example, how far does a person's right to dispose of his property as he thinks fit conflict with somebody else's right to a clean environment?[18] More generally, as far as their costs are concerned there is no sharp dividing line between 'positive rights', such as the right to subsidized education or income supports to single mothers, where the cost is direct and obvious, and the 'negative rights', such as the right to freedom of speech and association, where the costs are the costs of maintaining the required institutional infrastructure. Nevertheless, the basic human rights with which we are concerned here, such as freedom of expression, freedom from arbitrary arrest, or torture, or execution, are mainly those that are violated by governments at some cost to themselves in terms of the forces of repression that they are obliged to maintain. In other words, although it is costly to protect some human rights, greater respect for basic human rights would also save resources.

While there is room for much debate concerning the extent to which human rights encompass certain aspects of economic and social welfare, therefore, our concern here is with those to which all humane people would subscribe and yet are obviously flouted on a massive scale in spite of national laws and international conventions. For example, as the late Judith Shklar (1989: 27) pointed out, contrary to the expectations held at the beginning of this century in most of the Western world, 'torture returned and has flourished on a colossal scale ever since . . . somewhere someone is being tortured

---

[15] This applies, for example, to some of the articles in the Draft Principles on Human Rights and the Environment, *Human Rights and the Environment*, (UN Doc. E/CN.4/Sub2/1994/9, 6 July, 1994).

[16] See an excellent recent discussion of this topic in Holmes and Sunstein (1999).

[17] 'No Such Thing as a Free Right', *Financial Times* (26/27 June 1999).

[18] See many examples of such conflicting rights affecting the environment in Merrills (1996: 37ff.).

right now, and acute fear has again become the most common form of social control'. Similarly, all Western school-children learn about the abolition of slavery. But it is still widespread today in many parts of the world, as in the case of mine-workers in Brazil, brick-workers in Pakistan, and prostitutes, including children, in many countries (Luttwak 1999).

In short, the violation of undeniably basic human rights is currently widespread and a threat to human rights will always exist. By comparison, there are reasons to expect that poverty and environmental degradation, taken as a whole, must eventually be eradicated. Various statistical surveys among different countries or social groups and at different times confirm that we do not know very much about what makes people happy. But we do know with certainty what makes them suffer most. And a reduction in existing suffering from the violation of human rights will also help us bequeath a more decent society to future generations.

6. The Importance of Tradition

In pursuit of the objective of increasing respect for basic human rights, the development of a tradition of justice and tolerance, as well as legal institutions, also has a crucial part to play. In the course of the last few centuries the divine right of kings to rule or of established religions to dictate one's beliefs has been challenged. But it has often been replaced by equally, or even more, authoritarian rule by tyrannical governments that did not feel any need to claim divine sanction for dictating peoples' beliefs in the name of some new ideology or other.

Legal systems that embody basic human rights such as freedom of political association and peaceful assembly are not enough by themselves to ensure that old authoritarian belief systems or ideologies are never replaced by new ones. The transformation of Germany, with its well-established liberal legal framework, in the course of one or two years after the Nazis came to power in 1933 should be a lesson to us all. Furthermore, it should be remembered that the Nazis came to power as a result of a democratic electoral process. And the last decade or so has witnessed the resurgence of strong extremist groups in other highly developed civilized countries in Europe.

Thus the struggle for toleration and basic human rights has to be a continuous one; and history has shown too many examples of legal systems that protected human rights being too easily dismantled in the name of some ideology. Kolakowski (1999: 34, 40) is surely right in saying that 'In order for the principle of toleration . . . to be accepted and applied, we need not only laws but also the right cultural conditions, and these cannot be manufactured by fiat . . . I repeat: toleration is best protected not so much by the law as by the preservation and strengthening of a tolerant society'. Only a firmly entrenched tradition of respect for basic human rights and human diversity, even more than legal provisions safeguarding human rights, can provide lasting protection of liberal values.

And in many, if not most, countries a tradition of toleration and respect for diversity of beliefs and of acceptance of basic human rights has never taken hold, or is still only fragile. It will take decades, or generations, before it begins to be firmly established, even in many of the more advanced democracies.

7. The Prospects for International Action

It will be a very long time before citizens of countries that lack the requisite laws and traditions can expect much protection for human rights from international laws and institutions. The year 1998 was the 50th anniversary of the Universal Declaration of Human Rights. Yet it has failed to prevent massive suffering and death in internal struggles that have proliferated all over the world. And it is difficult to see how far the United Nations, as presently constituted, can do much, if anything, to remedy its past impotence in the face of widespread abuse of human rights.

Bequeathing a more decent and just society to future generations will thus be an even far more difficult task than bequeathing some target level of biodiversity or freedom from all danger of harmful climate change. As argued in Chapters 10 and 11, even the pursuit of these objectives will require a very high degree of international cooperation. But there has been some experience of international action to deal with global environmental and health problems going back over a century—for example, from action to contain cholera in the nineteenth century to recent action to protect the ozone layer. By contrast, international action to protect human rights in the many countries where, in spite of numerous international conventions and declarations, they are abused, has hardly begun.

Until the end of World War II such action was generally seen as lying outside the responsibilities of international bodies. The obstacles to international action are immense and quick results were never to be expected. One of the major difficulties is that the UN Charter states that the United Nations is based on the 'sovereign equality of all its members'. Unfortunately, this principle is essentially inconsistent with international interference in the internal affairs of any sovereign member state in the name of protection of human rights. This conflict of objectives was strikingly demonstrated during the recent international intervention in Bosnia and in Kosovo.

Thus although it is true that 'If there is a global religion today, it is human rights' (De Waal 1999: 32), and many international conventions to protect human rights have been signed, progress in implementing them has been painfully slow and the conventions and treaties in question often treated with contempt by some of the signatories. 'For example, the sight of General Omer al Bashir, military rule of Sudan where government militia forces are known to enslave children, among the seventy-one heads of state signing the Convention on the Rights of the Child is hardly an encouraging example of sincerity' (De Waal 1999: 32).

The problem is that the international treaties and conventions in defence of human rights are designed to correct the weaknesses of internal national laws and institutions. They depend for their effectiveness in the first place, therefore, on the cooperation of those who are the perpetrators of human rights violations. Since this is usually unlikely to be forthcoming and since international institutions are most reluctant to violate national sovereignty, there is a terrible dilemma at the heart of international pressures to extend respect for human rights.[19] Nevertheless, as Kofi Annan (1999) recently put it, 'Nothing in the UN charter precludes a recognition that there are rights beyond borders'.[20]

There is thus a conflict between international action to protect human rights and the objective of respecting national sovereignty. But conflicting and incommensurate objectives are an unavoidable and ubiquitous feature of daily life and choices have to be made depending on the strength of the conflict in particular instances and the feasibility of pursuing one or the other. In the same way that one cannot rank broad incommensurate objectives one should not assume that one objective, whether it is protection of human rights or respect for national sovereignty, must always have precedence over another. Thus, while pessimism concerning the scope for rapid progress in the international protection of human rights may be justified, despair is not. For despair can lead to violence by the victims or inaction by those who could help them. And in spite of the constraints some small steps have been taken over the years in the direction of greater international pressure on countries or individuals who violate human rights.

First, however much the timing or operation of the measures adopted may be open to criticism, recent international intervention to prevent violations of human rights in instances where it seemed that such intervention could be effective, as in Kosovo or East Timor, have been landmarks in international recognition of fact that the objective of respect for national sovereignty must sometimes give way to the objective of protecting basic human rights. These

---

[19] Simpson (1999: 9) puts the dilemma clearly: 'The underlying problem can be stated in a paradoxical way—the function of international legal mechanisms is to establish the rule of law, but legal mechanisms only work satisfactorily when the conditions embodied in the notion of the rule of law already exist'.
[20] See a valuable review of the problems by Best (1999: 9), in the course of a review of a recent book on this subject by Gutman and Rieff.

interventions were a clear statement of a major new principle, namely, that certain crimes could no longer be regarded as purely matters of internal policy of sovereign states. 'Gradually recognition is growing that violations of national sovereignty may be justified to prevent genocide and other crimes' (Glover 1999: 42).

Second, there has been an unprecedented development in the body of international rights law, ranging from the 1945 UN Charter, which was soon followed by the establishment of the Human Rights Commission, to the agreement reached in Rome in July 1998 which set up a permanent International Criminal Court. It is true that the United States opposed the creation of the Court, in company with Algeria, China, Iran, Iraq, Libya, and the Sudan. The agreement has yet to be ratified by 60 countries before it has international legal standing. But this should not be too difficult given that its adoption was approved by 120 nations, against the seven that included the USA.[21]

Third, until recently the UN Commission for Human Rights, which was set up in 1946, was never allowed to play a significant part in monitoring international human rights abuses. But that seems to have changed now. The Commission's own officials have been sent to monitor a range of trouble spots, and its activities are now backed up by a large number of voluntary experts and non-governmental human-rights organizations.[22]

Fourth, over the past two or three decades hundreds of human-rights NGOs, of which Amnesty International and Human Rights Watch are the best known, have been formed. They play an important part in documenting and publicizing abuses, in campaigning for legal change, in chivvying governments, in delivering aid to local groups and to victims of human-rights violations, and in arousing public opinion. They now participate in international, and sometimes national, policy-making and play a part in some form or other in all international human rights activities. And they have become very skilled at public relations so that they are well placed to embarrass governments and private organizations, such as multinational companies. This is

[21] It is also true that it remains to be seen how effective the Court will be after it has been ratified. Like all institutions, in the end this will depend partly on the character and determination of the people involved, which in this case means the prosecutors and judges attached to the Court. But, judging by the high calibre of those attached to the ad hoc International Criminal Tribunals set up to deal with violations of human rights in Rwanda and Bosnia, this should not be a major problem. The important constraints are more likely to be certain provisions in the agreement, notably those restricting the type of case that the prosecutors can pursue. Another crucial constraint will, of course, be the adequacy of funds and the support of the international community.

[22] Many of the NGOs attend, together with other human-rights campaigners as well as diplomats, the Commission's deliberations in Geneva, which have now been made public. And at the public meetings of the Human Rights Committee—the monitoring body for the International Covenant on Civil and Political Rights—NGOs and others are able to question officials from individual countries about their official reports on their own compliance with the international treaties that they have ratified.

important work since many governments, as well as multinational companies, do seem to be vulnerable to the power of shame.[23]

Some countries are, of course, concerned with the effect that their public image has on activities that directly affect their interests. Certain influential voices are now arguing that 'morality is not the only reason for putting human rights on the West's foreign-policy agenda. Self-interest also plays a part'.[24] Many of the countries that have shifted towards more democratic regimes have done so on account of the manifest failures of their autocratic systems to maintain, let alone raise, the standards of living of their populations.[25] But others have been motivated by their international ambitions.[26]

8. Conclusions

It does not make much sense to group together large classes of issues, such as the environment, human rights, poverty, crime and violence, and so on, and then rank them in order of absolute priority. Nevertheless, we believe that, as time goes by, there are reasons to believe that problems of poverty and environmental damage will eventually become less common and generally less acute than will be the threats to basic human rights. This is because while poverty and environmental damage will never be totally eliminated, there are forces in society that tend, in the very long run, to reduce them. By contrast, on the human scale of time there are no forces tending to eradicate those

[23] For example, complaints and critical reports by the Inter-American Commission on Human Rights have led Argentina to repeal legislation that interfered with free expression, Mexico to introduce independent election monitoring, and Colombia to compensate the victims of an army massacre. Even highly respected countries, such as Canada, the Netherlands, and Japan have changed some of their laws or improved the treatment of prisoners in response to public criticism. And in countries where the governments ignore critical reports by the committee, ranging from Algeria and Libya in 1998 to the USA in 1995—criticized for poor legal representation of indigent defendants, anti-gay laws, widespread police abuse, and so on—human rights campaigners and pressure groups derive encouragement, political ammunition, and back-up support for their activities. Even in the private sector, companies such as Shell—as a result of the publicity concerning the treatment of the Ogoni people in Nigeria—Reebok, Nike and many others have now adopted a policy of consulting human-rights groups and examining the human-rights aspects of their business practices (*The Economist*, Special Supplement, 5 December 1998, 14).

[24] *The Economist* (12 April 1997), 15.

[25] The considerable increase over the last decade or more in the number of states that are democratic is shown in World Bank (1997: Fig. 7.1, 112).

[26] For example, Turkey's aspiration to eventual participation in the European Union is beginning to have some influence on the extent of Turkish respect for basic human rights. The declaration by the new government in Britain of a determination to pursue an 'ethical' foreign policy, and the British decision to incorporate the European Convention on Human rights into domestic law, are small steps, but are also in the right direction, and no doubt reflect a desire to be a 'good' member of the European Union as long as there are no major conflicting interests at stake. Even Britain, which may be said to have led the way, with Magna Carta, in the recognition and enumeration of human rights, might find its treatment of prisoners in Wormwood Scrubs will be condemned internationally as much as it has been condemned at home.

features of the human psyche that, one way or another, frequently lead some groups of people to impose intolerable suffering on others. The only protection against this is a permanently vigilant protection of basic human rights. This requires more than constitutional extensions of democracies, though this is the place to start. It also requires deeply ingrained traditions. Because of their predictable permanent importance, therefore, the extension of human rights, taken by and large, should be the central focus of our moral obligations to distant generations. Our most important bequest to future generations, therefore, is to bequeath a more decent society, one of the chief characteristics of which is a greater respect for basic human rights.

Far from involving a conflict with the objectives of poverty relief or environmental protection, greater respect for human rights is actually complementary to them. Indeed, democratic institutions are essential in order that conflicts over the environment or the distribution of incomes, which can never be totally eliminated, are dealt with justly and peacefully.

PART 2
Justice between individuals

8

The Intrinsic Value of the Environment

1. Introduction

In the previous chapters we have argued that, subject to the limitations on comparisons between broad, general concepts like 'the environment' or 'human rights', it is more important to bequeath to future generations a decent society characterized by greater respect for basic human rights than to preserve the 'environment' in some sense or other in its present state. Our conclusion was reached largely on negative grounds that various theories of intergenerational justice or equity or 'sustainable development' were seriously flawed. But it was also founded on a positive assessment of what, we believe, is likely to remain the greatest permanent threat to human welfare.

However, many environmentalist philosophers and others would argue that the 'environment', or, more particularly, that part of it which may be described as 'nature', has some intrinsic value which confers on it a greater claim to our concern than if it was just another instrumental component of human welfare, like more food or clothing.[1] In turn this is taken to mean that it should be given special privileged weight in assessing the contribution of environmental preservation to human welfare. This would affect both any comparison between the effect of alternative policies on the welfare of future generations as against the welfare of the current generation, and the assessment of how much the present generation should devote to environmental protection as against other claims on resources.[2]

Of course, we do not dispute the great impact of environmental conditions in determining human welfare. There is no doubt, as one of us has documented elsewhere, that poor environmental conditions—notably as regards clean drinking water, sanitation, and decent shelter—are a major cause of

---

[1] Among a very large number of publications setting out this view a recent very wide-ranging presentation of most of the main arguments that have been presented in its support is included in Foster (1997). A masterly and impartial survey of the way that the concept of intrinsic value is used in the environmental debate is contained in Bowman (1996). Bowman quotes The World Charter for Nature, which states in its preamble that 'Every form of life is unique, warranting respect *regardless of its worth to man* [emphasis added], and, to accord other organisms such recognition, man must be guided by a moral code of action' (Bowman 1996:18).

[2] See also reference to Matthews in Bowman (1996: 25).

misery, disease, squalor, and degradation for countless millions of people throughout the world (Beckerman, 1992*a*, *b*). To the urgent need to improve local environmental conditions in the Third World can be added the needs for expenditures to improve the urban environment almost everywhere, as well as some components of the global environment, notably the oceans and the atmosphere.

Hence, from any perspective, there are massive needs for legitimate environmental expenditures. This means large-scale competition with expenditures on other sources of human welfare, such as health, education, and shelter. Thus, some way must be found of allocating total resources between these competing objectives. How far such an allocation can be carried out within the framework of some comparative valuation of costs and benefits and how far, instead, some incommensurate 'intrinsic' value should be attached to 'the environment' is, therefore, an important question.

Most of the discussion in this book has referred to 'the environment', which we have been interpreting in a very wide and loose sense as covering a vast and heterogeneous collection of goods and services, including 'any aspect of the environment to which a positive value may be attached, whether a natural feature, a species of animal, a habitat, an ecosystem, or whatever . . .' (Miller 1999: 152). One must not overlook environmental 'bads' either, since many environmental goods are simply the reverse side of the coin: that is, clean air is the counterpart of polluted air, and so on. We use the blanket term 'environment' simply because it is the concept that is used in most current policy debate. We do also make occasional reference to 'nature' in particular. But while the provision of, say, better sanitation, clean water supply, transportation, and so on would come under the heading of environmental programmes, nobody would suggest that such activities were part of the preservation of 'nature'. However, when it comes to the question of attributing 'intrinsic' value to the environment, the focus of the debate is usually on the natural component of the environment. Hence, although we shall often continue to talk about the 'environment', it has to be understood that 'intrinsic value' is usually attributed to 'natural' components of the environment and not to, say, better sewerage systems or more beautiful lamp-posts.

We have to face two questions, therefore. First, how far is it right to regard the environment, or, more often, 'nature', as a bearer of some distinct intrinsic value? Second, if it is not right, does this mean that the ranking of environmental objectives against others can be settled by appeals to some systematic economic formulae, such as cost-benefit analysis? This chapter concentrates on the former question, namely, the intrinsic value of the environment. This sets the scene for the discussion, in the next chapter, of the validity of the cost-benefit analysis used by economists in evaluating the desirability of specific projects that have important environmental effects.

2. The Concept of 'Intrinsic Values'

The attempt to attribute 'intrinsic' value to the environment has probably been one of the central and the most recalcitrant problems of environmental ethics.[3] But one prominent contributor to the debate believes that it would be better to abandon the attempt altogether (Regan 1992). He may well be right, since the term 'intrinsic' value means different things to different people. So we shall simply state here how we shall interpret it before going on to consider its applicability to the environment in general or nature in particular. We use the term 'intrinsic' value—as in our earlier discussion, in Chapter 4, of intergenerational egalitarianism—to indicate merely one part of a twofold classification of values as being either 'intrinsic' or 'instrumental'.[4]By that we mean that objects of value are, respectively, either valued for their own sake or valued for the sake of the contribution that they make to some other objective.

Some objects may have both kinds of value. For example, beautiful music may be valued for its own sake and may also possess the instrumental therapeutic value of soothing the savage breast. Flowers may have intrinsic aesthetic value and also have the instrumental value of providing important sources of food for insects or medicinal beverages for herbalists. Similarly, a primeval forest would be *instrumentally* valuable insofar as it contains scientifically valuable information that can be potentially useful for, say, medicinal purposes. But some people would claim that it is also valuable in itself over and above its usefulness: that it is *intrinsically* valuable.

There are two main routes by which one can arrive at the conclusion that certain values are intrinsic. One is the 'objectivist' approach. On this approach, a valued object is valuable objectively, *independently of any human valuations*. It would be argued that some objects, such as nature, are valuable on account of some objective characteristics that they possess, such as beauty, integrity, or harmony, and not on account of the value that outside valuers may attach to them.

In 1903 the philosopher G. E. Moore, who is usually regarded as a strong advocate of this objectivist view, invited us to make a famous thought-experiment concerning beauty.He asked us to imagine two worlds, one in which all imaginable natural beauty exists: 'put into it whatever on this earth you most admire—mountains, rivers, the sea, trees, and sunsets, stars and the moon . . . And then imagine the ugliest world you can possibly conceive We

---

[3] Callicott (1985): 271). See an excellent discussion of this feature of environmentalism in Sober (1986).

[4] For example, Nozick (1981: 414) writes, 'The notion of value I wish to investigate is not the value of something for some other purpose or further effects or consequences (assumed to be valuable). It is not its instrumental value, but rather its value in itself, apart from these further consequences and connections. Philosophers have termed this type of value intrinsic value'. Sometimes, in the context of this sort of classification, 'instrumental values' are referred to as 'extrinsic values'.

then have to assume that neither of these worlds can ever possibly be seen by any human being. Moore goes on to ask 'is it irrational to hold that it is better that the beautiful world should exist, than the one which is ugly (Moore 1978: 83–4). The subjectivist would say that such a comparison would, indeed, be irrational. Moore, however, took the opposite view. If the choice was between the sheer existence of beauty and the sheer existence of ugliness, then, according to him, 'beauty must *in itself*, be regarded as a greater good than ugliness' and we must prefer its existence to that of ugliness (Moore: 1978: 84; emphasis added).[5]

But Brian Barry (1999: 114) is surely right in saying that 'I have to say that the whole question [that is, Moore's question] strikes me as ridiculous. In what possible sense could the universe be a better or a worse place on one supposition rather than the other? It seems to me an abuse of our language to assume that the word 'good' still has application when applied to such a context'.

In other words, it is difficult to imagine what beauty would be if it were not beauty as it presents itself to some consciousness. Thus Moore's experiment is fundamentally flawed. Imagining the world without humans is really imagining the world without their sense of beauty and other values. If, in Moore's experiments, we were allowed to be 'spectators', so to speak, but not 'actors' on the stage of the world, then of course it is plausible that as spectators we would choose a beautiful world rather than an ugly one. But if we are not allowed to be spectators either, then 'beauty' and 'ugliness' are terms that seem to be devoid of any significance.

The alternative route, which is the 'subjective' route, and which is the one that we followed in our discussion of intergenerational egalitarianism, is that values cannot exist without a valuer. In the example of Moore's two worlds, it does not make sense to talk about a beautiful world unless there is some valuer who perceives it as beautiful. But the subjectivist view of value by no means implies that the mere fact that something is valued by somebody means that it must be valuable to everybody.[6]

---

[5] At other points in the book, however, Moore appears to express doubts about this view. For example, he writes (1978: 28), without indicating any dissent, that 'It seems to be true that to be conscious of a beautiful object is a thing of great intrinsic value; whereas the same object, if no one be conscious of it, has certainly comparatively little value, and is commonly held to have none at all'. And he displays a certain amount of equivocation in writing 'I have myself urged in Chap. III that the mere existence of what is beautiful does appear to have *some* intrinsic value; but I regard it as indubitable that Prof. Sidgwick was so far right, in the view there discussed, that such mere existence of what is beautiful has value, so small as to be negligible, in comparison with that which attaches to the consciousness of beauty' (1978: 189). It is only the distinction between 'negligible' value in the absence of any consciousness and zero value that protects Moore from the charge of blatant inconsistency, and the distinction is very difficult to justify in the context.

[6] Many people value things that most of us would regard as abhorrent, but it is probably true that such people would probably prefer to keep their 'values' quiet or deny that they had them, and this is probably largely because they know that the things that they value do not really have any moral value.

Furthermore, this so-called *'subjectivist'* approach to valuation, that is, requiring the existence of a valuer, does not prejudge the issue of which sort of value the valuer would ascribe to the valued object. One can subjectively attribute either instrumental or intrinsic value to the object in question. For example, as explained in Chapter 4 in connection with egalitarianism, some people may believe that greater equality between people is intrinsically valuable, and others may believe that it is only instrumentally valuable, for example, as a means of increasing social harmony. But both ways of valuing equality will be values held by people and neither need rest on a claim that the values in question are 'objective' values that exist independently of valuers. Thus, the subjectivist approach to valuation still allows the valuer to attribute *intrinsic* value to something.

How far values can be objective or subjective has been the subject of extensive speculation among philosophers for centuries. One classic discussion of this issue, by the late J. L. Mackie, began with the blunt statement: 'There are no objective values'. But, as he went on to explain, to some people this proposition appears outrageous while to others it appears as a trivial truth (Mackie 1988). Thus the problem of the objectivity or otherwise of values in general is a vast and complex problem to which we would not presume to attempt to contribute. Here we are concerned chiefly with the question of whether the environment or some parts of it can be the bearer of intrinsic values, and, if so, in what sense. This is a question for subjectivists as much as for those who subscribe to objective values. For where the value comes from and what possesses value are two different questions. As John O'Neill has pointed out, some of the confusion in the debate about intrinsic values arises out of a failure to distinguish between the *source* of value, for example human valuers, and the *object* of value—O'Neill's terminology, or *locus* of value in other peoples' terminology (J. O'Neill 1993: 11). For instance a common mistake is to assume that if we follow the subjectivist path, we are committed to the view that is despised by preservationists, namely, that nature can have only instrumental value to us. But, in fact, nothing prevents a subjectivist from attributing intrinsic value to nature or the preservation of the environment.

However, many environmentalists would not be satisfied with, let alone welcome, a subjectivist defence of the intrinsic value of nature. They believe it is unduly anthropocentric, and hence sells a crucial pass in the struggle to justify the intrinsic value of nature. It makes the status of nature too dependent on changes in human tastes and fashions or on differences in cultural norms. As is well-known, one of the dangers in the subjectivist approach to valuation is that it can slip into moral relativism, that is, that what is morally 'good' may depend too much on the particular society or epoch with which we are concerned.

The same could apply to the valuation of nature. If all that matters is human appreciation of nature then one day our cultural ideals may change.

The human race could become so culturally depraved that whereas it had previously regarded magnificent trees or forests as intrinsically valuable it now denied them intrinsic value and regarded plastic trees as more beautiful than real ones. All real trees would then be cut down except those required to satisfy minority tastes for quaint, old-fashioned wooden furniture or other useful purposes. Many environmentalists also share the view that 'In our enlightened times, when most forms of chauvinism have been abandoned, at least in theory, by those who consider themselves progressive, Western ethics still appears to retain a fundamental form of chauvinism, namely human chauvinism' (Routley and Routley 1979: 36)

3. The Objectivist Defence of Nature's Intrinsic Value

A widely-used argument that brings out the character of the objectivist case for attaching objective intrinsic value to nature is the 'last man argument', which closely resembles Moore's famous thought-experiment discussed above.[7] This takes a form such as 'Suppose you were the last man on earth and knew that you were about to die as well, but you had it in your power to press a button that would destroy all the beautiful things that would otherwise be left behind—the mountains, the forests, the beautiful scenery, the animals, and so on. Would you do so?' Those who claim that the items in question have *objective* intrinsic value would argue that it would be immoral to do so even in the absence of human beings. It is not a question of whether such an act of wilful and pointless vandalism would be stupid and contemptible, about which we can all agree. The question is whether the beautiful things that would be left behind if the last person to leave did not destroy them would be valuable on account of their beauty or integrity or whatever.

A clear illustration of the weakness of the 'last man' argument is exposed if one pushes the thought-experiment a bit further. Suppose that after the last man has departed, leaving behind the mountains and trees, and so on, perhaps in due deference to their intrinsic value and beauty, some aliens from outer space arrive on earth one day who have very different tastes from ours. They much prefer flat surfaces and find all these mountains and trees sticking up all over the place to be very ugly. Any philosophers among them who had previously espoused the 'last man' argument would be looking rather silly.[8]

Other arguments put up in defence of the objective view as applied to nature are equally unconvincing. For example, some environmental philosophers have argued that value is a concept that is applicable to any being that

---

[7] This was set out very forcefully by Richard and Val Routley (1980).
[8] See also Elliott Sober's (1986: 190–1) powerful critique of the 'last man' argument.

has a good of its own—for example, bamboo is 'good' for pandas, mild winters are 'good' for greenfly.[9] But this is a glaring example of the fallacy of equivocation: the word 'good' is being used in two entirely different senses. For even if certain inputs may be instrumentally 'good' for certain animals or inanimate objects in the sense that they may be necessary or sufficient conditions for them to flourish, this is a sense of the term 'good' that has nothing to do with being intrinsically morally 'good'. The mere fact that some living organism, like the tse tse fly or the HIV virus, or a more complex entity like an ecosystem, may flourish in particular conditions does not impose any moral obligation on humans to protect and promote those conditions.

There are other prominent avowedly objectivist defences of the intrinsic value of nature, but when it comes to the crunch they seem to sell crucial passes in that human interests and valuations enter by the back door. For example, Arne Naess, the founder of deep ecology, states that 'Richness and diversity of life forms . . . are also values in themselves. Humans have no right to reduce this richness and diversity *except to satisfy vital needs*' (emphasis added).[10] But the 'vital needs' to which reference is made are, presumably, the vital needs of humans.

Similarly, 'deep green' theory adopts the principle that 'there should be no substantially differential treatment of items outside any favoured class or species of a discriminatory sort that *lacks sufficient justification*' (Sylvan and Bennett 1994: 142, emphasis added). Again, it is presumably humans who are to decide what is 'sufficient justification' and to weigh this against the value of the environment. Thus the qualifications about the moral legitimacy of sacrificing nature in the interests of satisfying vital human needs, or when there is sufficient justification, means that, in the end, humans are entitled to weigh up the claims of the natural environment against any other claims that they think are vital. So we are once again relying on humans to weigh up competing claims on resources. In that case the concept of objective values outside the valuations made by humans can have no place.

All in all, therefore, the common environmentalist claim that nature is the bearer of some objectively intrinsic values seems difficult to defend. Indeed, the difficulty seems so great that those environmentalists who want to claim a privileged status for the environment would probably be on firmer ground if they defended the intrinsic value to the environment from a subjectivist point of view (O. O'Neill 1997: 128). In the end, objectivism may prove to be a liability to them rather than an asset, and some other, less metaphysically demanding view, such as that set out here and in the next chapter, may better serve the cause of environmental protection.

---

[9] See a useful discussion of this assertion and its advocates in J. O'Neill (1993: Ch. 2).

[10] See Naess and Session's 'platform' quoted in Sikora and Barry (1978: 95).

4. The Inevitability of Human-Centred Values

The objectivist case for regarding the environment, or parts of it, as the bearer of intrinsic value is closely linked, as already indicated, to the belief that the value of nature should not be seen from a purely anthropocentric viewpoint. But, in some fundamental sense, even objectivists are no less anthropocentric than those who believe that nature has purely instrumental value. For it is simply inevitable that, to whatever view we subscribe about the value of nature, it will always be our human view. There is no other perspective available to us and there is no other perspective that can be adopted in our treatment of the non-human world. Since 'anthropocentric' simply means 'seen from the standpoint of a human being', then all views about the status and value of nature are equally anthropocentric.[11]

There is also a certain tension between notions like 'biological egalitarianism' or 'eco-impartiality' and insistence on treating the human species on an equal footing with the other species. For if all species are to be treated equally why is the human species not allowed to act in the way that other species do, namely, in their self-interest? No other species respects the 'intrinsic' value of other forms of life. But we are expected to be different and, instead of safeguarding our own interests by displaying natural 'human chauvinism' in the way that lions display 'leo chauvinism', we are expected to overcome this natural inclination of all species, and adopt what might be called 'species impartiality'.

Now the demand that human beings should cultivate sensibilities such that they treat 'nature' with due respect—but not more—seems to be perfectly legitimate. But it is so because of a clear affirmation of human superiority. No other species would be capable of conceiving of such a grand idea as the equality of species which requires it to rise above the natural limitations of its own species. As Bernard Williams points out, it is one of the stranger paradoxes in many peoples' attitudes to nature that

while they supposedly reject traditional pictures of human beings as discontinuous from nature in virtue of reason, they remind us all the time that other species share the same world with us on (so to speak) equal terms, and they unhesitatingly carry over into their picture of human beings a moral transcendence over the rest of nature, which makes us uniquely able and therefore uniquely obliged, to detach ourselves from any natural determination of our behaviour. Such views in fact firmly preserve the traditional doctrine of our transcendence of nature, and with it our proper monarchy of the earth; they merely ask us to exercise it in a more benevolent manner. (Williams 1992: 65)

[11] As Luc Ferry (1995: 131) puts it in his criticism of deep ecologists. 'imagining that good is inscribed within the very being of things they forget that all valorization, including that of nature, is the deed of man and that, consequently, all normative ethic is in some sense humanistic and anthropocentrist'.

As Bernard Williams (1992: 65) writes, 'a self-conscious concern for nature is not itself a piece of nature: it is an expression of culture'. And he goes on to explain that 'nature which is preserved by us is no longer a nature that is simply not controlled. A natural park is not nature, but a park; a wilderness that is preserved is a definite, delimited, wilderness. The paradox is that we have to use our power to preserve a sense of what is not in our power. Anything we leave untouched we have already touched'. And finally Williams warns us that in order to avoid self-deception we must not forget 'the inescapable truth that our refusal of the anthropocentric must itself be a human refusal' (1992: 68).

But being anthropocentric does not necessarily mean that we are 'human chauvinists', as is suggested in much environmentalist literature. For the term 'chauvinism', as usually employed in connection with attitudes to national or racial differences, suggests narrowness of sympathy, ruthlessness, and a callous indifference to the feelings of people of different national or racial affiliation. However, the philosophical position represented by, say, Passmore, which is commonly described as anthropocentric, can hardly be accused of narrowness of sympathy. Passmore (1974: 187) openly admits that 'I treat human "interests" as paramount. I do not apologise for that fact'. But he strongly defends the need for the preservation of nature.

His humanism is of the hospitable, friendly type, as opposed to what Mary Midgley (1999: 111) calls 'exclusive humanism', or 'human chauvinism', which would be characterized by narrowness of sympathy. Her support for the friendly kind of humanism is unequivocal: '. . . there is a sense in which it is right for us to feel that we are at the centre of our own lives. Attempts to get rid of that sense would be doomed in the same way as stoical attempts to tell people not to care especially about themselves, or about those dear to them' (1999: 110). But, she adds, 'We need, then, to recognise that people do right, not wrong, to have a particular regard for their own kin and their own species' (1999: 111).

Thus, a concern with non-human components of the natural world—for example, other animal species, and plants—or with environmental preservation is by no means incompatible with an anthropocentric approach. Indeed, it may well be that an anthropocentric approach in terms of human obligations provides a stronger basis for environmental protection than does the ecocentric appeal to objective intrinsic values in the environment or the rights of the non-human world. For since obligations can be only human obligations, the anthropocentric approach seems to be unavoidable. Hence, it is argued, the benefits of diversity of species, as distinct from concern with individual animals or insects on the basis of other considerations, such as simple 'compassion', must be evaluated from a basically anthropocentric point of view. How they should be evaluated, however, is the subject of a later chapter.

5. Is There a Subjectivist Case for the Intrinsic Value of Nature?

We have adopted the widespread subjectivist view that values do not exist in the absence of a valuer so that there cannot be some 'objective' value provided by the environment independent of human valuations. However, as we have pointed out, a subjectivist approach does not necessarily preclude our believing that the environment or 'nature' is the bearer of 'intrinsic' values. But are there sound reasons for doing so? In other words, can one legitimately claim that concepts such as 'the environment' or 'nature' encompass some special category of goods that are bearers of intrinsic values in a way that does not apply to other goods? Such a claim might justify according the environment or nature some trumping power over competing bearers of values, such as improvement in the growth of knowledge by means of more education and research, or greater priority to music and the arts, or more protection of human rights by greater expenditures to keep down crime. However, such a claim seems difficult to defend.

It is true that the environment in general, or nature in particular, may be a source of top-level—that is, intrinsic—values such as aesthetic or spiritual satisfaction. But so may many other goods or services, such as works of art, musical performances, and books. And many ordinary goods and services, such as hospitals, schools, the institutions of law and order, or dwellings, may contribute to other equally important—and often far more important—top-level intrinsic values, such as personal well-being, justice, liberty, and knowledge.[12] Furthermore, the environment will share with most other ordinary goods and services the capacity to provide us with instrumentally useful, or even vital, goods and services, such as those we need for our nourishment or shelter or entertainment.

In other words, the concept of 'environmental values' to which reference is often made is a rather misleading one. The environment is a major bearer of many values, of physical well-being, such as food and clothing, as well as aesthetic or spiritual. But there seems no place for any separate category of 'environmental values'. For example, it would be very confusing to have a classification of values that had a separate category for 'environmental values' and another one for, say, 'aesthetic values'. For some environmental goods would have value only because they were part of the latter. It would be

---

[12] Sometimes the latter two categories may overlap. For example, for many years the main quadrangle in Balliol College, with its beautifully kept lawns and herbacious borders, its trees, and the Waterhouse-designed dining hall at one end and the sixteenth-century library at the other end has been part of the environment of one of us. It is far more aesthetically satisfying than would have been the open field that was there before the college was founded in the thirteenth century. The college is not part of nature, but contributes much more to the top-level value of aesthetic experience than would the nature that it replaced.

mixing up a classification of values with a classification of objects some of which bear one value and others that may bear other values.

In a heroic attempt to say 'Why Nature—Every Last Drop Of It—Is Good', Alan Holland endorses the argument, attributed to Robert Goodin, that the appeal of the natural world is that it 'serves to set our lives in a larger context, thereby providing them with some sense and pattern' (Holland 1997: 132). Now this is a very strong claim, since there are many strong rivals for this position. In French literature, for example, ranging from the Turk in Voltaire's *Candide* to Dr Rieux in Camus' *La Peste*, it is our work that gives a form to our existence and makes sense of our lives. In British literature work does not rate so high, of course, and most people would rank love or personal relationships or their religious faiths higher.[13] The proposition that it is nature that provides a sense and pattern to our lives is thus not one that would be universally accepted or that even seems prima facie plausible.

At a slightly less abstract level it is widely assumed that nature is not merely intrinsically beautiful but that nature and natural process are somehow intrinsically admirable or even morally superior to human artefacts or events. For example, it is thought that there is nothing wrong about species wiping each other out during the natural course of evolution, but the same process is believed to be immoral if carried out by one particular species, namely, human beings. Similarly, if a forest is destroyed by lava from an erupting volcano or natural climate change this is just unfortunate. But it is often believed that, in the absence of some other powerful reason, such as that the area is required to feed otherwise starving people, it is immoral if it is destroyed in order, for example, merely to use the timber for furniture or housing or some other human purpose.[14]

The difficulty with this view is that, in some basic sense, we, too, are part of nature. So the distinction between natural and artificial collapses. One cannot simultaneously claim that we are part of nature and that what we do is artificial. If we are part of nature, then logically everything we do is natural in that primary sense. So the cutting down of trees by humans in order to build a dam is no less 'natural' than the cutting down of trees by beavers in order to build a dam—though the consequences may be incomparably greater. And what is morally wrong about converting some wilderness into beautiful landscaped gardens or converting stone into beautiful cathedrals? Conversely, why should the apparently natural instinct in some men to rape lots of women be more morally defensible than an artificially cultivated taste for beautiful music or even an educated mastery of the art of seduction?

---

[13] See also Miller's critique of this Holland/Goodin view in Miller (1999:164).
[14] See reference in Bowman (1996: 22).

6. Different Classes of Environmental Goods

The fact that 'the environment' is such a loose and vague term that it embraces all sorts of goods, some having intrinsic value and some having only instrumental value, not only runs through much of the debate about the status of 'the environment' but also enters into the very practical policy question of how specific environmental assets should be valued when making decisions concerning expenditures on environmental preservation.[15] Some of the environmentalist criticisms of the conventional economists' approach to such decisions would have been much less confused if they had taken account of the distinction between different classes of environmental 'goods' suggested by David Miller.

One class comprises those environmental goods that are essential to human existence. Tolerably clean atmosphere, habitable climate, adequate water supply, and so on fall into this category. It may well be that it is in this sense, and this sense only, that the environment could be seen as a *unique* supplier of some top-level intrinsic value, namely, the value of human life itself. Whether or not this is the case, it is clear that there is a compelling need to ensure that these life-serving environmental assets are not destroyed and that collective action to protect these assets will be justified.

At the other extreme are environmental goods that are valued by individuals as part of their general private pattern of preferences. For example, some people may be greatly attached to the rural scenery in many parts of their country, or to the possibility of seeing some interesting wildlife. Other people may prefer to spend their leisure time listening to music or going to the theatre or talking to friends or reading books like this one or cultivating their gardens and so on. Here, it is far from obvious that theories of justice can support imposing the particular preferences of one group of people on others by making other people pay for them.[16] Thus, for example, it may be difficult to justify taxing everybody in order to preserve the scenery or the wildlife that some people may value highly rather than to support the activities that other people may value highly. On the other hand, there is something to be said for supporting certain minority tastes through communal action in certain cases, such as those discussed below.

[15] The discussion of this section follows very closely the classification proposed by David Miller (1999: esp. 157,159 and 171). Our departures from his classification are, we believe, of negligible importance, and have been made only on account of one or two minor considerations that are not worthwhile spelling out here.

[16] It may be argued that we are not concerned here merely with private preferences for a collective good but with an obligation of 'justice' to bequeath certain environmental assets to posterity in the same way that, as Dworkin (1985: 233) has argued, 'We inherited a cultural structure, and we have some duty, out of simple justice, to leave that structure as rich as we found it'. However, since we have argued at length in Chapters 2 through 4 that 'justice' is inapplicable between generations we see no need to discuss this argument here afresh.

Economists distinguish certain classes of goods or services where there is a prima facie case for concluding that some collective action will be necessary in order that they should be supplied to the socially optimal amount. First, there are the environmental goods, and bads, that give rise to what economists call 'externalities'. An example of a 'bad' or—in the jargon—'negative' externality would be when an incidental by-product of some industrial process is pollution by some factory that emits smoke or other pollutants from the chimneys or dumps undesirable pollutants in the effluent flowing into public rivers or the sea. Unless an appropriate payment is made, the polluter is depriving other people of some asset, such as clean air or water, without this being part of some mutually agreed transaction. In such cases incomes or welfare are being redistributed between people in a way that will not satisfy the criteria of a 'just' method of sharing out the costs and benefits of cooperation within the society in question. Some collective action, such as pollution charges, is hence needed in order to reduce the pollution to whatever is the socially optimal level. But it is not this sort of public economic activity that is of interest to us here, although it does call for public action.

More relevant here are what economists call 'public goods'.[17] To the economist this does not refer to goods that happen to be provided in the public sector. It refers to goods that have certain technical characteristics. 'Public goods' have the characteristic of 'non-rivalness' in consumption insofar as once the good is provided for one or more people it costs no more to society, *up to a point*, to allow additional people to use it. For example, there may be no extra cost to society if an extra person is allowed in to look at the paintings in a museum or to admire the flowers in a park. Of course, beyond a point, congestion may set in so that the extra utility enjoyed by the marginal person may reduce the utility enjoyed by others. But up to that point it would be wasteful to restrict admission, for example by making an admission charge. Hence, although such goods can technically be supplied in the free market— there are, indeed, restrictions on entry or entry charges for many museums and parks—they could not be profitably supplied up to the socially optimal level.

There is a second class of asset, sometimes known as 'commons', that do not have the characteristic of non-rivalness but that cannot be easily preserved or protected by any market mechanism on account of a technical characteristic known as 'non-excludability': that is, it is not technically possible to prevent other people from using—and often over-using—the assets in question. This applies, for example, to the oceans or the atmosphere. Overfishing, or using the sea as a dumping ground for waste matter, are common examples of the problem of the 'commons'.

---

[17] A very clear analysis of the conventional economics classification of the types of good or service in question here and its relevance to environmental goods is contained in de-Shalit (2000: 198–9).

There is yet another category of goods, often known as 'collective goods', that exhibit both non-rivalness and non-excludability. Examples of this are national defence, lighthouses, radio broadcasts, and the institutions of what passes for law and order. Once military forces are established to protect Britain from invasion by French farmers, it is impossible to exclude any inhabitant of Britain from this protection and it costs no more to allow an extra person to enjoy this protection. Similarly, once a lighthouse is operating it is both impossible to prevent an additional ship's crew from looking at the light and it costs no more to allow them to do so. In such cases, the private sector could not be counted on to supply the good to the socially optimal amount, if at all, on account of the non-excludability characteristic.

Thus, for one reason or another, it is generally agreed that the socially optimal supply of such goods will not usually be supplied through the free market and that some collective action is required in order to remedy these potential sources of market failure. And it happens that some of the private preferences for environmental goods or services are preferences for goods that would fall into one or other of the above three categories. For example, if, for some reason or other, some area of natural beauty or some species of wild animal is preserved, be it some species of whale or tiger or butterfly, in order that some people can see it or just enjoy the knowledge that it exists and is being preserved for posterity, society would not incur any extra cost by allowing anybody else to share the same experience.

So it is true that although most of the environmental goods and services to which many people are attached may reflect their private preferences, some of them will be private preferences for goods that will not be optimally supplied by the free market and so may constitute a prima facie case for collective action. Of course, they are not unique in this respect. Private preferences for, say, national defence, or better sanitation, or public health systems, or even better roads—up to the point of congestion—will also be preferences for goods that are not easily supplied to the socially optimal level through the private sector.

Thus the case for collective action to remedy market failure in the supply of environmental goods is not necessarily any stronger, in general, that the case for remedying market failure in the supply of many other goods and services. But given that there is a constraint on the total resources available to us, some choices—often painful—have to be made. One procedure would be to put such choices to the vote. It might appear that in a democratic society a majority vote in favour of, say, spending money to preserve some piece of rural scenery would be perfectly legitimate.[18] But there would probably also be an overwhelming majority vote in favour of spending more on schools,

---

[18] Such a view would, as Miller (1999: 157) points out, conflict with Rawls's view that 'There is no more justification for using the state apparatus to compel some citizens to pay for unwanted benefits that others desire than there is to force them to reimburse others for their private expenses'.

hospitals, housing, roads, and even private consumption! So such a procedure does not help us allocate resources between the competing uses.

But this is just another example of the common tension between the requirements of a democratic society and the importance of protecting minority interests and avoiding the tyranny of the majority. The usual economist's way of resolving this conflict is twofold.

First, one has to concentrate on marginal adjustments. That is to say, it would be a mistake to give absolute priority either to the dictates of majority rule or to the sanctity of minority interests. In a large society is must be accepted that innumerable public decisions will be taken that benefit particular groups but that may not command universal assent. But as long as the decisions are taken over a wide range of issues affecting different groups and *as long as, in each case, the benefits to the particular beneficiary groups seem to outweigh the social costs of providing them,* in the end the benefits of all the projects taken together will, hopefully, be spread around society so that all groups will stand to benefit, on balance. A member of a club might not object to the purchase of some periodical that she never reads since she knows that all the other members will also be contributing to the costs of goods or services from which she, perhaps with only a few other members, will benefit. This is a feature of social behaviour that can be generalized from local clubs and communities to whole nations.

But the second condition in the economist's approach is that, as indicated above, in each case, the benefit the beneficiaries will actually obtain must exceed the cost to society of supplying them. If the benefits were to fall short of the costs in many cases then the presumption, in the above argument, that, in the long run and taking all possible public projects together, everybody will finish up being a net beneficiary, will not hold. This is where we have to call up some help from cost-benefit analysis. This is designed to provide precisely the required comparison of benefits and burdens. It is an essential ingredient into democratic decision-making. And it cannot be brushed aside on the grounds that there is something sacred about some particular preferences for certain environmental assets which requires that other people be morally obliged to finance the satisfaction of these private preferences.

However, cost-benefit analysis brings its own problems. One of these is that the benefits accruing to some people from the provision of the service or asset in question are not necessarily confined to their personal use of these services. Contrary to popular caricatures of *homo economicus,* for which some economics text-books are partly responsible, economists do not assume that peoples' preferences are totally egotistical. People's preferences also extend to the provision of public goods from which they may not expect to derive any personal benefit. For example, many people are also proud to feel that the community to which they belong possesses some asset—be it a site of natural beauty, an opera house, the preservation of some beautiful old building, or even a prestigious education institution—even if they do not expect ever to benefit from the asset in question themselves, or, as in the Club example, regard expenditures on such assets as part of the quid pro quo of membership of a community that will, on balance, provide net benefits for them. For example, it is quite possible that a survey of the population as a whole would show that many people supported subsidizing some national opera house even though they do not expect that the patrons of the opera will then be more inclined to support the particular activities that they prefer.[19] It is quite possible that similar considerations apply to public expenditures on environmental preservation. This raises questions that are discussed in more detail in the next chapter.

---

[19] This does not mean that there may be no other way to maintain the opera without a state subsidy. For example, it is possible that a sufficiently high price would suffice, particularly given the high proportion of tickets that are sold to corporations who use most of them for corporate entertainment. But the public might feel that this solution would unfairly exclude large numbers of genuine opera lovers who ought not to be priced out of the market. Whether such an excuse for subsidies is justified is, of course, highly debatable, but the ramifications of the argument lie outside the scope of this book.

9

Plural Values and Environmental Valuation

1. Introduction

However highly one may value environmental 'goods' nobody would maintain that the whole of national product should be sacrificed to preserving the 'environment'—which, as we may remind the reader, is the shorthand term we are using to indicate the whole range of environmental assets or the benefits and satisfactions that one may derive from them. Everybody would agree that society has to make some choices between allocating resources to the 'environment' and allocating them to other objectives. These other objectives may range from, say, miscellaneous private consumption, housing, or cultural and leisure activities, to services, such as health and education.

At a personal level very few people would be able or willing to value a loved one or a close friend in monetary terms. This may be because the relationship to the valuer is of a deeper and more significant kind—of love, loyalty, and so on—than is the valuer's relationship to, say, his car—except in Italy—or to his dog—except in England, perhaps—or to his firm—except in Japan. In that case it may be perfectly normal for the valuer to make some enormous financial sacrifice to protect the loved one from danger or to provide the required medical attention. But one would not expect these personal valuations to be respected by the rest of society. For example, even if most people were prepared to make enormous financial sacrifices in an attempt to save the life of their loved ones, few of them would argue that society should devote a large proportion of national product, if that is what would be required, to reduce the risk of saving one more unidentifiable 'statistical life'.[1]

Consider a country, such as Britain, where, on the average, about ten people a year are killed in railway accidents. To simplify the arithmetic, suppose that about one billion train journeys are made each year in Britain so that the probability of a train passenger being killed on a train journey is one

[1] The *locus classicus* on this topic is Thomas Schelling (1968).

in 100 million. Suppose that, by spending a certain amount on improving safety the fatalities could be halved. This would reduce the probability of any one passenger being killed in a train accident from one in a 100 million to one in 200 million. How much would people be prepared to pay for this? If one knew that these expenditures would save one's own life or that of a loved one, one might be willing to pay a very large amount, and it is this judgement that usually underlies public knee-jerk reactions after some disaster, such as a train accident. But, if people realized that the extra expenditures are merely making infinitesimally small reductions in the probability of their own life or the life of a loved one being saved, few of them would be willing to make large contributions. Of course, even the very small contributions that individuals might be prepared to make for such small personal advantage could add up to large sums for society as a whole. Thus some method must be used to estimate what the total value is that people would be willing to put on some facility when it cannot be seen just by looking at any actual figures of how much they do spend on it. In other words, one needs to estimate, however roughly, how much people value some good or service that does not pass through the market and that, in some cases, may not yet be available at all.

2. Contingent Valuation

One technique often used to fill the gap in our information about how much people value certain goods is what is known as 'contingent valuation' (CV). This is basically a method of obtaining some estimate of the monetary valuation that people would put on the facility in question. In the case of the environment, for example, a representative sample of people might be asked how much they would be willing to pay (WTP) in order to have some nearby lake or river cleaned up, or how much they would be willing to accept (WTA) in compensation if it became polluted by some factory. Estimates of this kind have often been used in the USA for assessment of the damage done to the environment by various activities, although in the last few years it has given way to the 'public trust' doctrine, which equates the damages to whatever it costs to restore the environment to its original state where this is feasible. So far CV has played little or no role in planning disputes, but is used in decisions concerning environmental regulations, and could well be used increasingly insofar as the use of cost-benefit analysis (CBA) in environmentally-sensitive projects has become increasingly mandatory in US and UK legislation concerning environmental policy.

But CV, and hence the CBA estimates that have relied on it, together with other techniques for attaching monetary value to environmental costs and benefits, has been subjected to sharp criticism from many environmentalists, and also from a few philosophers. Some economists have also criticised CV, albeit not necessarily for the same reasons. For example, a panel co-chaired by Arrow and Solow voiced serious criticisms of CV as usually carried out, although they were optimistic that further refinements could overcome the main weaknesses and proposed guidelines that valid CV estimates should follow in order to do so (NOAA 1993). Diamond and Hausman (1994: 63) go much further than this and argue that there is little basis for such optimism and that 'CV is a deeply flawed methodology which does not estimate what its proponents claim to be estimating ... Thus, we conclude that current contingent valuation methods should not be used for damage assessment or for benefit cost analysis'.

3. Contingent Valuation and Commensurability

The Concept of Commensurability

One major criticism of CV is aimed at what many environmentalists and others believe is a central assumption of economic analysis, namely, that people allocate their resources—time, money, and so on—among various options that are all regarded as merely instruments for providing them with utility. We shall discuss later why this belief is, in our view, mistaken. But meanwhile let us follow up the nature of the criticism and its bearing on the use of CV in environmental valuation. According to the usual criticism, consumers are assumed in a CV analysis to behave in a manner designed to give them the maximum possible total utility, which can be seen as some simple, homogeneous top-level value. This requires that the different options can be made *commensurate* with each other in units of utility, sometimes called 'utils', that contribute to the single 'super-value', total utility, which they are seeking to maximize. For one cannot rank various possible combinations of apples and pears in order of their combined utility unless one can convert them, however unconsciously, into some common units of utility.

Critics of this model of the optimizing utility-maximizing consumer have now caught up with what has long been recognized in economics, namely, that such a model is a useful simplification of the way that consumers behave in respect of choices in general. Relatively recent criticism of the economist's paradigm follows a long tradition of theories of plural values, particularly those deployed by critics of utilitarianism.[2] A central feature of this criticism

---

[2] For example, according to Bernard Williams (1976: 105), even if utilitarians, and CBA practitioners also, do not necessarily believe that every social value should eventually be amenable to treatment by something like cost-benefit analysis and that 'the common currency of happiness is money', then 'they are committed to something which in practice has those implications: that there

is that some of the options facing consumers or respondents in CV surveys are not commensurate with each other, or are not commensurate with ordinary marketable goods and services and hence cannot be valued in monetary terms.

There is no one universally agreed definition of 'commensurability'. The definition of commensurability, together with the definition of 'comparability', and the related problems of rational choice under conditions of incommensurability and incomparability have recently been the subject of analysis by many eminent philosophers and we do not think they need any help from us.[3] For purposes of cost-benefit analysis and CV it is the commensurability of environmental goods with marketable goods and services that is relevant.[4] This requires that the options satisfy what is sometimes called 'strong commensurability', which requires quantitative comparability.[5] This corresponds to Sunstein's (1995: 5) definition of incommensurability: 'Incommensurability occurs when the relevant goods cannot be aligned along a single metric without doing violence to our considered judgements about how these goods are best characterized'.[6]

It may be possible to compare some goods in terms of some single metric that is irrelevant to the way that they are 'best characterized' for the purposes of allocating resources between alternative uses. For example, it may be possible to compare two lakes in terms of the volume of water they contain without this having much bearing on the relative value that people will place on their environmental services and hence on the choice that should be made between them for recreational purposes. What is required is a context-specific concept of incommensurability. The 'covering value'—to use Ruth Chang's apt term—involved in any comparison must be one that is germane to the purpose for which the comparison is to be made. In fact, in the absence of a specification of a *relevant* context it does not make sense to say that X and Y are either commensurate or incommensurate with each other. For example, it makes no sense to say that Beethoven and Titian are incommensurate *tout court*. For there are innumerable dimensions in which they may be perfectly commensurate: for example, how long ago they were born, to what age they

are no ultimately incommensurable values'. Some contributions that have a particular bearing on the subject of discussion here include E. Anderson (1993), Nagel (1979), Sen (1979; 1987), Raz (1986; 1991), Stocker (1990), Taylor (1991), Williams in Smart and Williams (1973), and the various contributions to Chang (1997), including the important Introduction by Chang herself. Sen (1987: 24) points out that Adam Smith reproached philosophers for trying to reduce every value to some single virtue. It is not only economists who have been guilty of this error—if error it be.

[3] An example of the different senses of the term 'incommensurability' is that in the philosophy of science it refers to the alleged impossibility of comparing the merits of theories belonging to different scientific paradigms.

[4] This proposition is, however, disputed by Chang (1997: 2).

[5] J. O'Neill (1993: 103). See also Griffin (1986), Stocker (1997), and Sunstein (1997).

[6] See also Chang (1997: 1), who refers to one of two traditional concepts of incommensurability as being when 'incommensurable items cannot be precisely measured by a single "scale" of units of value'.

lived, how tall they were at some specific age, and so on. But they are no doubt incommensurate in terms of, say, creativity.[7]

The definition of incommensurability that we shall use, therefore, is that, *in any particular context*, options are incommensurate if they cannot be compared in terms of any metric *that is relevant to that context*. In the present context a relevant metric would be one, such as the monetary costs, that permits the inclusion of the options in an economic comparison of the value to society of the environmental services in question relative to other competing uses of resources. Thus, our definition of incommensurability is context-specific.[8] Options may be comparable while still being incommensurate on the 'strong incommensurability' definition that we, like many others, adopt. It is possible to believe that Picasso was a greater artist than Piper without being able to compare them along a relevant common metric.

For most choice purposes—for example, choosing between spending the evening at the theatre and sitting at home reading a book—incommensurability may not matter much and comparability may well be the more significant requirement. But for purposes of using CV in environmental decision-making what matters is incommensurability. This raises various questions. First, does the mere fact that people do succeed in making choices in all sorts of situations in which they may appear to be faced with incommensurate options mean that all options must be commensurate after all, so that there is really no problem in theory though there may well be in practice? And, if we have to accept incommensurability in some form, is the environment one of the characteristic bearers of incommensurate values, so that it may often be impossible to value environmental assets in monetary terms? And if so, how far can society make rational choices in environmental policy in the face of incommensurability? In the rest of this section we shall consider the first two of these questions.

Does Choice Imply Commensurability?

As regards the first question, it is fairly obvious that people are constantly making choices between different kinds of options that are not commensurate. Consider, for example, somebody weighing up the pros and cons of taking one job rather than another. The 'covering value' would be something like 'the attractiveness of the career options'. She may weigh up various

---

[7] As Ruth Chang (1997: 6) puts it in her recent important work on this subject, 'Just as it makes no sense to say that one thing is simply greater than another, it makes no sense to say that one thing is simply better than another; things can be better only in a respect . . . Just as a comparison must be relativized to a covering value, so must its failure'.

[8] This is one, but not the only, way in which our definition differs from that proposed by Raz (1986: 322): that 'A and B are incommensurate if it is neither true that one is better than the other nor true that they are of equal value'. This definition is used by Raz as if it were synonymous with 'incomparability'.

considerations, such as the pay, the job security, the time to be spent commuting to work, the prospects of promotion, the degree to which the work will be interesting, the scope for personal responsibility, the attractiveness of the location, the probability of meeting members of the opposite sex or the same sex, and so on. Some of these considerations, such as the salary, the travel time, or the prospects for promotion, can be quantified and converted into monetary values and hence they can be made commensurate across the alternative careers. But others in the list will appear to be unquantifiable. So it is not possible to put a figure on the overall 'attractiveness' of the career options under consideration. Nevertheless, choices of this kind are constantly being made.

Similarly, people often make choices between options that may relate to different top-level values of the kind often included in lists of intrinsic values, such as loyalty, integrity, justice, personal welfare, and compassion.[9] In fact in such cases people apparently do not need units at all, let alone common units, to make comparisons between options.[10] Whether or not such options are even comparable is highly debatable and has been much debated, but there seems little doubt that they are not commensurate on our definition.

Thus the answer to the first question appears to be 'no'. The frequency of incommensurate values in the choices made in daily life seems to demonstrate that there is not, after all, some single end-value behind all our decision-making. Outside the realm of ordinary market transactions, therefore—and maybe even inside it—we do not have to accept the conventional economics assumption that 'revealed preferences' in the act of choosing must prove that some unique super value is being maximized.[11] As Griffin (1986: 32) puts it, 'The values a person holds are not unified in anything other than being his values'. So although the person making the choice may well be able to reach a decision, in the end it would never be on the basis of attaching comparable numerical values to each of the options.

This brings us to the second question: are the choices made between incommensurate options 'rational'? It may well be the case that the incommensurability of options does not prevent people from making choices between them. They do not remain in a state of permanent indecision, like

---

[9] See, for example, Bernard Williams's example of George's problem of whether to take a job in a laboratory engaged in chemical or biological warfare in order to provide for his family, where choice cannot be based on some 'super scale' of prudential values. See Smart and Williams (1973: 98). See also Sunstein (1995: 6) and Stocker (1990: 168–77; 1995: 9).

[10] Stocker (1990: 166–77). Aldred's suggestion (1994: 395) that the act of choice shows that agents have an ex post, but not an ex ante, utility function the domain of which included the options in question is not, however, very convincing and would not be very helpful to a utility maximizer.

[11] Most Chicago economists would dissent from this view, as would, perhaps, many, if not most, utilitarians, according to Bernard Williams (1976).

Buridan's ass. Nor do they usually just toss a coin.[12] But in what sense can whatever procedure they follow be described as rational?

In the more simplified models of consumer behaviour used in traditional neo-classical economics, rational choice is interpreted in a particularly narrow sense of *instrumental rationality*: the selection of means to maximize some clearly defined goal.[13] But this does not necessarily require strict commensurability. As long as options are comparable, and so can be ranked, it is possible to select the 'best' one in a consistent and rational manner. The ranking, or 'ordering' as it is often called in economics, need not be numerical. Thus the ubiquity of choice in daily life between apparently incommensurate options does not imply that choice between them must be irrational. In any case, few economists outside Chicago assume that a narrow sense of rationality—that is, the maximization of some single value, such as personal utility—governs all aspects of individual judgement and decision-making. Instead, rationality is usually interpreted more widely and is allowed to encompass choices that go beyond the 'maximization' of some simple quantifiable goal, such as utility.[14]

A wider concept of rational choice would merely require that rational appraisal plays a key role in the valuation of the options and that there is a logical connection between our valuation of the options and our choices between them, where appropriate. If we believe that there are good reasons for believing both that proposition P is true and that proposition P implies proposition Q it would be irrational to reject Q. Similarly, if we believe that there are strong reasons to value X highly while there are only weak reasons, or none at all, to value Y, it would be irrational then to value Y more than X. Of course, one may be mistaken in both cases. P may be false, and the apparently strong reasons for valuing X may in fact be flawed. But the original justification for believing Q or for valuing X more highly than Y, was rational.

By comparison, a simplified 'maximizing' model of rational behaviour would require one to search for 'a reason which defeats all others', in other words, to make a choice which is 'the best one'. By contrast, according to Raz,

[12] Of course, it may well be that the choices they make in these circumstances are mistaken, though it is not obvious, in such a situation, in what sense a choice could be the wrong one (Raz 1991: 86).

[13] See a detailed discussion of the concept of rationality in economics in Sen (1987: 12ff), and an excellent survey of concepts of rationality in economics by Hargreaves Heap *et al.* (1992).

[14] It may even mean sometimes discarding the usual criteria of consistency and transitivity, which are well-known to be, at best, necessary but not sufficient criteria of rationality. Otherwise one would have to regard many mad people as behaving rationally simply because they behaved in a consistent manner although they might not be using their reason at all as a guide to their behaviour. For example, Scanlon's (1998: 25) definition—'Rationality involves systematic connections between different aspects of a person's thought and behaviour'—could apply to mad people all of whose actions were consistent with some totally false image that they hold of the world and/or their place in it. It is for this reason that, as Scanlon (1998: 27) says, 'we normally draw a distinction between an attitude's being irrational and its being mistaken or "open to rational criticism" '. See also, for example, Sen (1979; 1987: 12ff).

'Rational action is action for (what the agent takes to be) an undefeated reason. It is not necessarily action for a reason which defeats all others'.[15] In some circumstances, then, in order that our actions qualify as 'rational', it suffices if we make a choice which is a good one—that is, is well justified given the conflicting reasons—and not the best reason which defeats all other reasons. In many cases this may be possible without the options being commensurate. Most of us would agree, for example, that Titian was a greater artist than, say, Sisley—great artist though he was too—without being able to quantify the difference. But in cases where we are obliged to attach numbers—for example, to say how much we would pay to preserve some environmental asset—we could not always be sure of making 'the best choice' in the absence of commensurability.

4. Are Environmental Goods Incommensurate with Marketable Goods?

The next question is how far environmental assets are particularly likely to be bearers of values that are incommensurate with ordinary marketable goods, so that they could not be included in a CV. We have argued in the previous chapter that there is little case for identifying some special kind of 'environmental value', since many of the satisfactions that most people derive from the environment are the same as, or similar to, those that are derived from a wide variety of sources. For example, people can derive aesthetic satisfaction from music or paintings or literature, most of which can be obtained in the form of privately appropriated marketable goods. Nevertheless, various general modes of valuation that defy commensurability and that are allegedly particularly likely to be born by environmental goods have been suggested by different philosophers.[16] One that deserves special attention here on account of its explicit bearing on cost-benefit analysis and environmental valuation is what Elizabeth Anderson (1993) calls, in her recent contribution to the theory of values in ethics and economics, 'higher' modes of valuation. Her concept of 'expressive valuation' emphasises the way that people play roles in society that are influenced by their view of how other people in society will expect them to behave, or of social norms, and how their valuations express these influences.

For example, our valuation of 'objects'—goods, people, animals, and so forth—are often affected by our relationships to the goods or people concerned. Simple examples of this given by Anderson are the way in which

---

[15] Raz (1986: 339). Much the same point is made by Sen (1987: 67–8).
[16] See the authoritative summary of some of them in Chang (1997: 9–10).

we may value an ugly useless gift from a friend on account of our relationship to the friend, or the way in which parents' adoration of certain features of their children that they would not expect other people to find adorable, expresses their love for the children. Thus what people regard as an appropriate valuation will depend partly on the ideals of the valuer and her social relationship to the object of her valuation (E. Anderson 1993: 24–5).

By contrast, in most ordinary market transactions the relationship between buyer and seller is usually irrelevant—with the exception of markets such as the labour market. Both buyer and seller are primarily, if not always exclusively, concerned solely with their own interests in the transaction and not with any other aspect of their relationship. We walk into a shop, we buy something, we stagger out. In most cases buyer and seller do not expect to meet again, and even if they do they will still assume that each other's behaviour is essentially egoistic, however 'highly' valued may be the objects involved. And we are also often buying the product for our personal satisfaction, though not necessarily for our own personal use.

Elizabeth Anderson (1993: 144) also argues that the fact that marketed goods are valued by purchasers as appropriate objects of use restricts the mode of valuation that is appropriate to them, since 'use' subordinates the objects to one's own ends, which she contrasts with higher modes of valuation such as respect and recognition of intrinsic values. By contrast, the valuation one places on public environmental assets is influenced by relationships—of obligation, or duty, or fairness—to other people, including possibly future generations. It may also express the satisfactions that one obtains from shared experiences. According to this 'expressive valuation' view, people will regard goods as incommensurate 'if they are not candidates for the same mode of valuation'. Something may be valued higher than something else if it makes 'deeper, qualitatively more significant demands on the attitudes, deliberations, and actions of the valuer' (E. Anderson 1993: 70).

But all these influences on people's market transactions are fully recognized by economists; and CV estimates do not rule them out. In fact, the view that economic analysis must rule them out is based on a totally mistaken interpretation of the concept of *homo economicus*, namely, that he is motivated entirely by egotistical considerations. In the above example of the purchase in the shop, the fact that the buyer and the seller are both trying, in respect of that particular transaction, to make the best deal they can tells us absolutely nothing about their motivations. The shop assistant may be going out to work solely in order to supplement her income so that she can help maintain her widowed aunt or make a bigger contribution to some worthy charity. The buyer may be buying the object in order to donate it anonymously to some museum.

Furthermore, the fact that prices may influence how much one buys or sells anything, including one's own labour, does not mean that it is the *only* variable that one takes into account. One may be influenced by all sorts of other considerations, many of which may have little to do with narrow self-interest (Robbins 1935: Ch. 4; Hahn and Hollis 1979: 45). The fact that somebody may work in a shop in order to help support his widowed aunt does not mean that he ought to charge less for his goods than he can obtain. It happens that in most transactions prices will play a part and seem to influence the outcomes in a manner that is predicted fairly accurately by standard economic models. It is the job of economists to analyse such models. It is the job of others—behavioural psychologists, perhaps—to analyse the other variables that influence consumer preferences. Critics should not be misled by the central role of prices and the way that they are determined in economics into believing that the preferences that people are expressing when they react to price variations are necessarily entirely self-interested. It is true that the notion that the influences on people's market choices are fully explained, in economic theory, in terms of narrowly defined self-interest has been encouraged by some economists and textbooks, but it has also been challenged for over a century by many authoritative economists (see Sen 1979: 95ff).

Furthermore, the explicit allowance in economists' CV estimates for 'option values' and 'existence values' is designed precisely to include the value that people attach to the preservation of assets for possible use by other people, including future generations. Thus the varying and widely ranging motivations behind the valuations that people may indicate in reply to a CV survey no more invalidate the results than do the differences between people with respect to the reasons why they are prepared to pay the same amount to buy a specific model of automobile or toothpaste invalidate an estimate of how much, in total, people value them. All that matters for the CV is that enough people can attach some rough monetary value to the environmental object in question.

Of course, this may often differ considerably from its market value, if it has any, precisely on account of the wider range of considerations, such as a feeling of common heritage or concern for future generations, of the kind allowed for by CV. But this is a merit, not a defect, of CV. For example, suppose that the famous Canova sculpture, 'The three Graces' was attacked and smashed beyond repair by some tourist, who then cheerfully offered to pay £8 million, which was, say, just above its latest market price. If one then accepted that this left the country no worse off one would, indeed, be treating the sculpture as substitutable with any other objects that could be bought for the £8 million in question. In that case one would have been equally ready to do a deal with any vandal who offered to pay £8 million for the pleasure of smashing up the Canova.

Many people, however, would feel some sense of loss irrespective of the price that the tourist offered to pay in compensation. It would be thought that £8 million worth of, say, automobiles or other goods that could be bought with the money could not replace the Canova. Preserving and protecting the Canova in Britain may have some significance for many people who never aspire to visit it, let alone be in the market for it. It may symbolise to them the attachment of the nation or community to unique works of art that aroused different kinds of satisfactions than those provided by ordinary marketed goods and services.

But this merely indicates that if, before it was smashed, a properly conducted CV had been carried out of what people were willing to pay to preserve the Canova, based on a representative sample of the population— which means including people who might never expect to see the Canova and who might, nevertheless, value it for the sort of reasons set out above— it ought to have arrived at an estimate of the public's willingness to pay (WTP) to preserve the Canova that would be greater than £8 million, and possibly very much greater. In other words, in such instances it would not be the CV estimates that would be misleading on the grounds that, for reasons such as those Elizabeth Anderson enumerates, they cannot correspond to market values; it would be the market values that may sometimes be misleading because they cannot encompass all the motives for valuation that CVs attempt to cover.

Of course, some respondents in CV surveys may genuinely be unable to attach monetary values to some things that they value. For example, most people would be unable to attach a monetary valuation to personal relationships, because this would express a view of some relationship that would conflict with their conception of what the relationship really involves. The most commonly cited extreme example would be that most people would find it impossible to put a monetary equivalent on, say, the life of somebody dear to them.[17] Where choices have to be made involving such values, Lukes (1996: 47) is right in suggesting that we may need a religious metaphor, such as a 'sacrifice', rather than the economic concept of a 'trade-off'.

A somewhat less extreme, and hence perhaps more illuminating, example is the one given by Raz (1986: 349) in a comparison between two situations. In one situation a person is offered a certain sum of money on condition that he leaves his wife for a certain amount of time. In the other situation the same person is offered a job somewhere that will take him away from his wife for a similar length of time but for which he will be amply paid. Many people would think that it would be perfectly legitimate, subject to his wife's consent, for him to accept the latter proposition but totally inappropriate for him to accept the former. In the latter case, although the wife would still be deprived of her husband's company for the same period of time, this would not be the intended object of the transaction, even if it is a predictable consequence. But in the former case he is simply treating his wife like a

---

[17] See an excellent, balanced discussion of this in Lukes (1996).

commodity and is willing to dispense with her for a period of time if suitably compensated. Such behaviour might be rightly regarded by the wife as contemptible.[18]

But CVs carried out in connection with environmental assessments are not usually concerned with such personal relationships, or with the value that one may attach to personal objects on account of their relationship with some other person, such as the donor. On the other hand, some environmental projects, particularly large-scale projects that may involve serious dislocation of established communities, might well involve damage that cannot be readily evaluated in monetary terms by the many people affected. Nevertheless, this merely reinforces the point that practitioners of CV and environmental CBA invariably make, namely, that such estimates can be only one input into the decision-making process. No advocates of CBA, whether based on CV or not, would claim more than that.

So the real question is how far the CV input into the decision-making process is a reasonably good approximation to how much people are willing to pay for some environmental asset, irrespective of their motives and of the range of the considerations that underpin their valuations. And it is possible that, however much a CV survey may, in principle, leave it open to people to include all sorts of considerations in their expressed willingness to pay— such as citizenship, solidarity with a community, respect for a tradition or for some unique aesthetic asset or work of great artistic or natural integrity, the desire to leave open to other people, including even future generations, and the possibility of benefiting from environmental assets—many people are unable to attach monetary valuations to these properties. Some of these considerations could be ethical considerations that related to top-level intrinsic values, such as loyalty to others or fairness to future generations. A plurality of intrinsic values implies that some of the things that contribute to one of them cannot be made commensurate with some other intrinsic value. For example, most people would regard, say, fairness or integrity or liberty or other values as distinct top-level intrinsic values that cannot be made commensurate in terms of some common numeraire. In the same way, without having to appeal to some special unique class of environmental values, some people may attach ethical properties to environmental preservation that will be genuinely incommensurate with the satisfactions they will derive from ordinary marketable goods. They might experience a similar

---

[18] On the other hand, her judgement might depend on how much the husband was being offered, and how much of it he was going to share with her! One is reminded of the no-doubt apocryphal, but well-known, story about Bernard Shaw's conversation with some lady sitting next to him at a dinner party and to whom he offered £100—this was many decades ago—to sleep with him. The lady indignantly replied, 'My dear sir! How dare you! What sort of woman do you think I am!' Shaw then offered her £10,000, which the woman promptly accepted. At that point Shaw is reported as saying,'Well, now we know what sort of woman you are we can start negotiating over the price'.

difficulty in evaluating the satisfactions they would derive from better provision of other collective goods, such as health or educational facilities. But this does not undermine its applicability to some environmental assets; it merely means that some of the satisfactions that people would derive from a good public health or education service would be equally incommensurate with ordinary marketable goods.

If this were true of many people the weakness of CV would not be a mere technical limitation that could easily be remedied by further refinements of the technique. It would be a more fundamental weakness. Inviting such people to value an environmental asset in the same terms as their valuations of ordinary marketable goods would appear to them to be a simple category mistake. It would be like asking them 'How much does the colour blue weigh?' They would not be able to answer the question because colours are not in the same category of characteristics as is weight. But whether or not some people are justified in distinguishing between their different final intrinsic values in such a way that they put some of the characteristics of environmental assets into different categories from those reserved for marketable goods is not a matter that can be settled on theoretical grounds. Nevertheless, reasons have been given in the previous chapter for questioning the force of the arguments put forward in support of the concept of separate 'environmental values', particularly those that are claimed to constitute some objective feature of nature.

How difficult or impossible it is, in practice, for some people to attach monetary values to environmental assets is a matter of dispute. Some critics of CV maintain that this difficulty is widespread and is demonstrated by some surveys designed to elicit people's valuations of the environment as well as by many other experiments concerning people's behaviour.[19] For example, critics of CV allege that many respondents approached refuse to attach monetary values to environmental assets at all or are often indignant at the suggestion that the environmental asset in question should be brought into relationship with the sordid measuring rod of money—to slightly modify Pigou's famous definition of economic welfare (Pigou,1932:11). Brian Barry (1995: 156), for example, reports that 'many respondents—up to a half in some surveys—become very angry when asked how much they would take in return for some degradation of the environment, saying that they are not in the business of accepting bribes. Quite a few are so indignant that they throw the interviewer out as soon as the question is asked'. But, as Miller (1999: 162) argues, it may simply be that some people are often unwilling to make hard choices and shelter behind protestations that they are shocked to be asked what monetary value they would put on priceless environmental assets.

But the evidence for the view that such surveys display a widespread

---

[19] Diamond and Hausman (1994: 15), Sagoff (1994: 298–9), Kahneman and Knetsch (1992).

inability, on ethical grounds, to attach a monetary valuation to environmental assets is conflicting. Some surveys report that this inability is, indeed, widespread (for example, Hausman 1993). But other researchers who are actually engaged in large numbers of CV exercises report that such instances are rare. And in good CV exercises respondents who say that they are unable to attach a monetary value to the environmental asset in question are usually pressed to give their reasons and these usually turn out to be little to do with the sort of considerations that Elizabeth Anderson emphasizes, let alone 'ethical' considerations and 'higher modes of valuation'. The reasons given are usually that they—the respondents—believe that they ought not to have to pay anything since it is the duty of the government or somebody else to incur the costs, or that they cannot afford to pay, in which case a figure of zero for their valuation should quite properly be included in arriving at the average for the whole sample. [20]

5. Limitations on Consumer Sovereignty

In addition to reservations about the model of the way consumers choose that is implicit in conventional welfare economics, and that is consequently believed to be mirrored in CV, its basic ethical assumptions have been powerfully criticized. The most important criticism is the assumption that society should seek to maximize the satisfactions of people's preferences. This is derived, in turn, from two prior assumptions. The first is the psychological assumption that, with very few exceptions known as 'merit goods', people's preferences—as reflected in their expenditures—are the correct guide to what is in their 'interests' or what adds to their 'welfare'. The second is the value judgement that society *ought* to maximize the satisfaction of consumer preferences. In other words, it is assumed that society's priorities should mirror the amounts that people are willing to spend on different goods. This value judgement has been subjected to powerful criticism by various economists such as Amartya Sen.

Their criticisms have been directed mainly at the morally restrictive character of normative conclusions based solely on 'utility information' without much attention paid to the moral aspects of the underlying preferences.[21] After all, the practice in ancient Rome of throwing Christians to

---

[20] Personal communication from Professor David Pearce, a co-Director of the Centre for Social and Economic Research on the Global Environment, which has been involved in hundreds of CV exercises. See also discussion of the concept and frequency of 'protest votes' in Jorgensen *et al.* (1999) and Lindsey (1994). But for a different view, albeit based on far less direct knowledge of CVs, see Barry (1995), Sunstein (1997), Vadnjal and O'Connor (1994).

[21] Sen (1982*a*) collects together some of his main contributions, but see also the chapters by Barry, Goodin, and others in Elster and Hylland (1986).

the lions might well have been justified on the basis of a cost-benefit analysis. For reasons that we have enumerated in chapter 1, the 'benefits'—in terms of the amount spectators were prepared to pay to see the spectacle—would have outweighed the 'costs' (excluding the suffering of the Christians). This does not mean that it was morally justified. There is the little matter of violating the basic human rights of the Christians. Of course, the dangers of overriding people's preferences always have to be borne in mind, since doing so in the name of some higher 'social good' always brings one to the brink of a slippery slope that can too easily lead to tyrannical contempt for democratic procedures. Nevertheless, it must be conceded that the ethics of certain preferences as expressed in market valuations should at least be the subject of public debate and discussion.

Furthermore, the results of CV, and hence of any CBA in which they will be incorporated, depends on the distribution of incomes. For since the CV technique still weighs people's preferences by the amount of money they would sacrifice in order to satisfy them, it gives more weight to the preferences of rich people than to poor people. Of course, this applies to all private goods as well and we may feel that some people's preferences for certain goods or activities are strange, distasteful, or even contemptible. But as long as they merely affect their own patterns of expenditure we may not feel any need to go out on the streets and persuade them to 'culture up'. We may object to the way incomes are distributed and may prefer greater equality. But given the income distribution we may not care much if richer people spend their higher incomes on wine, women, or song.

But when it comes to expenditures on public goods, such as the environment, we may object to the degree of our, and everybody else's, enjoyment of the environment being determined largely by the preferences of those members of society who happen to be the wealthiest. With private goods, the consequences of one's choice fall on oneself. With public goods one is affected by the consequences of other people's choices, which, if they are reflected in CV, will also depend partly on who has the highest incomes.[22]

Furthermore, even if one does not object to the existing distribution of income and, hence, to richer people having a bigger influence on the allocation of resources than poorer people, one may not accept that the amount of money people are willing to sacrifice is the relevant criterion for judging the social value of any project. Some critics of CV would argue that this would be like judging the relative merits of rival scientific theories, such as Darwinism as against creationism, by the intensity of people's preferences for one or the other.[23] Instead, they argue, rival scientific theories should be evaluated in terms of the sort of criteria that are appropriate in such cases, such as their

[22] This point is well developed in Jacobs (1995).
[23] A collection of articles criticizing CV and devoted to 'Values and Preferences in Environmental Economics' was published in a special issue of *Environmental Values*, 3/4 (1994).

explanatory power, their simplicity, the degree to which they rely on numerous unverified assumptions, their consistency with the evidence, and their logical properties.

What is required in such cases, it is argued, is discussion and debate designed to find 'the truth', not techniques to estimate which theory arouses the most intense preferences among its advocates (J. O'Neill 1993: 68–71; Keat 1994: 337–8). The same would apply, *mutatis mutandis*, to decisions concerning somebody's guilt or innocence of some criminal offence, or which person would make the best prime minister. In some cases, as with many public activities ranging from throwing Christians to the lions to expenditures to preserve the environment for posterity or for the use by other people, the relevant criteria may be ethical.

And, for reasons set out above, rejection of CV in favour of some other method, such as public debate, does not mean abandonment of 'rational choice'. The choice is not between 'a unified but artificial system like cost-benefit analysis, which will grind out decisions on any problem presented to it' and 'romantic defeatism, which abandons rational theory because it inevitably leaves many problems unsolved' (Nagel 1979: 139, 137). For in many fields of public life somebody has to make choices between various options without being able to fit them into the model of rational choice that is attributed to consumers in conventional welfare economics. Nevertheless, although it may be true that rational choice does not always require reference to quantifiable comparisons between commensurate options, it does not preclude consulting evidence of people's willingness to pay for the various options. Informed debate can be better only if it is more informed rather than less. Furthermore, for reasons set out in the next section, the comparison with debates over the issues such as the relative merits of competing scientific theories is highly misleading.

6. The Case for the Defence

The Correct Interpretation of 'Economic Man'

We have pointed out above that some of the criticism of CV has been based on an over-simplified view, for which the economics profession is partly responsible, of the psychological assumptions lying behind the standard model of choice used in economic analysis. This model does, indeed, analyse economic behaviour largely in terms of how people respond to price signals, whether as sellers—including sellers of their labour—or buyers. But this is not intended to tell us anything about *all* the variables that influence their behaviour in these capacities. It is concerned with the way that they will usually react to changes in *one* particular variable, namely, price. It is not denied that their preferences will be influenced by all sorts of considerations, including altruism, civic responsibility, pride in collective facilities or achievements, personal relationships, social mores, and so on. Most economists do not exclude the influence of all such variables on people's preferences. Hence, many of the criticisms of the economist's standard model of consumer behaviour are based on a mistaken interpretation of how, in fact, economists do view this behaviour.

The Crucial Role of the Resource Constraint

Whether or not environmental causes have some special moral status, the fact remains that many other pressing claims on society's resources do. Difficult and often painful choices have to be made, and refusal to make them by sheltering behind some vague rhetorical assertions about the sacred or intrinsic values of nature, the 'rights of future generations', and so on is a form of evasion, however understandable it may be in many situations.

But is public debate really the best way of making painful choices between environmental causes and other worthy objects of public expenditure? Is it, as critics of CV allege, like choosing between rival scientific theories or rivals candidates for political office? The answer depends on what exactly is to be debated and what happens after the debate. Here, the critics of CV are mostly silent, with a few notable exceptions.[24] Much of the criticism of CV in environmental valuations ignores the crucial difference between, on the one hand, debates about issues such as the truth of alternative scientific theories or the morality of abortion, and, on the other hand, the best way to allocate resources between, say, environmental protection and other uses.

For whatever decision is reached concerning the truth of evolution as against creationism, or the age of the universe, it has no effect on resource allocation and does not reduce the amount of resources that can be devoted to building hospitals, schools, public infrastructure, concert facilities, and so on. By contrast, in the absence of resource limitations, what would there be to debate as regards environmental protection? Everybody would be in favour of it, in the same way that everybody is against sin. *The only problem is that devoting resources to environmental protection means fewer resources are available for other uses.*

And for reasons set out in the previous chapter, the preferences that many people have for most environmental goods have no more moral status or claim on resources than other people's preferences for, say, higher standards

---

[24] Elizabeth Anderson (1993: 210–16) clearly recognizes the problem of resource limitations but does not go far into the precise type of institutional arrangement that would reconcile them with the requirements of appropriate modes of valuation, and Brian Barry (1995: 143–59) is chiefly concerned with showing that a referendum does not necessarily imply a return to 'want satisfaction' as distinct from 'ideal satisfaction'.

of living for themselves or their families, better housing or holidays, more churches, improved public services in the field of health or education or transport or the arts, and so on. It is not enough for the well-known environmentalist Bryan Norton (1994: 323) to proclaim that 'Environmentalists are moralists, and one of the ways they show this is by taking an active concern for both the options for experiences and the values of future people'. Are people who may have stronger preferences for other expenditures, such as those listed above, to be regarded as devoid of moral sentiments? Thus while public debate about the pros and cons of environmental projects are a valuable element in forming people's preferences and promoting informed decisions, they should not play a decisive role in a democratic society that is reluctant to impose the private preferences of, perhaps, vocal minorities or even majorities on citizens who have different tastes.

There is also the danger that the people who will be most influential in advocating environmental protection or renovation are likely to be, on the whole, local elites.[25] The ordinary person in the street is likely to be less able to spend time on such issues and probably less likely to be passionately concerned with them. Those who criticize CV on account of its giving more weight to people with more money should hesitate before giving much authority to debates at which the more affluent or leisured members of society are likely to be even more heavily represented.

The Democratic Character of Cost-Benefit Analysis

Furthermore, the main implication of the resource constraint issue is that, if some people benefit from extra environmental expenditures, other people— those who would benefit from alternative expenditures or lower taxes or higher national income—will lose. And, unfortunately, while most of the beneficiaries of environmental protection can usually be more or less identified and organized, those who bear the burdens cannot. For example, suppose it would cost £x million to carry out some environmental preservation project, like restoring and protecting some area of potential scenic beauty, that would give much satisfaction to local residents or to other people not too far away who would enjoy visiting the site in question if suitably restored or protected. Most of these beneficiaries can be identified and, indeed, often organize themselves into pressure groups that can participate effectively in the debate and the subsequent vote, and even organize demonstrations, chain themselves to railings, lobby members of Parliament, and so on. By contrast, it is virtually impossible to identify the people who will lose on account of the resources that might otherwise have been devoted to, say, schools or hospitals, or museums, or housing, and so on, being devoted instead to environmental preservation.

---

[25] This point is recognized by some critics of CV and CBA, including E. Anderson (1993: 215) and J. O'Neill (1993: 80–1). It is one of the points that Pearce rightly emphasizes (1994: 1330–6).

Since it is usually impossible to identify those who bear the cost of environmental projects, the best assumption to make in most cases is that the resources devoted to the environmental project are taken away from individual components of national final expenditures in the same proportion that they bear to the total. This would mean that about 65 per cent of the cost would fall on private consumption—since this makes up about 65 per cent of total final expenditures—and the rest on investment and public expenditures on health, education, law and order, housing, and so on. None of these alternative uses of resources should be despised by those in favour of the environmental project, or be assumed to be less worthy of respect than the beautiful countryside to be preserved. Some of the other uses of resources may be for purposes that would be regarded as equally desirable in terms of 'ideals' or 'higher modes of valuation' as is the environment. [26]

Thus the great contribution of CV and CBA is its democratic character; it represents all the unknown losers. By taking account of the costs of carrying out any environmental project all other rival claims on resources will be represented.

Democratic Decision-Making and 'Informed' Preferences

An old problem that is inherent in any procedure, including CV, for assessing the public's preferences is the problem of how far one should accept their preferences as they stand or try to rely only on *informed* preferences. After all, for the vast majority of the public, who expect their own voice to carry an almost infinitesimally small weight in public decision-making, it is not obviously rational for them to spend much time and effort making sure that they are well-informed about every public issue on which they may be required to express an opinion. In ancient Greece, the Athenians attempted to solve the problem by a system of random selection of limited numbers of citizens—500 or more in some cases—who constituted various key bodies involved in governing the city. By this means the persons appointed knew that their voice carried weight and they had both a duty and an incentive to make sure that they were well-informed about the issues on which they took legislative decisions.

Similar representative institutions based on more or less random samples of the population are being increasingly set up in various countries.[27] The objective is to confront groups of people with a presentation of the arguments bearing on any decision and an opportunity for them to debate the issue in a forum small enough for them to feel that their opinion counts so that it is worth their while trying to absorb the information and master the arguments.

---

[26] This point has been well put in *The Economist* (3 December 1994), 106.

[27] 'Citizens juries' in Britain and the USA, 'planning cells' in Germany and Switzerland, and 'consensus conferences' in Denmark (Fishkin and Lushkin 1998).

A closely related experiment, known as 'deliberative polling', has been carried out in recent years under the direction of James Fishkin and Robert Luskin, in both Britain and the USA, and which aims at improving on these existing institutions. [28] The idea is to use a sample of people who would be given the opportunity and incentive to familiarize themselves thoroughly with some issue and then see how they would vote on various questions put to them.[29] Experiments such as these are interesting and could possibly lead to important, if marginal, improvements to methods of democratic control. But their main value may be their demonstration of how much divergence there can be between a poll carried out among a group of reasonably well-informed people and a poll conducted among the same people before they had had an opportunity to acquaint themselves with the topic in question. This finding has great negative value. It shows how far one should mistrust polls! This highlights the danger that the findings of polls carried out among samples of people who have been exposed to the issues would be given too much legitimacy. Even confronting the sample of selected people with experts in an adversarial mode by no means guarantees a correct outcome, as many losers in court cases will justifiably testify.[30]

Society's Need for Transparency

While there is something to be said for public debate and discussion and for the 'deliberative democracy' innovations, this does not mean that there is no room for cost-benefit analysis as part of the decision-making process. If environmental decisions are taken behind closed doors by selected groups of people, whether selected through the ballot box or by means of some deliberative polling sample, society is denied transparency in decision-making. To reach decisions that have widespread social consequences and that will inevitably mean that there are some 'losers', society may have a much greater need for what appears to be an objective and impartial formula for trading off one option against another. For many types of decision, society needs some precise and publicly transparent 'algorithm' as an input into the decision-making process that is widely accepted by the population as a whole as being 'fair' and 'sensible' because it is based on explicitly stated methods that leave very little scope for individual interpretation by, for example, officials, politicians, single-issue organizations, or local pressure groups.

Some of the objections to CV can be overcome, and are being overcome, to some extent, by better framing and design of the CV survey. And while

[28] For an up-to-date discussion of what is known as 'deliberative democracy' in environmental decision-making, see de-Shalit (2000: 141ff).

[29] See Fishkin and Lushkin (1998) for a succinct account of the philosophy underlying the experiment and the manner in which it has been conducted.

[30] See also discussion of the limitations on public debate in Elster (1998).

there may be no fully satisfactory solution to the incommensurability problem, this may merely mean that there is no neat 'ideal' method by which society, or even an individual, can choose between incommensurate options. But rough justice that gives due weight to transparent and objective criteria may often be preferable to a suspicion, often justified, that decisions are being taken behind closed doors on the basis of criteria that are not openly and clearly defined. Those who can make a valid argument in favour of, say, ignoring the relationship between the costs and benefits of some environmental project, should, at least, be forced to do so explicitly and in the face of full exposure of the consequent burden on the community at large.

7. Conclusions

The validity of using CV surveys in the assessment of environmental projects is often thought to depend on various assumptions that may be valid only as regards ordinary marketable goods and services. Two assumptions, in particular, are at issue here. First, there is the value judgement, already much disputed among economists, to the effect that normative value resides in the expenditure patterns by which people 'reveal' their interests. Second, there is the positive assumption that individuals can value the environment in a manner that is commensurate with their valuations of ordinary marketable commodities. This is not a matter that can be settled on theoretical grounds. As we have argued in Chapter 8, some of the characteristics of environmental assets that critics of CV often allege represent 'higher' values that are incommensurate with market valuations are shared by many other claims on public resources as well as by many ordinary goods and services. Nevertheless, it is theoretically possible that some people are genuinely unable to put the characteristics of some environmental assets that they value into the same category as goods and services to which they can attach monetary values. But there is little evidence that this is a genuine difficulty for a significant proportion of people covered in most CV surveys.

Furthermore, while the criticisms of CV lead to the conclusion that what is required is some role for public debate and discussion concerning environmental policies in order to facilitate the emergence of a view as to which policies are 'right', it is far from clear what kind of institutions can fulfil this function properly without some input from a CV or some form of CBA. Public debate may be the obvious means for reaching decisions on the rightness of policies concerning, say, abortion or the legalization of cannabis: policies that do not turn on resource constraints. But it is less obvious that it can operate effectively when the whole problem is that there are resource constraints, so that the greater satisfaction of some people's preferences for wildlife or rural scenery means less satisfaction of other people's, and perhaps even their own, preferences for better housing, longer holidays, improved health and education services, and innumerable other preferences for ordinary marketed goods and services. And even in public health or other public policy issues, there are few areas in which public debate is not enriched by reference to relevant quantitative data.

It may well be that some economists, who prefer to rely on a rigorous approach to decisions on public expenditure that is firmly rooted in some underlying theory, do not give the criticisms of CV and cost-benefit analysis the attention they deserve. But until both sides to the dispute recognize what is valid in their opponents' arguments little progress can be expected. As Steven Lukes (1997: 195) puts it, 'The point, perhaps, is not to ask which side has the better of the argument that continues to divide them, but rather to fear and resist the advent of a world in which either has won it'. The economists need to accept, however much it goes against deeply ingrained habits of thought, that some people may not be able to attach monetary values to certain characteristics of some environmental assets for perfectly legitimate reasons of incommensurability. The environmentalists need to recognize the full significance of the fact that the resource constraint enters into environmental choices in a way that is absent from issues such as abortion, assessing the validity of a scientific theory, or the election of a prime minister.

PART 3
Justice between nations

10

International Justice and Sharing the Burden of Environmental Protection

1. Introduction

This book has concentrated mainly on justice between generations and its implications for environmental policy. But there are other major ethical dimensions to environmental policy. One of these is the way in which the costs and benefits of any policy should be shared out between rich and poor countries. Are there any principles of distributive justice that can provide guidance? Most discussions of global environmental problems seem to assume that there are. This assumption is also embedded in various international agreements as have already been reached to deal with global environmental problems. For example, the 1987 Montreal Protocol, which set the framework for control of ozone layer depleting substances, and its subsequent amendments specifically differentiated between rich and poor countries. And there is widespread agreement among commentators that considerations of international equity will have to play a part in climate change negotiations (Barrett 1992; Kverndokk 1992; Grubb and Sebenius 1992; Rose 1992).

Indeed, such considerations have already been reflected in international agreements. 'The Framework Convention on Climate Change' agreed at the 1992 Rio de Janeiro World Environmental Conference stated that, 'the parties should protect the climate for the benefit of present and future generations of humankind, *on the basis of equity* and in accordance with their common but differentiated responsibilities and respective capabilities' (INC 1992; emphasis added).[1] In similar vein the 1992 Convention on Biological Diversity refers

---

[1] In the subsequent (1997) Kyoto agreements the developed countries committed themselves, as a bloc, to reduce their emissions of six greenhouse gases below their 1990 level by 5 per cent by between 2008 and 2012, whereas no commitments were imposed on the developing countries even though no international action will have any significant impact on the future increase in global carbon emissions unless they reduce their emissions substantially. This is one of the reasons why even the modest commitments agreed at Kyoto will almost certainly be rejected by the US Senate, in view of the Byrd-Hagel resolution of July 1997, which ruled out any ratification of any international treaty to reduce carbon emissions that was not accompanied by similar commitments by developing countries.

to the need for 'equitable sharing', or 'fair' and equitable' sharing, of the benefits at least four times (Yamin 1995: 541). It also includes various substantive provisions designed to give effect to this concern with 'fairness' in the international distribution of the costs and benefits of biodiversity preservation. In a list of 'many profound ethical questions' that one authoritative commentator, enumerated as arising in connection with the Biodiversity Convention negotiations is the question of 'on what basis are developing countries entitled to financial assistance for undertaking conservation?' (Yamin 1997).[2]

The operative word here is 'entitled'. This chapter will be concerned chiefly with whether there are any principles of distributive justice between countries that tell us how much poor countries, as distinct from poor individuals, are 'entitled' to receive as a matter of justice. We shall argue that there is none.[3] We shall argue that it is almost as difficult to identify any compelling principles of distributive justice between countries as it is to identify principles of distributive justice between generations. But, as in the latter case, this does not relieve us of any moral obligations to take account of the interest of people living in other countries and to give special weight to the position of the poorest among them. And, as have we argued in earlier chapters, this has to be based on a concern to give priority to the worst off individuals along the lines we have espoused in Chapter 4 and to which we return in section 5 below.

2. Obstacles to a Theory of International Justice

The absence of any compelling theory of international justice might seem slightly surprising. But it ought not to be. Justice is a matter of relationships between individuals. Nations can claim moral legitimacy only insofar as they protect and defend the basic human rights of the individuals composing those nations. This imposes on nations a duty to defend their nationals against foreign oppression. But it also imposes on governments a duty to respect the basic human rights of their nationals within their own jurisdiction. Governments that fail to do so or, as in so many cases, are the chief violators of the human rights of their nationals, have no moral legitimacy and so have little claim to considerations of justice between nations.[4]

---

[2] Farhana Yamin, Director of the Foundation for International Environmental Law and Development, School of Oriental and Asian Studies, University of London.

[3] According to Stanley Hoffmann (1995: 52), 'John Rawls is the only prominent contemporary philosopher I know of who is trying to construct a theory of international affairs'.

[4] In the sphere of distributive justice within a country, a legitimate question raised by Nozick (1974: 190) is why the participants in Rawls's 'original position' should apply the difference principle to 'groups', that is, the 'worst-off groups', as they do in Rawls, rather than to the worst-off individuals.

As Hoffmann (1981: 156) has put it,

One has to keep in mind that states exist only as communities of people; states are not divinities; their rights are rooted in the presumption of a fit between them and their people; and this does put a kind of damper on the demands of the Third World governments for absolute sovereignty, for impermeable state rights. We may feel that we have a duty to share some of our wealth with them, but only if that wealth is used toward justice for those communities of people. This also means that equity claims presented by Third World states are in a sense conditional on their doing something for their people.

During the emergence of the calls for a 'New International Economic Order' (NIEO) in the early 1970s, the leaders of the developing countries were primarily demanding justice between sovereign states, not between their inhabitants. They were demanding equality of respect, greater developing countries' participation in world economy, and greater Third World control over international institutions and global resources. The leaders of the nations pressing for a NIEO were also demanding significant wealth redistribution between nations. It was claimed that all such demands were 'just', that is, that they could be grounded in some theory of justice or, at least, in some compelling and universally acceptable ethical theory that had implications for international justice. But at the same time they insisted that internal equality was their own affair. But, as Little (1998: 342) put it, 'One cannot convincingly say at the same time "you have an obligation to help our poor" and "our poor are our own concern" '. In any case, the problem of justice between individuals across national boundaries applies also to potential donors, as well as beneficiaries. Extracting the required transfers from them would require a further erosion of national sovereignty.

Thus there is little point in proposing that we redistribute wealth between *individuals* on an international scale without explaining how this can be reconciled with principles of national sovereignty. Some recent international military interventions in sovereign states—for example, Bosnia, Kosovo, East Timor—have given rise to widespread questioning of the legitimacy of such violations of national sovereignty. But if it has proved difficult to violate national sovereignty in order to protect large numbers of innocent civilians from being persecuted and driven from their homes, it would be eccentric to demand that it can be violated in order to protect some thousands of species of beetles threatened with extinction in tropical forests.

Thus principles of *inter*national justice cannot be simple extensions of principles of *intra*national justice. Indeed, historically, the idea that *distributive* justice might apply between countries as well as between people within a country is relatively new. International justice has traditionally been confined largely to the problem of peace and war between nations. For example, among the developments that have brought the issue of international justice on to the stage have been the global environmental issues mentioned above. There have also been economic and political developments that gave rise to an understandable and perfectly justified move by the poorer nations of the world to assert their rightful place on the international economic and political scene. Nevertheless, we shall argue below that there is little scope for a theory of international distributive justice that goes beyond the moral obligations of beneficent concern to improve the position of the worst off individuals in society.

3. The Limited Scope for Theories of International Distributive Justice

One of the currently widespread political theories is libertarianism. The essence of this is that even inequality of wealth between individuals within any country does not provide, by itself, a compelling ethical basis for the redistribution of wealth between them, unless the inequalities have been the result of illegitimate procedures. Otherwise, any such redistribution would violate the individual's rights to liberty, notably the freedom to dispose of freely, or keep, any goods that one has acquired legitimately and to which one is then 'entitled'. That right is fundamental and must not be violated even if its violation would lead to more equality. Nozick, for example, in a book that is rightly famous and influential, even though he later regarded it as being in some respects 'seriously inadequate,'[5] referred to these liberty rights as 'side constraints' upon action.[6]

According to Nozick, the degree to which any given distribution of resources is 'just' is not to be assessed in the light of what that distribution looks like at any point of time—what he calls an 'end-state' theory. It was to be assessed according to the route by which it was reached. If it was arrived at as the outcome of a series of transactions and activities that were legitimate, notably those that were freely entered into, then the owners of resources were justly *entitled* to them. In place of an end-state theory of justice Nozick proposes an 'entitlement' theory.

It is true that the rich nations may have owed their position to previous unjust exploitation of poorer nations or people, or plain theft of their resources. The wealth of the richer may be partly the result of *illegitimate* acquisitions, and so may not be justified in terms of an entitlement theory

---

[5] Nozick (1989: 17). He was referring, of course, to his 1974 book *Anarchy, State, and Utopia*.

[6] Nozick (1974: 31) derived them from the Kantian moral imperatives that a person should never be treated solely as a means, but always as an end. Since individuals are to be treated as ends they are inviolable. They may not be used or sacrificed without their consent for the achievement of some other end, for example, the promotion of the objective of greater equality.

(for example, Shue 1995). How far this is the case can, of course, be the subject for indefinite speculation about the course of historical events.

But in any case the current citizens of any country are hardly morally responsible for illegitimate actions of their predecessors. For example, the citizens of, say, some rich country today may enjoy high levels of income as an indirect consequence of some forcible conquest of other nations or exploitation of other nations' resources in the distant past. But quite apart from the dubious morality of holding anybody to be morally guilty of actions taken before they were even born, and hence over which they had no choice, many citizens of rich countries today do not even have their roots in those countries. It would be ironic, for example, if poor Hispanic immigrants into the USA had to incur any sacrifice, such as being unable to afford adequate heating in winter or air conditioning in summer, on account of the fact that their ancestors in Latin America may have been exploited in the past by powerful US companies.

Another very widespread theory in the English-speaking Western world, to which most of us probably subscribe in some circumstances but that appears to leave no room for distributive justice between nations, is utilitarianism. For utilitarianism, like justice, is concerned with individuals. It is the utility of *individuals* that counts, not the utility of nations. Nations are not units that can enjoy utility (see for example Little 1998: 342). But, given the enormous disparities in per capita incomes between individuals throughout the world, the utilitarian injunction to maximize total utility would imply a massive redistribution of wealth from wealthy individuals to poorer individuals in the world. However, redistribution between governments cannot be relied upon to achieve this objective. There are too many despotic governments in 'kleptocracies' who may appropriate outside aid to help prop up their repressive regimes, fight wars against their neighbours, or build palaces or overseas bank accounts for their rulers.

Furthermore, even without aiming at the ludicrously over-ambitious aim of redistributing world wealth up to the point where total world utility was maximized, the adverse effects on incentives of any major redistribution would be impossible to assess. In view of this O. O'Neill (1991: 283) goes as far as to say that, as regards international justice, consequentialism is a nonstarter. For we are not sure which decisions would maximize utility.

Another currently popular political theory, known as 'communitarianism', would also have little time for any significant international redistribution of wealth on grounds of 'justice'. For communitarianism is based on the view that distributive justice presupposes a bounded world of a political community. It is a world of a common language, culture, and history, which produce a collective consciousness that is essential for investing the concept of justice with common meaning (for example Walzer 1983: 28). As one leading communitarian (Walzer 1997: 19) puts it, 'International society is an anomaly

... because it is obviously not a domestic regime; some would say that it is not a regime at all but rather an anarchic and lawless condition'. To make sense, international justice would require the whole world to be a single political community. Since it is not, communitarianism could be interpreted as implying that international justice is an illusion

4. Rawlsian Theory and Its Extension

Strictly speaking, the Rawlsian theory of justice has no more place for a theory of distributive justice between nations than those political theories mentioned above. In fact, Rawls did not apply his distributive principle, the famous 'difference principle', between nations any more than he applied it between generations. Indeed, Rawls's 1972 treatment of international justice was extremely cursory. In 1993, in a series of lectures in Oxford, he returned to the question of international justice and made a far more detailed study of what such principles should consist of. He still used the procedural device of an original position, in which notional delegates of democratic 'peoples' would agree on principles of international justice.[7] But although he then articulated the basis for his conclusions in much greater detail, the main conclusions did not change substantially.

In 1993 Rawls still excluded any principle of distributive justice between nations. In 1972 Rawls had stated that 'The original position is fair between nations; it nullifies the contingencies and biases of historical fate' (1972: 378). And in 1993 he did not modify his position on this issue. The Rawlsian theory of justice between nations, therefore, provided adequate grounds only for those parts of the NIEO that called for in increase in the status of poor nations in international institutions and so on, but not for those parts that claimed an international redistribution of wealth.

Rawls appears to have excluded distributive justice from his theory of international justice for reasons that resemble the way we have characterized the communitarian approach above. That is to say, he did not believe that international society had sufficient institutions and powers for it to make sense to talk about *distributive* justice between just states. After all, for Rawls justice is the first virtue of social institutions, so that it presupposes a society. And while there may be enough of an international society for some rules of

---

[7] In 1993 Rawls referred to the participants in the original position as if they were representatives of 'peoples' who are defined as 'corporate bodies organized by their governments' (Rawls 1993b). But, as Stanley Hoffmann (1995) shows, in a wide-ranging critique of Rawls's 1993 Amnesty Lecture, this only creates new problems, since the concept of a 'people' is far more ambiguous than that of a nation state, particularly in the present state of the world, in which we witness numerous attempts by different ethnic or other groups of 'people' to split off from the particular nation-state to which they happen to be attached.

international behaviour—for example, outlawing agression, enforcing treaties, and so on—there may not be enough of an international society to provide the basis for any rules of international distributive justice (Little 1998: 340).

But suppose, in an attempt to cling to the notion of 'fairness' between nations, one persists with Rawls's device of the original position but abandons his link between principles of justice and their being limited to the context of a given political community, typically a Western-style liberal democracy. In that case could the participants in 'the original position' still find room for some sort of international distributive justice, based on the notion of 'fairness', in certain situations?

After all, as Barry (1973: 129–30) pointed out, participants in the 'international' original position should take account of the fact that the situation of the worst-off people in the world will be improved best not through the application of the difference principle within countries but through its global application: '. . . the question of distribution between societies dwarfs into relative insignificance any question of distribution within societies. There is no conceivable internal redistribution of income that would make a noticeable improvement to the nutrition of the worst-fed in India or resourceless African states like Dahomey, Niger or Upper Volta'.

So since Rawls believed that contingencies, such as being born with particular talents, should work for the good of the least fortunate, he should perhaps have made a similar claim about the international distribution of resources. In fact it can be argued that the natural distribution of resources is a purer case of something being 'arbitrary from a moral point of view' than the distribution of talents.

All this may be perfectly true, but it still does not demonstrate that the participants in the original position could have reached agreement on some international counterpart of the difference principle. Any attempt to demonstrate that they would do so runs into formidable difficulties, which is probably why Rawls did not make the attempt. In the first place, there is the above-mentioned problem of whether the unit to which the theory of international justice is supposed to apply is the individual or the nation. How far could the participants form a view as to the feasibility of international transfers between individuals throughout the world in a world of nation states, or their effects on improving the situation of the worst-off groups? And how far would the participants in the original position be willing to accept some global difference principle that could operate amid the vast economic and social inequalities that exist today between rich and poor countries? This would require such a major transfer of resources from rich to poor countries that it would be totally impossible politically in the absence of an effective world government that can only exist in some absurdly idealized situation, requiring a totally implausible surrender of national sovereignty. Given the impossibility of arriving at compelling answers to these questions it seems that this 'original position' path leads nowhere.

Perhaps in the ideal world in which countries were internally 'just', Beitz's (1988) proposal to apply the difference principle to nations rather than to individuals might indeed be an attractive 'second best' solution. But in the real world, where most poor countries are far from internally just, international transfers might not be used for the improvement of the lot of the worst-off people. For example, it might often require the transfer of resources from a country that is already reasonably 'just' to a poorer country that is manifestly not. It would be difficult for the government of any democratic country to impose taxes on its citizens in order to help despotic governments maintain power.

5. The Kantian Contribution

If, however, rich countries could attach conditions in providing aid to poorer countries designed to ensure that it is the poorest inhabitants of those countries that benefit—rather like the conditions recently imposed in connection with the cancellation of the debts of poor nations—this would constitute a 'first best' solution to the distributional problem. And it would be along the lines that would be required by a Kantian moral system.

Of course, nobody would expect to find detailed guidance in Kantian moral philosophy—or in any moral philosophy, for that matter—to the solution of real-life practical problems. The most one can hope for is some clarification of basic principles and problems that ought to be taken into account. And, indeed, in turning to Kant, even in respect of the relatively new problem of international justice, as long as one does not start with unjustifiably exaggerated expectations, one is not disappointed.

As is well-known to anybody interested in ethical theory, Kant's famous 'categorical imperative' is a fundamental concept in Kantian ethics. Even allowing for the scope for varying interpretations of Kantian rules, the essence of this is that, in arriving at a view as to how everybody should behave, we should all abstract ourselves completely from our own particular situation and see the operation of the selected rule from the standpoint of anybody else that may be affected. That is to say, in considering what rule should govern assistance to needy people a rich person should take account of the point of view of needy people even if he had every reason to assume that he would never be needy, so that the rule he would adopt would not be one that would necessarily be in his interests at all. Similarly, a poor person would take account of the consequences of any such rule for rich people even if he had no hope of ever becoming rich himself (see also pages 37–38 above).

Thus the Kantian categorical imperative, which is meant to help us decide which actions are morally right, makes impartiality a central requirement. In deciding what is morally right I ought to abstract from what lies in my own interest. The categorical imperative, in the first of its three formulations, says, 'Act only on that maxim through which you can at the same time will [that is, would like] that it should become a universal law' (Kant 1964: 88). In one of Kant's examples he considers whether it is morally right to borrow money if we know we will not be able to pay it back. If we did judge that we were morally entitled to borrow money in such a situation we would be following a maxim such as 'It is morally right to borrow money if you are short of it although you know that you will never be able to pay it back'. For Kant this rule or 'maxim' has to be rejected as it cannot be wished that it should become a universal law, although it may work to my advantage and be 'quite compatible with my own entire future welfare'. The reason why it cannot be wished to become a universal law is that it would make 'the very purpose of promising impossible, since no one would believe he was being promised anything, but would laugh at utterances of this kind as empty shams'(Kant 1964: 90). Indeed, Kant could hardly be more emphatic in insisting that what is morally right cannot be determined by what lies in one's own interests.[8]

For the reasons set out in the next chapter, concerning two major global environmental problems, it is impossible to find a formula to deal with sharing out the burden of global environmental protection that would take into account all conceivable, and often conflicting, points of view. Nevertheless, although in most cases the categorical imperative will not allow us to identify a single formula that correctly embodies it, it often helps us to eliminate some extreme 'wrong' formulae that are inconsistent with it. In other words, the categorical imperative can often fulfil a useful, if mainly negative, function. In such cases we may not learn which solution would be morally right but do seem to learn which ones would be morally wrong.

For example, Nagel (1991: 49) asks how much assistance to the poor the Kantian ethic would expect ordinary individuals to provide. At one extreme there is some maximum level of sacrifice above which a rich man's assistance to the poor cannot be expected to be morally obligatory. And at the other extreme there is a minimum level of assistance that a well-off person should expect to give to the poor and below which he should not fall 'because he cannot will such tight-fistedness as a universal law'. Thus the limits set by the Kantian perspective, however imprecise, do strengthen the moral claim of a beneficent concern for the worst off people in the world on which we have insisted right through this book.

And the guidance provided in this interpretation of Kant for present

---

[8] At one point he states that the categorical imperatives, in the three formulations of which we have presented one, 'did by the mere fact that they were represented as categorical, exclude from their sovereign authority every admixture of interest as a motive' (Kant 1964: 99).

purposes would also be very much in line with the Rawlsian injunction to be concerned with the position of the worst off group in society, or the 'Threshold Prioritarian' view advocated in Chapter 4. For it is clear that a Kantian approach would imply that, within the boundaries of what is feasible, priority ought to be given to assisting the worst-off people in the world. Kant would say that no one who applied the categorical imperative would wish to adopt a universal law that denied help to those who 'struggle with great hardships' (Kant 1964: 90–1).

6. Conclusion

It appears that there is little to which one can appeal in theories of justice that can guide us in the area of distributive justice between *nations*. This is largely because of the conflict between the desire to reduce some of the inequalities between individuals irrespective of national boundaries and the desire to respect national sovereignty. Existing theories of justice either rule out distributive justice between nations altogether or impose tight limits on its scope.

However, some approaches, including those of Kant or Rawls, provide theoretical frameworks that can justify concern for the worst off *individuals* in society and for the avoidance of policies that condemn individuals to poverty. While they are based on relatively fully articulated ethical 'systems', their conclusions are consistent with our appeal, in the *intergenerational* context, to concentrate on a humanitarian concern with the reduction, or avoidance, of poverty. In the next chapter we discuss how one should apply this approach—it cannot be dignified by the term 'principle'—to the real world problems of climate change and the preservation of biodiversity.

11

International Justice and the Environment: Global Warming and Biodiversity

1. Introduction

In the previous chapter we pointed out that while certain ethical principles, such as those in the Kantian tradition, imposed certain limits on the way resources ought to be distributed between individuals, they did not apply much, if at all, to whole nations. Hence, there were no principles of international distributive justice on which one could base the case for richer countries to help poorer countries tackle global environmental problems. Consequently, the case for richer countries to shoulder most of the burden of global environmental protection may have to be based mainly on considerations of common humanity, or virtue, or beneficence, or whatever word we want to ascribe to that part of morality that lies outside the domain of justice and that is relevant to the particular problem in hand. At the same time, there are also some specific global environmental problems that could adversely affect richer countries but that can only be solved by international cooperation. In such cases richer countries may feel motivated to participate in their own interests. In the rest of this chapter we shall consider how far these two considerations should play a part in finding solutions to two particular major global environmental problems. These are climate change and biodiversity.

2. Climate Change

The Case for International Cooperation

The per capita energy consumption of China and India is about one tenth of that of the USA. So when it has reached only one half of that of the USA this will represent a fivefold increase in their per capita energy consumption. The combined population of these two countries alone is over 2 billion, and it is still rising. Similarly, the annual per capita emissions of carbon in the 'least developed countries' of the world as a whole is only 0.2 metric tons, as against 2.0 metric tons in all developing countries and 11.4 metric tons in the industrialized countries (UNDP 1998: Table 47). Given that both China and India have very large coal reserves, they have a big incentive to meet the inevitable enormous increase in their energy demand by using coal, which is, of course, the most carbon intensive of the fossil fuels used in energy production. And, as is well known, it is chiefly the increase in carbon emissions resulting from the burning of fossil fuels that seems to be largely responsible for climate change.

Unless something is done, therefore, to induce poorer countries to moderate the rise in their demand for energy in general and, in particular, their use of coal, all the efforts by the rich countries to curb their own carbon emissions—which are not rising fast anyway on account of the different structure of their economies—are totally futile. Windmills could cover the whole of Britain, which accounts for only about 2 per cent of world carbon emissions, and surround the entire coastline of Denmark without making a significant dent in world carbon emissions.

This might appear to constitute a good example of where the richer countries have to cooperate to help the poorer countries moderate the inevitable increase in their carbon emissions, for example, by free transfer of technology or by compensating them for other measures they may need to take to curb their emissions. Human-induced climate change might appear to be a paradigmatic example of a 'global commons' situation, that is, one in which unrestricted access to some limited communal facility makes everybody worse off in the end. But, in fact, typically 'global commons' situations do differ significantly from each other so that there is no one general compelling method for dealing with them.[1] In the global warming instance some countries may actually benefit from the climate change and even those that may lose somewhat from it may have little incentive *from a purely short-term self-interest point of view* to incur burdens now in order to cooperate in action to reduce carbon emissions. Enforced cuts in carbon emissions will almost certainly be a burden on any country's economy, particularly those that are already heavily dependent on energy use. And the benefits of such cuts—that is, the extent to which global warming would harm them—vary greatly between countries according to how much harm global warming would otherwise do to them.

In particular, in most rich countries the enormous technical changes that have taken place over the course of the last century—for example, in the form of heating, refrigeration, modes of transport, building construction, and the decline in the importance of agriculture—have greatly reduced their vulnera-

---

[1] See, in particular, the discussion in some of the contributions to Dasgupta, Mäler, and Vercelli (1997).

bility to climate differences (Ausubel 1991). As mentioned in Chapter 6, the worst that one recent study of the effect of climate change on a region of Britain could come up with was the possible need for longer tea-breaks for employees (Jones 1998). However, this study does not seem to have made due allowance for the possibility that climate change-induced melting of Arctic ice could divert the Gulf Stream and bring about a dramatic fall in temperatures in Western Europe.

Similarly, it is sometimes asserted, for example by insurance companies, that the damage done by storms will increase. But, as pointed out in Chapter 6, there is neither theoretical reason to believe that the incidence of storms will rise as a result of global warming, nor any evidence of an upward trend in such events over the past few decades.[2] Meanwhile, the increase in the damage done by storms of similar magnitude in similar areas over the past is probably simply the result of the increase in the population and the number and value of buildings and other artefacts. It is true that some floods and storms that have attracted a lot of publicity lately have done terrible damage in some poor countries. But that is largely because they lack the infrastructure to protect themselves or to cope with the consequences. This is an aspect of their poverty.

Of course, given the uncertainties of the science of climate change, account should be taken of the possibility, however small, that even the rich countries will lose enough from global warming to make it worth their while cooperating on global measures to reduce it. Evidence accumulated over the last few years, while still far from decisive, does seem to strengthen the possibility that climate change could be significant over the course of this century and possibly even more so during the course of the subsequent century or more. On the other hand, the evidence that such climate change as is predicted by the IPCC does major damage, on balance, to the economies of the rich countries is still very fragmentary indeed, and the best estimates so far suggest that such damage is likely to be negligible, at least over the course of this century.[3]

One of the few things that is probably known with a high degree of probability about the effects of global warming is that they will be mainly on agriculture. In some countries these will be favourable—longer growing seasons, less frost, more rainfall, and higher carbon concentrations in the atmosphere. But in others they could be unfavourable. In such cases the damage would affect countries heavily dependent on agriculture. On the whole these happen to be poor countries. But it is still questionable how far such countries would be willing and able to make any sacrifice today, for example by reducing their carbon emissions, in order to benefit the inhabitants of their

[2] See Chapter 6, section 4, for more detailed discussion of such possibilities.
[3] See a very thorough and detailed survey of results by various scholars in Mabey *et. al.* (1997: 73ff and Table 3.6).

countries in perhaps 50 to 100 years' time, by which time they will probably be very much richer than those alive today.

Thus we are faced with a situation where, on the whole, the countries that can afford to bear a really heavy burden as part of global cooperative action to combat climate change may have little incentive, from a narrow self-interest point of view, to do so, while the countries which would suffer most from climate change in the longer run will be unable to do so. Indeed, whether they could afford it or not, it may not even be rational for poor countries to incur any sacrifice now in order to raise even further the standards of living that their descendants can be expected to enjoy later in this century. Effective international action to curb climate change is only likely to be taken, therefore, if the rich countries shoulder most of the burden of limiting carbon emissions. Hence, if, as seems increasingly likely over the next few years, the need for action is established with as much reasonable certainty as can be expected, beneficence as much as, if not more than, self-interest would have to play an important part in any international cooperative action. But many powerful countries are most reluctant to entrust international organizations with the authority to enforce action that may be unwelcome to them. Furthermore, there are serious conflicts of interests over this issue *within* many countries.[4] The prospects for effective international action must seem very slight, therefore, unless and until compelling evidence is forthcoming to demonstrate that climate change will do really serious damage to most countries in the world.

'Ethical' Rules for Sharing the Burden of Combating Climate Change?

Suppose that such evidence is eventually forthcoming and it is clear that the world is not faced with a zero-sum game but with one in which cooperation is essential in the general interest. What ethical principles have a bearing on the terms of such cooperation?

Developing countries often maintain that the rich countries have a moral obligation to bear the brunt of the burden in this matter, as in other global environmental problems, because (1) the greater wealth of the rich countries is often the product of past exploitation of the people and natural resources of the developing countries, and (2), more specifically, the only reason there is an apparent need to curb future emissions of carbon is that the present level of carbon concentration in the atmosphere is so high, and that that, in turn, is the result of the past high level of emissions by the developed countries throughout the last century.[5]

---

[4] See a summary of the manner in which divergent political interests within a country—the USA—can override the scientific considerations as far as climate change policy is concerned in Skolnikoff (1999).

[5] See references to these arguments that are not necessarily shared by the authors in question

But it would be unwise to put much weight on this 'natural debt' argument. For it relies on the notion that the current citizens of rich countries are morally responsible for the decisions made by earlier citizens. The notion of moral responsibility is closely linked to the notion of being a free agent, voluntarily acting in knowledge of the consequences. Choice and reasonably expected knowledge of the consequence are two essential ingredients of moral responsibility. As regards the latter, very few people alive during the first half of the twentieth century, for example, could possibly have known what effects their burning of fossil fuels might have on the global climate. And as regards the former, it is difficult to see how the present inhabitants, particularly immigrants, of any country can have had any choice as regards the amount of fossil fuels burnt by earlier inhabitants. For both reasons, therefore, it is difficult to see why the existing citizens of any country should feel any guilt on account of their predecessors' consumption of fossil fuels.[6]

Nevertheless, even if the present inhabitants of rich countries cannot be held morally responsible for the decisions of earlier inhabitants, the fact remains that they owe their present wealth to the burning of fossil fuels by the earlier inhabitants. It is this that enabled these countries to enjoy rapid growth. It is this that enabled the present inhabitants of the advanced countries to enjoy very high standards of living. They would not then be in a strong moral position in asking the current poor countries to sacrifice their own prospects for future economic growth in order to help solve a global problem. The current inhabitants of rich countries have been 'lucky' in having inherited advanced economies. Luck does not impose duties of justice, but it does sometimes impose a moral obligation to share that luck with other members of the community, or, at least, not to expect those who have not shared in that luck to contribute equally to remedy the consequences.

This is one of the reasons why we have some reservations about another, and probably the most popular, 'ethical' rule that has been suggested for sharing out the burden of cutting carbon emissions, namely, that emission quotas or permits should be shared out between countries in proportion to population. This rule was explicitly proposed in an early draft of the United Nations Framework Convention on Climate Change that was put to the 1992 Rio 'Earth Summit'. According to this proposal, emissions were to converge to a

---

in, for example, Shue (1995) and Yamin (1995). A new source of dispute between countries as to the 'equitable' allocation of permits has been the recent estimate that, on account of growth of forests and other forms of biomass carbon sequestration, North America is actually a major net 'sink' of carbon, which may help explain why a large proportion of global carbon emissions does not show up in a corresponding rise in the carbon concentration in the atmosphere even after allowing for the carbon believed to be absorbed in the oceans (Fan *et al.* 1998). These estimates have, however, roused considerable criticism, and, anyway, increasing forest cover cannot, of course, provide a permanent sink for carbon emissions, as some of the critics of these estimates have pointed out (Kaiser 1998).

[6] The difficulties surrounding such a claim are well set out by Sher (1981).

common per capita level over the course of the years (INC 1992). More recently, a report by the (British) Royal Commission on Environmental Pollution (RCEP 2000: 2) stated that 'The most promising, and just, basis for securing long term agreement is to allocate emission rights to nations on a *per capita* basis—enshrining the idea that every human is entitled to release into the atmosphere the same quantity of greenhouse gases'.

One of the foremost experts on the international negotiation of conventions to reduce carbon emissions, Michael Grubb (1989: 37), says of this rule that 'The moral principle is simple, namely that every human being has an equal right to use the atmospheric resource'. Later, in co-authorship with Sebenius, he stated that 'For many analysts . . . and much of the international community that will be involved with greenhouse negotiations, per capita allocations probably have the strongest, if not the only, claim to an ethical basis . . . Its basic presupposition—that each human being should have an equal right to an as-yet unallocated, scarce, global commons—has considerable appeal' (Grubb and Sebenius 1992: 205). This rule is also what Rose (1992: 61) calls the 'egalitarian' principle, of which he says that 'it emanates from basic precepts of human equality as embodied in the constitutions of many countries'.[7]

The ethical basis for this rule is not, however, as straightforward as it may seem. Insofar as people have basic human rights they presumably include rights to liberty, compatible with respecting the liberty rights of others, and to the minimum standards of living needed to take advantage of their right to life. The latter would include, notably, a right to a minimum of food, shelter and *clean air* to breathe. But everybody breathes the same amount of clean air whatever method is used to share out rights to pollute the air. This is because how much one is damaged by carbon emissions depends on how much carbon everybody else is emitting. Because of its 'public good' character a country's national defences defend everybody in the country equally irrespective of how the taxes to pay for the defence are distributed among the population. Similarly, we all gain equally in terms of clean air to breathe by measures to reduce air pollution irrespective of who bears the burden of cutting the pollution.

But consider the case of a room in which there are several people, all of whom would like to smoke, but they all know that smoking over a certain limit will harm them all equally, so that the total amount of smoking must be restricted. [8] This would correspond to the climate change situation, in which

---

[7] See also similar views expressed by Kverndokk (1992).

[8] If some people are smokers and some non-smokers, the two possible solutions to the problem that would appeal to economists would be to either (1) give smoking rights to the smokers but allow the non-smokers to pay the smokers to reduce their smoking; or (2) give non-smokers the rights to clean air and allow the smokers to pay them for the right to use up some of it by smoking. The final equilibrium amount of smoking will generally differ according to which party—the smokers or the non-smokers—is given the rights, and how far they have different incomes. In the climate change case, however, it can be assumed that everybody is in the situation of the smokers.

everybody has some need to pollute the environment by using energy, ranging from primitive societies where fuel is obtained from biomass, to high-tech societies using lots of energy for transport, lighting, heating, air conditioning, and so on. In the smoke-filled room example, everybody has an equal claim to smoke and the most equitable solution, therefore, would be to allocate 'smoking rights' equally among them. The argument would be that, as many people would claim, 'fairness' requires that equal claims are satisfied equally.[9] Of course, some people may be more addicted to smoking than others, in the same way that some nations may have a bigger need to use energy than others. This means that people should be allowed to 'trade' their smoking rights among each other. Similarly, although everybody has an equal right to emit carbon, people should be allowed to trade their emission permits according to their respective situations. And in the interests of minimizing world abatement costs—that is, cutting carbon emissions in the countries in which it is cheapest to do so—such trading of emissions quotas should be encouraged. Thus, the per capita rule for distributing tradable carbon emission quotas or rights has some merit.[10]

But it also suffers from one important limitation arising out of our earlier argument concerning the moral obligation not to inhibit the development of poor countries by expecting them to share equally in the burden of limiting total carbon emissions. For a simple per capita rule does not take sufficient account of the need to help the poorest countries. For example, two countries with equal populations could differ greatly with respect to their incomes. So there might be a case for giving more permits per capita to poor countries than to rich countries. Furthermore, given the conflict between respect for national sovereignty and the objective of helping the poorest *individuals*, rather than their governments, it is undesirable to share out all the tradable permits among governments. Instead, some of them should be given to some international agency in a way that represented some compromise between these two objectives.

Thus although the outcome of the previous discussion is that there are no general principles of international justice that can tell us how much rich countries should help poor countries deal with the climate change threat, some principles seem to emerge that should be taken into account in any system for allocating carbon emission permits.

First, if other things were equal carbon emission permits should be allocated among countries in proportion to their populations. But other things are not equal, notably per capita incomes. And a principle that has long been accepted as equitable in distributing the burden of taxes amongst people within a country is that account should be taken of capacity to pay. Hence,

---

[9] See our discussion of Broome's theory of fairness in Chapter 4.

[10] This differs from the conclusion that we reached in an article on this subject published some years ago (Beckerman and Pasek 1995).

rich countries should receive fewer permits per capita than poor countries. Without our wishing to suggest that the present inhabitants of rich countries are, in any way, morally responsible for the carbon emissions of their prede-cessors, the fact remains that they have hugely benefited from them, so that it would be improper for them to insist now that poor countries should sacri-fice the benefits of future economic growth in order to help solve the global problem of climate change.

Second, we should be concerned with distribution among individuals rather than among nations, but other considerations, including those of *Realpolitik*, mean that, in general, national sovereignty should be respected. Hence, the total of permits should be split into two groups, not necessarily equal. In the interests of respect for national sovereignty, one group of permits should be allocated to governments according to the above principle. But in the interests of targeting assistance towards the poorest individuals, the other permits should be auctioned by some international agency that would be mandated to use the revenues from the sale of the permits only for projects that directly alleviate the most acute environmental needs of poor people in developing countries. Such projects might be entirely financed by the agency in question or carried out by the agency in conjunction with the authorities of the countries concerned so as to ensure that the funds are not simply substitutes for expenditures that the governments concerned would other-wise have carried out anyway.

As regards the first of these two principles, it should be noted that we differ in two respects from the suggestion in the recent RCEP report that there should be a gradual convergence over the course of the next few decades towards an equal per capita level of carbon *emissions*. First, for the reason given above, we believe that distributing emission permits on a per capita basis gives insufficient priority to poor nations. Second, assuming that trade among countries is allowed, there is all the difference in the world between equal per capita quotas or permits and equal per capita emissions. Only if trade were to be banned, or fail to take place—which is extremely unlikely—would the two things coincide, as implied in RCEP (2000: para. 4.51 and Table 4.1). In that case, it might well be true that countries would converge on equal per capita levels of emission only after several decades, if ever. But on the assumption that emission quotas are to be traded, there is no reason why they should not be distributed according to the above rules as soon as the precise formulae are agreed. Presumably, countries that start from very high levels of carbon emissions would have to be heavy net purchasers of permits, whereas countries with very low levels of emissions would be able to sell a lot of their permits. The trading patterns would change over time, of course. First, the total of permits issued would have to change over time. And second, tech-nological changes in different countries would lead them to adjust their economically optimal level of carbon emissions, so that they would be continually faced with the choice between buying or retaining their permits and incurring the costs of reducing their emissions.

3. Biodiversity

Most of the world's biodiversity is found in tropical or semi-tropical regions, which happen to be mainly in developing countries. In the past any loss of biodiversity caused by humans was the result of hunting. But in modern times it is caused almost entirely by the damage done to the habitat of millions of species that live in forests, particularly in tropical and semi-tropical countries. In many of these countries rapidly expanding populations and absence of alternative employment opportunities are partly or largely responsible for the destruction of forests. Deforestation is also often the result of the domestic policies of the countries in which the biodiversity loss is experienced. This may include the absence of clearly designed property rights so that poor farmers have no incentive to husband deforested areas in a sustainable manner, or subsidies and tax breaks that encourage excessive transformation of forests into other uses, or inadequate protection of the rights of indigenous people in the areas concerned. And in some countries government regulations designed to curtail logging are simply flouted or evaded on a massive scale.[11]

Deforestation is also sometimes caused by multinational companies engaged, say, in building roads and destroying forests in the course of logging or mining operations. In doing so they destroy the habitat of the species living in the forests without taking into account the possible potential value to the world as a whole of the species in question. Such companies may have little or no stake in the long-term sustainability of the environmental assets in question.

How much deforestation is actually going on and what rate species are being made extinct as a result is not yet amenable to anything like precise measurement. This is not so much on account of uncertainty about the former, although the rate of this destruction is often exaggerated.[12] The main reason for our ignorance about the rate at which species are becoming extinct is that we do not know (1) within an order of magnitude of ten how many species there are to begin with, or (2) the number of species becoming extinct each year. Sir Robert May, who is, as of September 2000, the Chief Scientific Adviser to the Government and who is a foremost authority on the question, suggested that the 'best guess' one could make about the number of species

---

[11] See, for example, a report in *The Economist* (3 April 1999), 68.
[12] See for example, a critique of some popular exaggerated notions of the rate of destruction of forests in Stott (1999).

in existence is about 7 million, though a possible range could be anywhere between 3 million and 100 million, and that some experts believe that the most plausible range is between 5 million and 15 million (May 1997: Table 4).[13] Estimates of extinctions are also inevitably very uncertain, since one does not actually observe the death of what is known to be the last pair of any species. Thus the fact that only 641 species have been certified as having become extinct since the year 1600 does not exclude the possibility that many more have become extinct without our knowing about it, particularly since the vast majority of species, including plants and animals, are insects, and about 40 per cent of these are beetles (May 2000). Thus estimates of species extinctions have to be based on statistical projections from scanty data. According to Sir Robert May (2000), one common method of estimating the rate of species extinction implied that species were becoming extinct, largely through the loss of tropical forests, at the rate of about 0.3 per cent per annum, which would correspond to about 6 per cent becoming extinct over the next 20 years. This figure is in sharp contrast to the figure proposed by Thomas Lovejoy, a well-known commentator on the subject, in the second of the BBC's Reith Lectures for 2000, on 'Respect for the Earth'. He predicted, as he has been doing for decades, that a quarter or more of all species would become extinct during the next 20 years: about four times the May 'guesstimate'. But his own figures do not match his prediction. Instead they tend to confirm May's much lower estimate of the current rate of species extinction. For according to Lovejoy, species are currently being made extinct at about 1,000 to 10,000 times the normal rate. He did not say what the normal rate was, but he is on record as accepting that the rate of species extinction from the beginning of the twentieth century to 1980 averaged about one species a year. So if this had been 'normal' we would now be losing between 1,000 and 10,000 species a year.

Suppose, to simplify the arithmetic, we take a figure near the middle of this range, namely, 5,000 species a year. This would amount to 100,000 species becoming extinct after 20 years. If we then take the mid-point of the estimated range of the number of species in existence mentioned above, that is, 10 million, this means that after 20 years only 1 per cent of all species would have become extinct, by comparison with Lovejoy's figure of 25 per cent. Even if we take the top figure of Lovejoy's estimate of the range for extinctions, that is, 10,000 a year, this would still imply a cumulative loss after 20 years of only about 2 per cent.[14] Thus, although we do not wish to dismiss the need for concern about loss of biodiversity, it must be noted that many of

[13] The eminent biologist, Edward Wilson (1992: 330) also surmised that the range could be between 10 million and 100 million and that 'No one can say with confidence which of these figures is the closer'.

[14] See Norman Myers (1979) and Lovejoy's predictions contained in US Council of Environmental Quality and Department of State (1980).

the alarming figures bandied about concerning rates at which species are becoming extinct, even on what was once regarded as a serious and prestigious BBC Reith Lectures series, appear to be vast exaggerations.

But whatever the facts about rate of loss of biodiversity the question here is how far it is the result of market distortions of one kind or another. These could include bad domestic policies, lack of property rights by indigenous people, or unequal bargaining power of the parties involved. Such market distortions would mean that even though rapid deforestation may confer short-run economic advantages on the developing countries in question or on some multinational corporations, the longer-run effects may be very harmful to the local economies and communities. How far is there also a longer-term loss for the world as a whole?

Some attempts have been made to estimate the value of biodiversity for the world as a whole. The two main estimates of the total value of biodiversity, one for the USA alone and one for the world as a whole, comprise valuations of a large number of components of 'biota' or components of 'natural capital', such as the oceans, forests, wetlands, grasslands, and so on (Pimentel *et al.* 1997; Costanza *et al.* 1997). But, as David Pearce (1998) has pointed out, it is difficult to see what the object of the exercise is. For the question 'what is the value of biodiversity as a whole?' seems a useless question to ask. This is illustrated in the methodology involved in one of the two estimates in question (Costanza *et al.*1997), which is an estimate of the value of the whole world's eco-system and natural capital, and which is basically an extrapolation to the whole world of estimates made for individual items of natural capital. This is a dubious method since it makes no sense to value how much poorer the world would be if the whole ecosystem was removed any more than it would make much sense to estimate how much poorer the world economy would be if we removed the whole of the labour force or the whole of the man-made capital. In all such cases world output would disappear entirely, so that if we added together the corresponding values of each source of output the total would come to three times the world's actual output.[15]

It makes sense to ask what the value is of this or that individual marginal environmental project, such as some local irrigation system, or reduction in some particular deforestation activity. These affect specific bits of biodiversity that may be of value to specific purposes or groups of people. Such questions are useful because it is at that level that decisions may be taken and also at that level that the valuation technique may be valid. But the question 'what is the value of the whole world's biodiversity?' makes no sense at all.

Preservation of specific items of biodiversity confers two main types of benefit on the world as a whole. First, they may be valued as a source of

---

[15] This is the old 'adding-up' problem in economics, which was the subject of considerable discussion among the Austrian economists around the end of the nineteenth century.

productive input into goods or services that contribute to human welfare, for example, as an actual or potential source of medicinal products. Second, people anywhere in the word may value the preservation of species for its own sake, obtaining satisfaction from the knowledge that species are being preserved, whether on the grounds of 'existence value' or 'option value' or the other sources of valuation discussed in Chapter 9. We shall begin by considering the former motive for valuing biodiversity.

One of the most widely-held arguments for believing that a loss of biodiversity is harmful for the whole of the human race is that the loss of certain species of plants may deprive the world as a whole, and future generations, of some medicinal benefits that would otherwise have been obtained from them. If the continued existence of these plants is believed to be potentially valuable to the whole human race then their destruction in country X harms other countries, if not now then in the future: that is, it is an example of the harmful 'externality' discussed in Chapter 8 above. And it is widely believed that tropical rainforests are full of potential major drug material just waiting to be discovered, a belief that has inspired the pharmaceutical industry ever since the discovery of quinine and of the properties of aspirin which is derived from willow bark.

But it is not clear how important this potential benefit may be compared with the progress in medical science that can be made by research and development in the laboratories. For example, between 1960 and 1982 the National Cancer Institute in the USA and the American Department of Agriculture examined and tested about 35,000 samples of roots, fruits, and bark from 12,000 species of plants. Only three of them were found to be of any significance. And, of course, large pharmaceutical companies have not been blind to the possibility that some of the species in tropical areas may have medicinal value. Indeed, some of them have long been carrying out major projects to screen species for this precise purpose.

But the success rate has been very low and some of them have been cutting down on these activities in favour of more laboratory research designed, essentially, with the same end-purpose in mind, namely, to identify the characteristics of substances, whether natural or synthetic, that have potential medicinal benefits. For example, Shaman Pharmaceuticals, which has been the leading proponent of the so-called 'ethnobotanical' approach to drug discovery, sent teams of physicians and botanists into the rainforests of Asia, Africa, and South America, where they collaborated with local healers in identifying plants with medicinal properties. But the results were very meagre and the company has now abandoned most of this research. Also, Merck, which is one of the world's largest drug companies, spent ten years trying to extract and develop the active principles from Chinese herbal remedies, without success. Other firms too are scaling down their activities in this area in favour of methods for screening the vast numbers of artificial products that have now been created by modern combinatorial chemistry.[16]

In other words, from a narrow economic point of view, it appears that pharmaceutical companies are probably best equipped to estimate the relative pay-off to the preservation of tropical forest areas as sites of research into species of potential medicinal value, and there is no reason to believe that they are not doing enough of this. There is certainly no presumption that they are not doing as much as is required in the interests of the world as a whole. The terms on which they carry out their research are, of course, complex and involve delicate issues such as property rights in the exploitation of the results. Some of the companies involved have behaved in an exemplary manner in respecting the 1992 Convention on Biological Diversity and guaranteeing to share the benefits with the host country should any of the plants examined turn out to be winners. But others have not. It is also true that some companies may have been able to strike harsh bargains. All this is to be greatly deplored. But it does not prove that the degree of preservation of biodiversity is inadequate from the point of view of the rest of the world.

But what about the value that people attach to biodiversity irrespective of its potential medicinal value? There may be a stronger case for restricting the loss of biodiversity on 'public good' grounds, rather like the public good case for the provision of familiar amenities, such as lighthouses, national defence, and so on discussed in Chapter 8, where once the facility is installed or provided it costs no more for additional users to take advantage of it. Similarly, the 'public good' character of the preservation of cherished species arises because if the species in question is preserved for the satisfaction of some people the satisfaction that others may derive from its existence imposes no extra cost on society. Consequently, there is a prima facie case for believing that the free market will not achieve the socially optimal level of preservation of all such species.

Insofar, therefore, as people all over the world may feel some sense of loss if species are made extinct in some countries, it makes sense for them to contribute to their preservation, and not leave the burden of doing so to the countries in which the species in question happen to live. But while there is some force to this argument it has to be recognized that it applies equally to the preservation of all sorts of 'public goods'. The preservation of works of art and ancient temples, for example, also no doubt gives great satisfaction to millions of people who may not expect ever to see them themselves. There is little reason, therefore, why people who do not share the particular preference for species preservation should be obliged, for example through the payment of taxes, to promote that particular private preference rather than their own.

---

[16] *The Economist* (20 February 1999), 107.

After all there is no legal obstacle to the formation of voluntary organizations to collect contributions to help preserve species in developing countries, like the ones that exist to raise contributions to help the humans living in those countries.

Thus it seems that the case for richer countries to make the biggest contribution to biodiversity preservation, like the case for their making the biggest contribution to moderating the growth of global carbon emissions insofar as this turns out to be necessary, has to be based largely on simple benevolence. Whatever doubts there may be about the net effects on the rest of the world of the pace of deforestation in some countries it is probably faster than is desirable in the longer-run interests of the countries themselves. As indicated above, poverty, rapidly increasing population, and misguided internal policies all lead to deforestation as a short-term solution that only aggravates longer-term problems in many poor countries. Help in this area would be a good example of an instance of an opportunity to take advantage of widespread support and concern in rich countries to help poor countries cope with a largely domestic environmental problem.

4. The Moral Obligation of Rich Countries to Shoulder the Burden of Global Environmental Protection

We have argued above that there is very little case, on grounds of either international justice or narrow self-interest, for rich countries bearing much of the burden of dealing with two global environmental problems, namely, climate change and the loss of biodiversity. But there are other grounds for their doing so.

First, throughout this book we have taken the view, shared by most philosophers, that justice does not exhaust the whole of morality. Instead we have appealed to a humanitarian principle of giving priority to the worst off groups in society within the limits of what is practical and up to a certain threshold. An example of the latter principle, in ordinary domestic policy, is what is known as 'specific egalitarianism'. This is a policy of providing, or subsidizing, some specific good or service for what are likely to be, on the whole, needy groups of people, even though more generally redistributive policies might be more economically efficient. For example, in theory the welfare of old-age pensioners would be raised more by increasing their pensions than by giving them free bus passes or television licenses. After all, some of them might not watch the TV or want to travel by bus; perhaps some of them prefer to use their cars, so that they would rather have the extra money to allocate in the way they think best, for example paying the high tax on petrol. But while the public might object to paying higher taxes to finance a general rise in pensions, many people take the view that one should not deprive 'the poor old dears' of the opportunity to ride on a bus rather than have to walk, or to pass the time watching the TV when they have few other sources of entertainment available to them. In such cases, 'specific egalitarianism' may not be the most efficient way of helping the worst off group but it is often better than the alternative, which, for lack of public support, could be to do nothing.

The same applies to international contributions to deal with global environmental problems. The likely loss to the human race of a reduction in biodiversity may well be exaggerated, and the likely damage that climate change would inflict on rich countries is probably very small indeed. Nevertheless, insofar as the better-off inhabitants of rich countries are genuinely concerned with poverty in the world and insofar as large sections of their public are concerned, rightly or wrongly, with these two global environmental issues, they provide an excellent opportunity to extend aid to some poor countries that they might otherwise not receive it at all.

But all that can be claimed is that this principle should be taken into account in deciding policy towards poorer countries. Like any ethical principle it cannot provide very precise guidance. After all, there are competing claims on the benevolence of rich countries and competing claimants. Many poor countries would resent their claims being ignored simply because they could not demonstrate that they were homes to endangered species or that they would be hard-pressed to meet carbon emissions standards.

The second reason why rich countries should shoulder most of the burden of dealing with the two global environmental problems discussed is that self-interest should not be interpreted narrowly. For the extent to which rich countries may need to cooperate with poor countries should not be approached case by case. It should be looked at taking into account the whole range of activities affecting all or most countries. Within any society, for example, individuals cooperate in the promotion and support of certain institutions or laws even where the practical consequences in specific instances may not be to their advantage. If cooperation were to be refused in such instances society would collapse. We all accept that we may need to cooperate in some spheres of social activity in which we do not benefit in order to be able to rely on cooperation in other spheres of social activity where we do benefit.[17]

Similarly, at the international level countries need to cooperate on numerous issues such as control of international crime, trafficking, migration, trade, the struggle against international terrorism, or the proliferation of weapons of

---

[17] In 'game theory', for example, it is well known that what may be a rational strategy in a one-off 'game' of a 'prisoners' dilemma' variety may not be the optimal strategy when the participants know that the game will be repeated. Cooperation may then be the best strategy even though, in specific isolated cases, it would be not be optimal.

mass destruction, as well as numerous environmental areas where rich countries may have as big a stake as do poor countries, such as preserving whale stocks, reducing dumping of oil at sea, dealing with the threats to the ozone layer, or trade in 'dangerous' waste material. Yet, again, while it is incumbent on rich countries to interpret national self-interest in a broad and far-sighted manner, there are limits to the extent to which rich countries should help poor countries cooperate in dealing with global environmental problems. For even rational, far-sighted self-interest does not require that one cooperates without limit in any activity that may be of interest to others but not to oneself. If a few members of a club want to spend a fortune on buying the last few dozen bottles remaining of some vintage wine it is not incumbent on the others to agree that the club's money should be spent this way simply because the club also subscribes to some weekly magazine that many of them may read.

In conclusion, therefore, if there is some case for rich countries to bear more than their share of the burden of dealing with global environmental problems it has to be on grounds of intelligent self-interest and common humanitarianism, rather than on the shaky grounds of some theory of international justice. At the same time, we have reminded readers at various points throughout this book of the fairly obvious point that ethical principles can never provide precise guidance to most practical policy problems. Hard and fast formulae, such as respecting the rights of future generations to inherit the environment as it stands or eliminating all undeserved inequalities between people, have to be treated with great suspicion and probably rejected. In the sphere of international action to deal with global environmental problems, the most that can be expected is a balanced allowance for such valid ethical principles that seem to be relevant.

12

Conclusions

This book is about certain ethical aspects of environmental policy. No attempt has been made to discuss all the major ethical issues arising in environmental policy. For example, we do not discuss animal rights or genetically modified foods. Our focus has been on distributional issues, namely the way in which the gains and losses from environmental polices are distributed among different people, whether they be different members of any community, or citizens of different nations, or members of different generations. It has been impossible at some point to avoid touching on more general ethical issues, such as the intrinsic value of nature, the incommensurability of plural values, and even the fundamental problem of whether there can be valid ideals that do not depend, in the end, on their being good for people.

But the ethical issues with which we have been mainly concerned lie in the domain of 'justice' or 'equity'. And we have paid particular attention to the problem of justice between generations. This is because some of the most intractable and high-profile environmental problems of today are the global problems, notably climate change and loss of biodiversity, and these are problems that can seriously affect the welfare of future generations. Public discussion of these problems and pronouncements about them from public figures, such as princes, pop stars and politicians, invariably refer to the moral constraints on our freedom of action in these matters arising out of the 'rights' of future generations or the dictates of intergenerational justice. But any policy to deal with these problems really effectively is likely to impose heavy burdens on the present generation. So how far is the present generation under a binding moral obligation to bear this burden, and how should it be shared out among different section of the present generation?

In the first few chapters of this book we argue that future generations cannot be said to have any rights. We then go on to argue that this means that the interests that they *will* have cannot be protected within the framework of any theory of justice. But we share the widely held view that rights and justice do not exhaust the whole of morality. There is room for virtue, or beneficence, or whatever term is to be used to describe the moral obligations that lie outside the domain of rights or justice. So we still have moral obligations to take account of the interests that future generations will have. But what exactly are these obligations?

Some people believe that guidance can be obtained from special theories, such as principles of intergenerational equity or equality, or the currently fashionable doctrine of 'sustainable development'. But in Chapters 4 and 5 we argue that these are fundamentally flawed. We argue that 'instrumental' egalitarianism—for example, greater equality as a mean of promoting social harmony—cannot apply between generations. And the view that greater equality has some *intrinsic* value is difficult to defend since, for example, there is nothing to be said for taking something away from better off people without improving the situation of worst off people, even though this must increase equality.[1] Instead of egalitarianism, therefore, we argue that the guiding principle should be the humanitarian principle of giving priority to the worst off people in society, at least up to a certain threshold level of wellbeing, above which differences between people have little or no moral significance.

As for sustainable development, this may well have provided a useful rallying point for alerting people to the ways in which market failures may lead to excessive environmental damage. It may also provide a useful reminder of the ethical dimension to development policy. But, unfortunately, it is so full of intellectual confusion and inconsistencies that, on the whole, the widespread uncritical genuflection in the direction of sustainable development may do more harm than good.

Hence, we conclude that we have to abandon the notion that future generations have any rights that 'trump' the interests of people alive today or that policies have to be constrained by any considerations of intergenerational justice, or equity, or sustainable development. Instead we have to fall back on an appraisal of what will be the most important interests of future generations and how they compare with the interests of people alive today. This requires us to try to predict what the most important interests of future generations are likely to be and which of them are most likely to be at most risk.

One obvious starting prediction has to be the prospect for the future rise in material well-being. For, in the light of our support for the humanitarian principle of giving priority to the worst off people, we need to avoid policies that might condemn future generations to poverty. But we give reasons, in Chapter 6, for supposing that the prospects for continued, and possibly even accelerating, technical progress are such that future generations are likely to be incomparably richer than people alive today. Nor is there any danger that economic growth will be hampered at all by any limit on the supply of so-called 'finite resources'. We expect that all the apocalyptic prophecies of this

---

[1] As explained in Chapter 4 where this issue is discussed in more detail, we are assuming here that insofar as the worst off may derive satisfaction merely from the reduction in the welfare of the better off this would constitute a form of envy that has no moral force.

nature will turn out to be falsified in the same way that all such prophecies have been falsified in the past.

On the other hand, research over the last few years suggest that there is more substance to the view that the climate is changing and will continue to do so. But there is still very little reason to believe that it will have a major impact on the material well-being of the world's population *taken as a whole*. Individual nations or groups of people may suffer, but some people, not necessarily the same ones, would also suffer if really effective measures were ever to be taken to moderate climate change. So this is not just a question of distribution between generations. It is a question of distribution between nations or between groups of people within any nation, and is discussed in more detail in later chapters of the book.

Following on our economic predictions we argue, in Chapter 7, that our main obligations to future generations do not lie in the material field at all but in the field of human relations or, more particularly, in the field of respect for human rights. In the very long run, the growth of material prosperity resulting from continued technical progress will, we believe, lead to a gradual and inexorable improvement in the environment and to the eradication of mass poverty in the longer run, although in the short-to-medium run the environment in many countries will be harmed by economic growth, and even in the very long run there will always be local environmental problems and pockets of acute poverty, even in rich countries. But, by contrast, there is no reason to assume that similar progress will be made in respect for human rights. As we said in chapter 7, human compassion does not seem to keep pace with technical progress.

In our view, therefore, the most important interests of future generations that will be under permanent threat will not be in the field of economic prosperity or environmental change. They will be in the field of human relations. This is because there will always be potential conflicts between peoples for all sorts of different 'reasons' and these conflicts are often the source of horrific violations of basic human rights and of widespread appalling human suffering. It may be difficult to predict relatively minor changes in the tastes and preferences of future generations, and impossible to predict technological developments of new or transformed products. But the fundamental needs of all human beings will always include not merely food, shelter, and so on, but security and self-respect. These can only be guaranteed in a decent society that protects basic human rights.

There is no need to give chapter and verse to substantiate the proposition that the twentieth century has been a century of unparalleled violation of human rights on a massive scale throughout the world, including many parts of the 'civilized' world, and that this has been accompanied by appalling suffering and brutality. Given the propensity for cruelty and intolerance that seems to be deeply embedded in the human psyche the need for constant vigilance in the protection and extension of human rights will never diminish and could even increase, if we judge by certain disturbing features of current societies. In our judgement, therefore, the most valuable bequest we can make to future generations would be a more decent society in which there is respect for basic human rights, tolerance for differences in conceptions of the good life, and democratic institutions and traditions that enable people to sort out their inevitable conflicts peacefully and free of fear of oppression and humiliation.

One of the tensions apparent in many environmental pronouncements, particularly by public figures or sincere and well-meaning members of the public who are comfortably off, is the emphasis on resource conservation and 'sustainable development' combined with the assertion that the trouble with modern civilization is its preoccupation with material prosperity. In this book we argue that this tension can be dispelled. For we argue that there is no long-run obstacle to the improvement in material living standards. But a major obstacle to the welfare of many people will always be the violation of basic human rights, greater respect for which is essential to enable all conflicts, including conflicts over shares in resources, to be settled in a peaceful and tolerant manner. It will not benefit future generations if they have plenty of resources but have to use them to build palaces for despots or finance the forces of oppression.

Nor does greater effort to promote and protect basic human rights conflict with other major objectives, namely, greater concern for the environment and the eradication of mass poverty. In fact, the objectives are complementary. For example, few countries did more to poison their air, water, and earth more than did the countries of the ex-Soviet bloc. In countries where democratic action is suppressed very little attention is paid to the environmental grievances of the inhabitants. Similarly, although there are exceptions, there is a close correlation between respect for human rights and democratic institutions on the one hand, and the relief of poverty on the other.

As Sen (1999) has demonstrated recently, greater freedom, which is the counterpart of greater respect for basic human rights, invariably helps promote other major objectives. Nor is there any conflict of interests between generations as far as the objective of increasing respect for human rights is concerned. The best, indeed the only, way to bequeath a more decent society to future generations is to start by extending and protecting human rights today. In this way we help reduce the suffering of countless millions of people alive today as well as increase the welfare of future generations.

But although we believe that, as far as the environment is concerned, there is no great conflict of interest between generations, we do believe that environmental policy creates serious conflicts of interest between individuals within any generation and between nations. 'Generation' and 'nation' are useful terms for collective entities, but their use should not blind us to the differences between the members. In the end, justice is concerned with the relationships between individuals. Whatever principles of justice or equity one adopts they are unlikely to justify a policy that may raise even further the prosperity of the average person alive in the year 2100, who is likely to be at least four times as rich as the average person alive today anyway, if, as a result, the poorest members of the current generation have to be denied their opportunity to escape from poverty. Thus we have to consider how far the costs and benefits of environmental policy are distributed between different people within any nation and between rich and poor nations.

Some difficult choices have to be made, therefore, between alternative uses of resources. This is traditionally supposed to be where the economist has to be brought in and asked to carry out some quantitative appraisal of the costs and benefits of alternative course of action. After all, Lionel Robbins's (1935: 16) famous definition of economics was that 'Economics is the science which studies human behaviour as a relationship between ends and scarce means which have alternative uses'.

However, as most professional economists have long been well aware, attempts to move from a more or less ethically neutral analysis of human behaviour towards guidelines for economic policy—that is, to go from 'positive' to 'normative' economics—immediately run into a host of ethical problems. These include, in particular, the question of how sacred consumer preferences are and whether moral aspects of consumer preferences ought to be taken into account. In particular, does this mean that environmental preferences have some special status that raises them above the allegedly materialistic preferences, based on self-interest, that are believed to dominate market valuations? These, and related, issues that have a bearing on environmental policy are discussed in more detail in Chapters 8 and 9. Our view is that, while the moral force of consumer preferences is not sovereign, (1) the determination of prices by market forces in no way means that consumer preferences are entirely egotistical and materialistic, and (2) the attempt to put so-called 'environmental values' into some special category that has superior moral claims is a 'category mistake', since many of the values of which the environment is a bearer are shared by other uses of resources, such as education and health. Furthermore, the economist's technique of cost-benefit analysis has an important, though by no means sole, contribution to make to the decision-making process insofar as it is more democratic than any alternative.

Finally, it is clear that some global environmental problems, such as the preservation of fish stocks, protection of the ozone layer, elimination of pollution of the oceans, climate change, and the protection of biodiversity, can be effectively tackled only by means of international cooperation. But this, too, raises the ethical question of how the costs and benefits of such international action are to be shared out among nations, especially between rich and poor nations. Chapter 10 asks how far there are any principles of international justice that help provide an answer to this question, and we conclude that one can expect very little guidance from that direction. This is largely because principles of justice are chiefly about relationships between people who need to agree on principles for distributing peacefully the fruits of their common endeavour. Principles of international justice are limited, therefore, largely to respect for national sovereignty, freedom from aggression, respect for treaties, and so on. Furthermore, many nations are not ruled by governments that are motivated chiefly, let alone solely, by the interests of their citizens. Rich countries may well be justified in believing that no principles of justice require them to give aid of any kind to governments that, at best, use it incompetently or, at worst, use it to finance their forces of repression or feather their overseas bank accounts. Hence, we conclude, as we did in connection with justice between generations, that one has to fall back on considerations of benevolence and a humanitarian concern with the worst off members of society that have to be applied on an *ad hoc* basis in individual instances.

In the light of this we examine, in Chapter 11, two major global environmental problems, namely, climate change and biodiversity. We begin by asking, in both cases, whether one can make out a case for rich nations to bear the burden of international action on grounds of their self-interest. We find that while some such case can be made it is not a strong one, and even then is must be grounded largely on the case for wider international cooperation in a number of different fields. Some members of a club may feel that although some of their club's activities are of little interest to them they are willing to pay their membership subscriptions because of the benefits they derive from its other activities.

In the same way it may benefit rich nations to cooperate in international action to curb climate change or preserve biodiversity in order to be able to call on other countries to cooperate with them in dealing with other problems, such as international trade conventions, protection of the ozone layer or of fish stocks, and the spread of terrorism, drugs, and crime. But the main reason why rich nations ought to bear the brunt of the burden of international action in these two fields is, again, the objective of giving priority to the worst-off sections of society, within the limits of what is practicable. Climate change, in particular, is a striking example of a mismatch between, on the one hand, countries that have little interest in doing much to prevent it, since they will suffer very little, if at all, from global warming, but who could afford to take action, and, on the other hand, countries that will be most harmed by climate change but who cannot afford to take any action to prevent it.

This brings us back once again to a prediction made by one of us—Wilfred Beckerman—in 1974 and to which we referred in the Preface, namely, that the most likely conflicts in the future would not be between Man and the environment but between Man and Man. Unlike the predictions of imminent exhaustion of raw materials or imminent worldwide starvation that he was criticizing at the time, this prediction has turned out, tragically, to have been borne out by events. The only amendment to this prediction that he feels might be warranted today, therefore, would be in the interests of political correctness, namely, to replace 'conflict between Man and Man' by 'conflict between Woman and Woman'. Or should it be 'between Man and Woman'? This will have to be the last unresolved question posed in this book.

REFERENCES

Aldred, J. (1994). 'Existence Value, Welfare and Altruism'. *Environmental Values*, 3/4: 381–402.

American Council on Science and Health (1997). *Global Climate Change and Human Health*. New York: American Council on Science and Health.

Anderson, D. (1998a). *Explaining Why Carbon Emission Scenarios Differ* (Report for the Working Group III of the Intergovernmental Panel on Climate Change). London: Imperial College of Science and Technology,.

—— (1998b). 'On the Effects of Social and Economic Policies on Future Carbon Emissions'. *Mitigation and Adaptation Strategies for Global Change*, 3: 419–53.

Anderson, E. (1993). *Value in Ethics and Economics*. Cambridge, MA. and London: Harvard University Press.

Anderson, M. (1996). 'Human Rights Approaches to Environmental Protection: An Overview', in A. Boyle and M. Anderson (eds), *Human Rights Approaches to Environmental Protection*. Oxford: Clarendon Press.

Appiah, K. (1997). 'The Multiculturalist Misunderstanding'. *New York Review of Books*, October: 30–5.

Aristotle (1976). *Ethics*. Harmondsworth: Penguin Classics.

Arrow, K. (1951). *Social Choice and Individual Values*. New Haven: Yale University Press.

Atkinson, A. (1970). 'On the Measurement of Inequality'. *Journal of Economic Theory*, 2: 244–6.

Atkinson, G., Dubourg, R., Hamilton, K., Munasinghe, M., Pearce, D., and Young, C. (1997). *Measuring Sustainable Development: Macroeconomics and the Environment*. Cheltenham: Edward Elgar.

Ausubel, J. (1991). 'Does Climate Change Matter?'. *Nature*, 350/6320: 649–52.

—— (1999). 'Five Worthy Ways to Spend Large Amounts of Money for Research on Environment and Resources'. *The Bridge*, 29/3: 4–16.

Baier, A. (1981). 'The Rights of Past and Future Persons', in E. Partridge (ed.), *Responsibilities to Future Generations*. New York: Prometheus Books.

Balling, R. C., Jr. (1992). *The Heated Debate*. San Francisco: Pacific Research Institute for Public Policy.

Barrett, S. (1992). 'Acceptable Allocations of Tradeable Carbon Emission Entitlements in a Global Warming Treaty', in UNCTAD (ed.), *Combatting Global Warming: Study on a Global System of Tradeable Carbon Emission Entitlements*. New York: United Nations.

—— and Graddy, K. (1997). 'Freedom, Growth, and the Environment' (draft paper). London: London Business School.

Barry, B. (1973). *The Liberal Theory of Justice*. Oxford: Clarendon Press.

—— (1977). 'Justice Between Generations', in P. Hacker and J. Raz (eds), *Law, Morality and Society*. Oxford: Oxford University Press.

—— (1986). 'Lady Chatterley's Lover and Doctor Fischer's Bomb Party: Liberalism, Pareto Optimality, and the Problem of Objectionable Preferences', in J. Elster and A.

Hylland (eds), *Foundations of Social Choice Theory*. Cambridge: Cambridge University Press.

—— (1989). *A Treatise on Social Justice. Volume I: Theories of Justice*. London: Harvester-Wheatsheaf.

—— (1995). *A Treatise on Social Justice. Volume 2: Justice as Impartiality*. Oxford: Clarendon Press.

—— (1999). 'Sustainability and Intergenerational Justice', in A. Dobson (ed.), *Fairness and Futurity*. Oxford: Oxford University Press.

Beckerman, W. (1972). 'Economists, Scientists and Environmental Catastrophe'. *Oxford Economic Papers*, 24/3: 327–44.

—— (1974). *In Defence of Economic Growth*. London: Duckworth.

—— (1979). 'Does Slow Growth Matter? Egalitarianism versus Humanitarianism', in W. Beckerman (ed.), *Slow Growth in Britain: Causes and Consequences*. Oxford: Clarendon Press.

—— (1980). 'Comparative Growth Rates of "Measurable Economic Welfare": Some Experimental Calculations', in R. Matthews (ed.), *Economic Growth and Resources* (vol. 2). London: Macmillan.

—— (1983). 'Human Resources: Are they Worth Preserving?', in P. Streeten and H. Maier, *Human Resources, Employment and Development*. London: Macmillan.

—— (1992a). *Economic Development and the Environment* (World Bank Background Paper No. 24 to the World Development Report. (1992). Washington, DC: World Bank.

—— (1992b). 'Economic Growth and the Environment: Whose Growth? Whose Environment?'. *World Development*, 20/4: 481–96.

—— (1994). ' "Sustainable Development": Is it a Useful Concept?'. *Environmental Values*, 3: 191–210.

—— (1995a). *Small is Stupid*. London: Duckworth. (US edition: *Through Green-colored Glasses*. Washington, DC: Cato Institute. (1996.))

—— (1995b). 'How Would you Like your Sustainability, Sir? Weak or Strong? A Reply to my Critics'. *Environmental Values*, 4: 169–179.

—— (1997a). 'Intergenerational Equity and the Environment'. *The Journal of Political Philosophy*, 5/4: 392–405.

—— (1997b) 'Warming to Global Change', *The Times*, 11 December: 22.

—— and Pasek, J. (1995). 'The Equitable International Allocation of Tradable Carbon Emission Permits'. *Global Environmental Change*, 5/5: 405–13.

—— —— (1997). 'Plural Values and Environmental Valuation'. *Environmental Values*, 6/1: 65–86.

Beitz, C. (1988). 'International Distributive Justice', in S. Luper–Foy (ed.), *Problems of International Justice*. Boulder and London: Westview Press.

Bentham, C. (1997). 'Health', in J. Palutikof, S. Subak, and M. Agnew, *Economic Impacts of the Hot Summer and Unusually Warm Year of 1995*. London: UK Department of the Environment, HMSO.

Bergson, A. (1938). 'A Reformulation of Certain Aspects of Welfare Economics'. *Quarterly Journal of Economics*, 52: 310–34.

Berlin, Sir I. (1997). *The Proper Study of Mankind*. London: Chatto and Windus.

Best, G. (1999). 'Might, Right and the Rule of Law'. *Times Literary Supplement*, 20 August: 9.

Blair, (Tony) A. (1997). 'Facing Up to a Climate of Change'. *Times*, 4 December: 22.

Bolin, Bert (1997). 'Scientific Assessment of Climate Change', in G. Fermann (ed.), *International Politics of Climate Change*. Oslo: Scandinavian University Press.

—— (1998). 'Key Features of the Global Climate Change System to be Considered in Analysis of the Climate Change Issue'. *Environment and Development Economics*, 3/3: 348–65.

Bowman, M. (1996). 'The Nature, Development and Philosophical Foundations of the Biodiversity Concept in International Law', in M. Bowman and C. Redgwell (eds), *International Law and the Conservation of Biological Diversity*. London and the Hague: Kluwer Law International.

Boyle, A. and Anderson, M. (eds) (1996). *Human Rights Approaches to Environmental Protection*. Oxford: Clarendon Press.

Broome, J. (1984). 'Selecting People Randomly'. *Ethics*, 95: 38–55.

—— (1989). 'What is the Good of Equality', in J. Hey (ed.), *Current Issues in Microeconomics*. London: Macmillan.

—— (1991a). *Weighing Goods*. Oxford: Blackwell.

—— (1991b). 'Fairness'. *Proceedings of the Aristotelian Society*, 91: 87–101.

—— (1992). *Counting the Cost of Global Warming*. Cambridge: The White Horse Press.

Bryant, B. (1995). *Environmental Justice: Issues, Policies, and Solutions*. Washington, DC: Island Press.

Burke, E. (1790/1968). *Reflections on the Revolution in France*. Harmondsworth: Penguin.

Callicott, J. (1985). 'Intrinsic Value, Quantum Theory and Environmental Ethics'. *Environmental Ethics*, 7/3: 257–75.

—— (1995). 'Animal Liberation: A Triangular Affair', in R. Elliot (ed.), *Environmental Ethics*. Oxford: Oxford University Press.

Chang, R. (ed.) (1997). *Incommensurability, Incomparability, and Practical Reason*. Cambridge, MA. and London: Harvard University Press.

Clark, H., Newton, P., Bell, C., and Glasgow, E. (1997). 'Dry Matter Yield, Leaf Growth and Population Dynamics in *Lolium Perenne/Trifolium Repens*–Dominated Pasture Turves Exposed to Two Levels of Elevated CO_2'. *Journal of Applied Ecology*, 34/12: 304–16.

Cohen, G. (1993). 'Equality of What? On Welfare, Goods, and Capabilities', in M. Nussbaum and A. Sen (eds), *The Quality of Life*. Oxford: Clarendon Press.

Cooper, R. (1985). 'International Economic Cooperation: Is It Desirable? Is It Likely?'. *Bulletin of the American Academy of Arts and Sciences*, 39/2: 11–35.

—— (1994). *Environmental and Resource Policies for the World Economy*. Washington, DC: Brookings Institution.

Costanza, R. *et al*. 'The Value of the World's Ecosystem Services and Natural Capital'. *Nature*, 387/May: 253–60.

Crafts, N. (1997). 'Economic Growth in East Asia and Western Europe Since 1950: Implications for Living Standards'. *The National Institute Economic Review*, No.162: 75–84.

Crisp, R. (1998). 'Equality and its Implications' (draft). Oxford: St Anne's College.

—— (2000). 'Equality, Priority, and Compassion' (draft). Oxford: St Anne's College.

Daly, H. (1995). 'On Wilfred Beckerman's Critique of Sustainable Development'. *Environmental Values*, 4: 49–56.

Dasgupta, P. (1974). 'Some Alternative Criteria for Justice Between Generations'. *Journal of Public Economics*, 3: 405–23.

—— (1995). 'The Population Problem'. *Journal of Economic Literature*, 33: 1879–1902.

—— and Maler, K.–G. (1994). *Poverty, Institutions, and the Environmental–Resource Base* (World Bank Environment Paper No. 9). Washington, DC: World Bank.

—— —— and Vercelli, A. (eds) (1997). *The Economics of Transnational Commons*. Oxford and New York: Clarendon Press.

—— and Weale, M. (1992). 'On Measuring the Quality of Life'. *World Development*, 20: 119–31.

De George, R. (1981). 'The Environment, Rights, and Future Generations', in E. Partridge (ed.), *Responsibilities to Future Generations*. New York: Prometheus Books.

de–Shalit, A. (1995). *Why Posterity Matters*. London and New York: Routledge.

—— (2000). *The Environment Between Theory and Practice*. Oxford: Oxford University Press.

De Waal, A. (1999). 'Honoured in the Breach', *Times Literary Supplement*, 2 July: 32.

Diamond, P. and Hausman, J. (1994). 'Contingent Valuation: Is Some Number Better than No Number?'. *Journal of Economic Perspectives*, 8/4: 45–64.

Dobson, A. (1998). *Justice and the Environment*. Oxford: Oxford University Press.

—— (ed.) (1999). *Fairness and Futurity*. Oxford: Oxford University Press.

Drèze, J. and Sen, A. (1989). *Hunger and Public Action*. Oxford: Clarendon Press.

Dunn, J. (1999). 'Politics and the Well–being of Future Generations', in T.–C. Kim and R. Harrison (eds), *Self and Future Generations*. Cambridge: White Horse Press.

Dworkin, R. (1975). 'The Original Position', in N. Daniels (ed.), *Reading Rawls*. Oxford: Blackwell.

—— (1981). 'What is Equality', Parts 1 and 2. *Philosophy and Public Affairs*, 10: 185–246 and 283–345.

—— (1983). 'In Defence of Equality'. *Social Philosophy and Policy*, 1/1: 24–40.

—— (1984). 'Rights as Trumps', in J. Waldron (ed.), *Theories of Rights*. Oxford: Oxford University Press.

—— (1985). *A Matter of Principle*. Cambridge, MA: Harvard University Press.

Easterlin, R. (1996). *Growth Triumphant: The Twenty–first Century in Historical Perspective*. Ann Arbor: University of Michigan Press.

Ehrlich, P. and Ehrlich, A. (1974). *The End of Affluence*. Rivercity, M. A.: Rivercity Press.

Elliot, R. (1989). 'The Rights of Future People'. *Journal of Applied Philosophy*, 6: 159–71.

—— (ed.) (1995). *Environmental Ethics*. Oxford: Oxford University Press.

—— and Gare, A. (eds) (1983). *Environmental Philosophy*. Milton Keynes: The Open University Press.

El Serafy, S. (1996). 'In Defence of Weak Sustainability: A Response to Beckerman'. *Environmental Values*, 5: 75–81.

Elster, J. (1998). *Deliberative Democracy*. Cambridge: Cambridge University Press.

—— and Hylland, A. (eds) (1986). *Foundations of Social Choice Theory*. Cambridge: Cambridge University Press.

ESRC (Economic and Social Research Council). (1997). *Newsletter of the ESRC Global Environmental Change Programme*, ESRC Global Environmental Change Programme, University of Sussex, Falmer, Brighton.

Fan, S. *et al.* (1998). 'A Large Terrestrial Carbon Sink in North America Implied by Atmospheric and Oceanic Carbon Dioxide Data and Models'. *Science*, 282: 442ff.

Faucheux, S., Pearce, D., and Proops, J. (eds) (1996). *Models of Sustainable Development*. Cheltenham: Edward Elgar.

Feinberg, J. (1970/1998). 'The Nature and Value of Rights'. *Journal of Value Inquiry*, 4:

603–14; reprinted in S. Cahn and P. Markie (eds) (1998), *Ethics: History, Theory and Contemporary Issues*. Oxford: Oxford University Press.

—— (1973). *Social Philosophy*. Englewood Cliffs: Prentice–Hall.

—— (1974). 'The Rights of Animals and Unborn Generations', in W. Blackstone (ed), *Philosophy and Environmental Crisis*. Athens, Georgia: University of Georgia Press. Reprinted in E. Partridge (ed.) (1981). *Responsibilities to Future Generations*. New York: Prometheus Books.

Feldstein, M. (1999). 'Reducing Poverty, Not Inequality'. *The Public Interest*, 137/Fall: 33–41.

Ferry, L. (1995). *The New Ecological Order*. Chicago: Chicago University Press.

Fishkin, J. and Luskin, R. (1998). 'Deliberative Polling and the Quest for Deliberative Democracy', paper presented to the annual meeting of the American Political Science Association, Boston, MA, September.

Foster, J. (ed.) (1997). *Valuing Nature? Economics, Ethics and Environment*. London and New York: Routledge.

Frankfurt, H. (1988). *The Importance of What We Care About: Philosophical Essays*. Cambridge: Cambridge University Press.

—— (1997). 'Equality and Respect'. *Social Research*, 64/1: 3–16.

French, A. (1964). *The Growth of the Athenian Economy*, London: Routledge & Kegan Paul.

Gauthier, D. (1986). *Morals by Agreement*. Oxford: Clarendon Press.

Gewirth, A. (1996). *The Community of Rights*. Chicago: University of Chicago Press.

Glover, J. (ed) (1990). *Utilitarianism and Its Critics*. New York and London: Macmillan.

—— (1999). *Humanity: A Moral History of the Twentieth Century*. London: Cape.

Goodin, R. (1983). 'Ethical Principles for Environmental Protection', in R. Elliot and A. Garde (eds), *Environmental Philosophy*. Brisbane: University of Queensland Press.

—— (1986). 'Laundering Preferences', in J. Elster and A. Hylland (eds), *Foundations of Social Choice Theory*. Cambridge: Cambridge University Press.

Graaff, J. de V. (1967). *Theoretical Welfare Economics*. Cambridge: Cambridge University Press.

Grainger, A. (1997). *Bringing Tropical Deforestation Under Control* (Global Environmental Change Programme Briefings No. 16). London: ESRC Global Environmental Change Programme.

Gray, H. (1997). 'Solar Fuel'. *Engineering and Science*, 3: 28–32.

Griffin, J. (1986). *Well–Being*. Oxford: Clarendon Press.

Grubb, M. (1989). *The Greenhouse Effect: Negotiating Targets*. London: Royal Institute of International Affairs.

—— and Meyer, N. (1993). 'Wind Energy: Resources, Systems, and Regional Strategies', in T. Johansson *et al.* (eds), *Renewable Energy: Sources for Fuels and Electricity*. Washington, DC: Island Press.

—— and Sebenius, J. (1992). 'Participation, Allocation and Adaptability in International Tradeable Emission Permit Systems for Greenhouse Gas Control', in OECD, *Climate Change: Designing a Tradeable Permit System*. Paris: OECD.

Hahn, F. and Hollis, M. (eds) (1979). *Philosophy and Economic Theory*. Oxford: Oxford University Press.

Harding, A. (1996). 'Practical Human Rights, NGOs and the Environment in Malaysia', in A. Boyle and M. Anderson (eds), *Human Rights Approaches to Environmental Protection*. Oxford: Clarendon Press.

Hare, R. (1997). 'Equality and Justice', in L. Pojmore and R. Westmoreland (eds), *Equality: Selected Readings*. New York and Oxford: Oxford University Press.

Hargreaves Heap, S., Hollis, M., Lyons, B., Sugden, R., and Weale, A. (1992). *The Theory of Choice*. Oxford: Blackwell.

Harris, J. (1975/1990). 'The Survival Lottery', in J. Glover (ed.) (1990), *Utilitarianism and Its Critics*. New York and London: Macmillan.

Hart, H. L. A. (1975). 'Rawls on Liberty and its Priority', in N. Daniels (ed.), *Reading Rawls: Critical Studies on Rawls' 'A Theory of Justice'*. Oxford: Blackwell.

—— (1982). 'Are There Any Natural Rights?', in J. Waldron (ed.), *Theories of Rights*. Oxford: Oxford University Press. (First published in 1955.)

Hausman, D. and McPherson, M. (1993). 'Taking Ethics Seriously: Economics and Contemporary Moral Philosophy'. *Journal of Economic Literature*, 31/June: 671–731.

Hausman, J. (ed.) (1993). *Contingent Valuation: A Critical Assessment*. Amsterdam: Elsevier.

Henderson–Sellers, A., *et al.* (1998). (1998). 'Tropical Cyclones and Global Climate Change: A Post–IPCC Assessment'. *Bulletin of the American Meteorological Society*, 79: 19–38.

Heyd, D. (1992). *Genethics: Moral Issues in the Creation of People*. Berkeley: University of California Press.

Hoffmann, S. (1981). *Duties Beyond Borders: On Limits and Possibilities of Ethical International Politics*. Syracuse: Syracuse University Press.

—— (1995). 'Dreams of a Just World'. *New York Review of Books*, 2 November: 52–6.

Hohfeld, W. (1923). *Fundamental Legal Conceptions*. New Haven: Yale University Press.

Holland, A. (1997). 'Substitutability: or, Why Strong Sustainability is Weak and Absurdly Strong Sustainability Is Not Absurd', in J. Foster (ed.), *Valuing Nature? Economics, Ethics and Environment*. London and New York: Routledge.

—— (1999). 'Sustainability: Should We Start From Here?', in A. Dobson (ed.), *Fairness and Futurity*. Oxford: Oxford University Press.

Holmes, S. and Sunstein, C. (1999). *The Cost of Rights: Why Liberty Depends on Taxes*. New York: W.W. Norton.

Howarth, R. and Norgaard, R. (1992). 'Environmental Valuation under Sustainable Development'. *American Economic Review*, 82/2: 473–7.

INC (Intergovernmental Negotiating Committee) (1992). *Annex 1 to the Report of the Intergovernmental Negotiating Committee for a Framework Convention on Climate Change: United Nations Framework Convention on Climate Change*, document A\AC.237/18 (Part 1) Add. 1. New York: United Nations.

IPCC (Intergovernmental Panel on Climate Change) (1990). *Climate Change: The IPCC Scientific Assessment*. Cambridge: Cambridge University Press.

—— (1996a). *Climate Change 1995, Impacts, Adaptation and Mitigation of Climate Change: Scientific–Technical Analysis* (contribution of Working Group II to the Second Assessment Report of the IPCC). Cambridge: Cambridge University Press.

—— (1996b). *Climate Change 1995: Economic and Social Dimension of Climate Change* (contribution of Working Group III to the Second Assessment Report of the IPCC). Cambridge: Cambridge University Press.

Jacobs, M. (1995). 'Sustainable Development, Capital Substitution and Economic Humility: A Response to Beckerman'. *Environmental Values*, 4: 57–68.

Jevons, W. (1865). *The Coal Question*. London: Macmillan.

Jones, S. (1998). 'Global Warming May Take Toll on North–West'. *Financial Times*, 12 December: 6.

Jorgensen, B., Syme, G., Bishop, B., and Nancarrow, B. (1999). 'Protest Responses in Contingent Valuation'. *Environmental and Resource Economics*,14: 131–50.

Kahneman, D. and Knetsch, J. (1992). 'Valuing Public Goods: The Purchase of Moral Satisfaction'. *Journal of Environmental Economics and Management*, 22: 57–70.

Kaiser, J. (1998). 'Possibly Vast Greenhouse Gas Sponge Ignites Controversy'. *Science*, 282: 386–7.

Kant, E. (1964). *Groundwork of the Metaphysics of Morals*. New York: Harper and Row. (tr. Paton)

Keat, R. (1994). 'Citizens, Consumers and the Environment: Reflections on *The Economy of the Earth. Environmental Values*, 3/4: 333–50.

Kofi Annan. (1999). 'Two Concepts of Sovereignty'. *The Economist*, 18 September: 81–2.

Kolakowski, L. (1999). *Freedom, Fame, Lying and Betrayal*. Harmondsworth: Penguin.

Kverndokk, S. (1992). *Tradeable CO$_2$ Emission Permits: Initial Distribution as a Justice Problem* (CSERGE Working Paper 92–35). University College London and University of East Anglia: CSERGE.

Landsea, C., Nicholls, N., Gray, W., and Avila, L. (1996). 'Downward Trend in the Frequency of Intense Atlantic Hurricanes During the Past Five Decades'. *Geophysical Research Letters*, 23/13: 1697–1700.

Lardy, N. (1999). *China's Unfinished Economic Revolution*. Washington, DC: Brookings Institution.

Laslett, P. and Fishkin, J. (eds) (1992). *Justice Between Age Groups and Generations*. New Haven and London: Yale University Press.

Leibenstein, H. (1976). *Beyond Economic Man*. Cambridge, MA: Harvard University Press.

Lerchl, A. (1998). 'Changes in the Seasonality of Mortality in Germany from 1946 to 1995: The Role of Temperature' *International Journal of Biometeorology*, 42: 84–8.

Lessnoff, M. (1986). *Social Contract*. London: Macmillan.

Lindsey, G. (1994). 'Market Models, Protest Bids, and Outliers in Contingent Valuation'. *Water Resources Planning and Management*, 120: 121–9.

Little, I. M. D. (1950). *A Critique of Welfare Economics*. Oxford: Clarendon Press.

—— (1998). *Collection and Recollections*. Oxford: Clarendon Press. Includes 'Distributive Justice and the New International Order' (originally 1980) and 'Ethics and International Economic Relations' (originally 1992).

—— and Mirrlees, J. (1974). *Project Appraisal and Planning for Developing Countries*. London: Heinemann.

Locke, J. (1965). *Two Treatises of Government*, ed. P. Laslett. Cambridge: Cambridge University Press.

Lukes, S. (1996). 'On Trade–offs Between Values', in F. Farina, F. Hahn, and S. Vannucci (eds), *Ethics, Rationality, and Economic Behaviour*. Oxford: Clarendon Press.

—— (1997), 'Comparing the Incomparable', in R. Chang (ed.), *Incommensurability, Incomparability, and Practical Reason*. Cambridge, MA. and London: Harvard University Press.

Luttwak, E. (1999). *Disposable People*. Berkeley, CA: University of California Press.

Lynch, M. (1998). *Crying Wolf: Warnings About Oil Supply*. Cambridge, MA: Center for International Studies, MIT.

Mabey, N., Hall, S., Smith, C., and Gupta, S. (1997). *Argument in the Greenhouse*. London and New York: Routledge.

Mackie, J. L. (1984). 'Can There be a Rights–Based Morality?', in J. Waldron (ed.), *Theories of Rights*. Oxford: Oxford University Press.

—— (1988). 'The Subjectivity of Values', in G. Sayre–McCord (ed.), *Essays on Moral Realism*. Ithaca, NY: Cornell University Press.

Macklin, R. (1981). 'Can Future Generations Correctly Be Said to Have Rights?', in E. Partridge (ed.), *Responsibilities to Future Generations*. New York: Prometheus Books.

MacLean, D. and Brown, P. (eds) (1983). *Energy and the Future*. Totowa, NJ: Rowman and Littlefield.

Maddison, A. (1995). *Monitoring the World Economy*. Paris: OECD.

Malakoff, D. (1997). 'Thirty Kyotos Needed to Control Warming'. *Science*, 278: 2048.

Margalit, A. (1996). *The Decent Society*. Cambridge, MA: Harvard University Press.

May, R. (1997). 'The Dimensions of Life on Earth', in P. Raven and T. Williams (eds), *Nature and Human Society: The Quest for a Sustainable World*. Washington, DC: National Academy Press.

—— (2000). Florence Nightingale Lecture. Oxford: St Anne's College, 26 May.

Meacher, M. (1997). 'Sustainable Way Forward'. *Financial Times*, 4 June: 13.

Meadows, D. H., Meadows, D. L., Randers, J., Behrens III, W. (1972). *The Limits to Growth: A Report to the Club of Rome*. New York: Universe Books.

Mendelsohn, R. and Nordhaus, W. (1996). 'The Impact of Global Warming on Agriculture—A Reply', *American Economic Review*, 86/5: 312–15.

Merrills, J. (1996). 'Environmental Protection and Human Rights: Conceptual Aspects', in A. Boyle and M. Anderson (eds), *Human Rights Approaches to Environmental Protection*. Oxford: Clarendon Press.

Midgely, M. (1999). 'The End of Anthropocentrism?', in R. Attfield and A. Belsey (eds), *Philosophy and the Natural Environment*. Cambridge: Cambridge University Press.

Miller, D. (1991/92). 'Distributive Justice: What the People Think'. *Ethics*, 102: 555–93.

—— (1999). 'Social Justice and Environmental Goods', in A. Dobson (ed.), *Fairness and Futurity*. Oxford: Oxford University Press.

Mills, M. (1999). *Getting It Wrong: Energy Forecasts and the End–of–Technology Mindset*. Washington, DC: Competitive Enterprise Institute.

—— (2000), *Renewable Energy and the Laws of Nature*. www.greeningearthsociety.org

Mirrlees, J. (1982). 'The Economic Uses of Utilitarianism', in A. Sen and B. Williams (eds), *Utilitarianism and Beyond*. Cambridge: Cambridge University Press.

MIT Workshop on Alternative Energy Strategies (1977) *Energy: Global Prospects 1985–2000*. Cambridge, MA: MIT.

Moore, G. E. (1978). *Principia Ethica*. Cambridge: Cambridge University Press.

Myers, N. (1979). *The Sinking Ark*. New York: Pergamon.

Naess, A. and Sessions, G. (1984). 'Basic Principles of Deep Ecology'. *Ecophilosophy*, 6: 3–7.

Nagel, T. (1979). *Mortal Questions*. Cambridge: Cambridge University Press.

—— (1991). *Equality and Partiality*. Oxford: Oxford University Press.

Narveson, J. (1967). 'Utilitarianism and New Generations'. *Mind*, 76: 62–72.

NOAA (National Oceanic and Atmospheric Administration) (1993). 'National Resource Damage Assessments Under the Oil Pollution Act of 1980' (a report of a panel co–chaired by K. Arrow and R. M. Solow, US Dept. of Commerce). *Federal Register*, 58/10 (15 January), Washington, DC.

Nordhaus, W. (1994). *Managing the Global Commons*. Cambridge, MA: MIT Press.

Norgaard, R. (1992). *Sustainability and the Economics of Assuring Assets for Future Generations* (Policy Research Working Paper WPS 832). Washington, DC: World Bank.

Norton, B. (1994). 'Economists' Preferences and the Preferences of Economists'. *Environmental Values*, 3/Winter: 311–32.

Nozick, R. (1974). *Anarchy, State, and Utopia*. Oxford: Blackwell.

—— (1981). *Philosophical Explanations*. Oxford: Clarendon Press.

—— (1989). *The Examined Life*. New York: Simon and Schuster.

Okun, A. (1971). 'Social Welfare Has No Price Tag'. *Survey of Current Business*, US Dept. of Commerce, July, part 2.

—— (1975). *Equality and Efficiency: The Big Tradeoff*. Washington, DC: Brookings Institution.

O'Neill, J. (1993). *Ecology, Policy and Politics*. London and New York: Routledge.

O'Neill, O. (1991). 'Transnational Justice', in D. Held, *Political Theory Today*. Oxford: Polity Press.

—— (1996). *Towards Justice and Virtue*. Cambridge: Cambridge University Press.

—— (1997). 'Environmental Values, Anthropocentrism and Speciesism'. *Environmental Values*, 6/2: 127–42.

Parfit, D. (1983). 'Energy Policy and the Further Future: The Identity Problem', in D. MacLean and P. Brown (eds), *Energy and the Future*. Totowa, NJ: Rowman and Littlefield.

—— (1984). *Reasons and Persons*. Oxford: Oxford University Press.

—— (1991). *Equality or Priority?* (The Lindley Lecture). University of Kansas.

Partridge, E. (ed.) (1981). *Responsibilities to Future Generations*. New York: Prometheus Books.

Pasek, J. (1992). 'Obligations to Future Generations: A Philosophical Note'. *World Development*, 20: 513–21.

—— (1993). *Environmental Policy and the 'Identity Problem'*. University College London and University of East Anglia: CSERGE.

—— (1994). 'International Justice and Environmental Policy', in P. Dunleavy and J. Stanyer (eds), *Contemporary Political Studies. 1994: Volume Two*. Exeter: Political Studies Association of the UK, Short Run Press.

Passmore, J. (1974). *Man's Responsibility for Nature*. London: Duckworth.

Pearce, D. (1994). 'Commentary'. *Environment and Planning*, 26: 1329–38.

—— (1998). 'Auditing the Earth'. *Environment*, 40/2: 23–8.

—— and Warford, J. (1993). *World Without End: Economics, Environment and Sustainable Development*. Washington, DC: Oxford University Press for the World Bank.

Pezzey, J. (1992). *Sustainable Development Concepts: An Economic Analysis* (Environment Paper No.2).Washington, DC: World Bank.

—— (1997). 'Sustainability Constraints versus "Optimality" versus Intertemporal Concern, and Axioms versus Data'. *Land Economics*, 73/4: 448–66.

Pigou, A. (1932). *The Economics of Welfare* (4th edn). London: Macmillan.

Pimentel, D. *et al.* (1997). 'Economic and Environmental Benefits of Biodiversity'. *BioScience*, 467/11: 747–57.

Plant, R. (Lord) (1991). *Modern Political Thought*. Oxford: Blackwell.

Pletcher, G. (1981). 'The Rights of Future Generations', in E. Partridge (ed.), *Responsibilities to Future Generations*. New York: Prometheus Books.

Pojman, L. and Westmoreland, R. (eds) (1997). *Equality: Selected Readings*. Oxford: Oxford University Press.

Rawls, J. (1972). *A Theory of Justice*. Oxford: Clarendon Press.

—— (1993*a*). *Political Liberalism*. New York: Columbia University Press.

—— (1993*b*). 'The Law of Peoples', in S. Shute (ed.), *On Human Rights: The Oxford Amnesty Lectures 1993*. New York: Basic Books.

Raz, J. (1986). *The Morality of Freedom*. Oxford: Oxford University Press.

—— (1991). 'Mixing Values'. *Proceedings of the Aristotelian Society*, Supp. Vol. 65: 83–100.

RCEP (Royal Commission on Environmental Pollution) (2000). *Energy—The Changing Climate*. London: The Stationery Office.

Read, P. (1994). *Responding to Global Warming: The Technology, Economics and Politics of Sustainable Energy*. London and New Jersey: Zed Books.

Regan, T. (1982). *All That Dwells Therein*. Berkeley, CA: University of California Press.

—— (1992). 'Does Environmental Ethics Rest on a Mistake?'. *The Monist*, 75: 161–82.

Reiter, P. (1998). 'Global Warming and Vector–Borne Disease in Temperate Regions and at High Altitude'. *The Lancet*, 351: 839.

Robbins, L. (1935). *The Nature and Significance of Economic Science* (2nd edn). London: Macmillan. Chapter 5 is reprinted in F. Hahn and M. Hollis (eds) (1979), *Philosophy and Economic Theory*. Oxford: Oxford University Press.

Robertson, A. and Merrills, J. (1996). *Human Rights in the World* (2nd edn). Oxford: Blackwell.

Roemer J. (2000). 'What We Owe Our Children, They Their Children, And...'. Paper presented to a conference on Intergenerational Justice, Department of Economics, University of California, Davis, May.

Rogner, H.–H. (1997). 'An Assessment of World Hydrocarbon Resources'. *Annual Review of Energy and the Environment*, 22: 217–62.

Rose, A. (1992). 'Equity Considerations of Tradeable Carbon Emission Entitlements', in UNCTAD, *Combating Global Warming*, New York: United Nations.

Rosenblum, N. (1989). *Liberalism and the Moral Life*. Cambridge, MA: Harvard University Press.

Routley, R. and Routley, V. (1979). 'Against the Inevitability of Human Chauvinism', in K. Goodpaster and K. Sayre (eds), *Ethics and Problems of the 21st Century*. Notre Dame: University of Notre Dame Press.

—— (1980). 'Human Chauvinism and Environmental Ethics', in D. Mannison, M. McRobbie, and R. Routley (eds), *Environmental Philosophy*. Canberra: Australian National University.

Sachs, J. (2000). 'A New Map of the Word'. *The Economist*, 24 June: 113ff.

Sagoff, M. (1994). 'Four Dogmas of Environmental Economics'. *Environmental Values*, 3/4: 285–310.

Scanlon, T. (1984). 'Rights, Goals, and Fairness', in J. Waldron (ed.), *Theories of Rights*. Oxford: Oxford University Press.

—— (1998). *What We Owe to Each Other*. Cambridge, MA: Harvard University Press.

Schelling, T. (1968). 'The Life That You Save May Be Your Own', in S. Chase (ed.), *Problems in Public Expenditure Analysis*. Washington, DC: Brookings Institution.

—— (1995). 'Intergenerational Discounting'. *Energy Policy*, 23/4–5: 395–401.

Schiesser, H. *et al.* (1997). 'Winter Storms in Switzerland North of the Alps'. *Theoretical and Applied Climatology*, 58: 1–19.

Schumacher, E. (1973). *Small is Beautiful.* London: Blond Briggs.

Sen, A. (1979). 'Rational Fools: A Critique of the Behavioural Foundations of Economic Theory', in F. Hahn and M. Hollis (eds), *Philosophy and Economic Theory.* Oxford: Oxford University Press.

—— (1982*a*). *Choice, Welfare and Measurement.* Oxford: Blackwell.

—— (1982*b*). 'Equality of What?', in A. Sen, *Choice, Welfare and Measurement*, Blackwell, Oxford.

—— (1987). *On Ethics and Economics.* Oxford: Blackwell.

—— (1992). *Inequality Reexamined.* Oxford: Clarendon Press, and New York: Russell Sage Foundation.

—— (1999). *Development as Freedom.* Oxford: Oxford University Press.

—— (2000). 'East and West: The Reach of Reason'. *New York Review of Books*, 20 July: 33–8.

Sher, G. (1981). 'Ancient Wrongs and Modern Rights'. *Philosophy and Public Affairs*, 10/1: 3–17.

Shklar, J. (1989). 'The Liberalism of Fear', in N. Rosenblum (ed.), *Liberalism and the Moral Life.* Cambridge, MA: Harvard University Press.

Shue, H. (1995). 'An Introduction to the Debate'. *International Affairs*, 71/3: 453–61.

Sikora, R. and Barry, B. (eds) (1978). *Obligations to Future Generations.* Philadelphia: Temple University Press.

Simon, H. (1982). *Models of Bounded Rationality.* Cambridge, MA: MIT Press.

Simon, J.(1996). *The Ultimate Resource.* Princeton, NJ: Princeton University Press.

Simpson, A. (1999). 'Rights Talk, Rights Acts'. *Times Literary Supplement*, 27 August: 9.

Skolimowski, H. (1995). 'In Defence of Sustainable Development'. *Environmental Values*, 4/1: 69–70.

Skolnikoff, E. (1999). 'The Role of Science in Policy: The Climate Change Debate in the United States'.*Environment*, 41/5: 16–20, 42–5.

Smart, J. and Williams, B. (1973). *Utilitarianism: For and Against.* Cambridge: Cambridge University Press.

Sober, E. (1986). 'Philosophical Problems for Environmentalism', in B. Norton (ed.), *The Preservation of Species: The Intrinsic Value of Nonhuman Species.* Princeton: Princeton University Press.

Stott, P. (1999). *Tropical Rain Forest: A Political Economy of Hegemonic Mythmaking.* London: Institute of Economic Affairs.

Steiner, H. (1983). 'The Rights of Future Generations', in D. MacLean and P. Brown (eds), *Energy and the Future.* Totowa, NJ: Rowman and Littlefield.

Sterba, J. (1980). 'Abortion and the Rights of Distant Peoples and Future Generations'. *Journal of* Philosophy, 77: 424–40.

—— (1998): *Justice for Here and Now.* Cambridge: Cambridge University Press.

Stocker, M. (1990). *Plural and Conflicting Values.* Oxford: Oxford University Press.

—— (1997). 'Abstract and Concrete Value: Plurality, Conflict and Maximization', in R. Chang (ed.), *Incommensurability, Incomparability, and Practical Reason.* Cambridge, MA. and London: Harvard University Press.

Streeten, P. (1986). 'Mankind's Future: An Ethical View'. *Interdisciplinary Science Reviews*, 11/3: 248–56.

—— (1996). 'Population Stabilizes, Economic Growth Continues? A Review Essay on

Richard Easterlin's *Growth Triumphant: The Twenty–First Century in Historical Perspective'. Population and Development Review*, 22/4: 773–80.

Sunstein, C. (1997). 'Incommensurability and Kinds of Valuation: Some Applications in Law', in R. Chang (ed.), *Incommensurability, Incomparability, and Practical Reason*. Cambridge, MA. and London: Harvard University Press.

Sylvan, R. and Bennett, D. (1994). *The Greening of Ethics*. Cambridge: The White Horse Press.

Tawney, R. (1964). *Equality* (5th edn). London: Unwin.

Temkin, L. (1993). *Inequality*. Oxford: Oxford University Press.

—— (1995). 'Justice and Equality: Some Questions About Scope'. *Social Philosophy and Policy Foundation*, 12/2: 72–104.

—— (forthcoming). 'Equality, Priority, and the Levelling Down Objective', in M. Clayton and A. Williams (eds), *The Ideal of Equality*. London and New York: Macmillan and St Martins Press.

UK Department of the Environment (1996). *Indicators of Sustainable Development for the United Kingdom*. London: HMSO.

—— (1997). *This Common Inheritance: UK Annual Report*. London: HMSO.

UNDP (United Nations Development Programme) (1991). *Human Development Report*. New York and Oxford: Oxford University Press for the UN.

—— (1998). *Human Development Report*. New York and Oxford: Oxford University Press for the UN.

US Council of Environmental Quality and Department of State (1980). *The Global Report to the President* (vol. 2). Washington, DC: Government Printing Office.

Vadjnal, D. and O'Connor, M. (1994). 'What is the Value of Rangitoto Island?'. *Environmental Values*, 3/4: 369–80.

Vlastos, G. (1984). 'Justice and Equality', in J. Waldron (ed.), *Theories of Rights*. Oxford: Oxford University Press.

Waldron, J. (ed.) (1984). *Theories of Rights*. Oxford: Oxford University Press.

Wallas, G. (1914). *The Great Society*. London: Macmillan.

Walzer, M. (1983). *Spheres of Justice: A Defence of Pluralism and Equality*. Oxford: Robertson.

—— (1997). *On Toleration*. New Haven: Yale University Press.

Warren, M. (1981). 'Do Potential People Have Rights', in E. Partridge (ed.), *Responsibilities to Future Generations*. New York: Prometheus Books.

WCED (World Commission on Environment and Development) (1987). *Our Common Future* (the Brundtland Report). New York and Oxford: Oxford University Press.

Weiss, Edith Brown (1989). *In Fairness to Future Generations: International Law, Common Patrimony, and Intergenerational Equity*, New York: Transnational Publishers, Inc.

WHO (UN World Health Organisation). (1998). *World Health Report 1998: Life in the 21st Century – A Vision for All*, Geneva.

Wigley, T. (1998). 'The Kyoto Protocol: CO_2 CH_4, and Climate Implications'. *Geophysical Research Letters*, 1 July: 2285ff.

Williams, B. (1976). *Morality: An Introduction to Ethics*. Cambridge: Cambridge University Press.

—— (1992). 'Must a Concern for the Environment be Centred on Human Beings?', in C. Taylor (ed.), *Ethics and the Environment*. Oxford: Corpus Christi College.

Wilson, E. (1992). *The Diversity of Life*. London and New York: Penguin Books.

Wissenburg, M. (1999). 'An Extension of the Rawlsian Savings Principle to Liberal Theories of Justice in General', in A. Dobson (ed.), *Fairness and Futurity*, Oxford: Oxford University Press.

World Bank (1992). *World Development Report 1992: Development and the Environment*. Washington, DC: World Bank, and Oxford: Oxford University Press.

—— (1993). *World Development Report 1993: Investing in Health*. Washington, DC: World Bank, and Oxford: Oxford University Press.

—— (1997). *World Development Report 1997: The State in a Changing World*. Washington, DC: World Bank, and Oxford: Oxford University Press.

Yamin, F. (1995). 'Biodiversity, Ethics and International Law'. *International Affairs*, 71/3: 529–46.

—— (1997). 'Environmental Ethics'. Paper presented to the 38th meeting of the group of advisers on the ethical implications of biotechnology, June, European Union, Brussels.

INDEX